CRM
in Real Time

Praise for *CRM in Real Time* ...

"*CRM in Real Time* is a must for any company, nonprofit, or government agency that wants to ensure the success of its CRM initiative."

—Terry Delongchamp
CIO/Director IT Systems
Sigma Financial Corporation

"*CRM In Real Time* gets to the heart of what a successful CRM implementation is all about—people, process, and technology—and makes the powerful case for doing CRM in real time. You can save hundreds of hours and thousands of dollars by reading this book before taking on a CRM initiative."

—Bob McLaughlin
Senior VP (retired)
McGraw-Hill

"In *CRM in Real Time,* industry leader Barton Goldenberg shares his proven recipe for success."

—Michael E. Shelly
VP Business Technology Management
Raymond James Financial Services, Inc.

"*CRM in Real Time* provides an inside look at how your organization can achieve meaningful ROI on its current and future CRM investment."

—John Caputo, President
Maximizer Software Inc.

"Barton Goldenberg shares his proven CRM Roadmap and his analysis of CRM in an always-on digital ecosystem. *CRM in Real Time* is a winner!"

—Tim Bajarin, President
Creative Strategies, Inc.

CRM
in Real Time

Empowering Customer Relationships

Barton J. Goldenberg

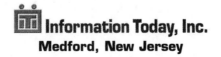

Information Today, Inc.
Medford, New Jersey

First Printing, 2008

CRM in Real Time: Empowering Customer Relationships

Copyright © 2008 by Barton J. Goldenberg

Library of Congress Cataloging-in-Publication Data

Goldenberg, Barton J.
  CRM in real time : empowering customer relationships / Barton J. Goldenberg.
    p. cm.
  Includes index.
  ISBN 978-0-910965-80-4
  1. Customer relations--Management. 2. Customer realtions. I. Title.
  HF5415.5.G652 2008
  658.8'12--dc22

                                                          2008005276

Printed and bound in the United States of America

President and CEO: Thomas H. Hogan, Sr.
Editor-in-Chief and Publisher: John B. Bryans
Managing Editor: Amy M. Reeve
Project Editor: Barbara Brynko
VP Graphics and Production: M. Heide Dengler
Book Designer: Kara Mia Jalkowski
Cover Designer: Laura Hegyi
Proofreader: Dorothy Pike
Indexer: Beth Palmer

www.infotoday.com

Dedication

CRM in Real Time: Empowering Customer Relationships is dedicated to my father. Thanks for the inspiration you provided me throughout life. May you forever rest in peace.

Contents

Preface

Welcome to *CRM in Real Time: Empowering Customer Relationships.*

During the past 23 years of my career, I have worked with and helped set up more than 400 enterprise-class customer relationship management (CRM) systems.

In this book, I have shared some of the lessons that I've learned in the process. In addition, I have focused on the important trend of CRM as it moves toward the Real-Time Enterprise (the process of interconnecting a company's entire operations via internal and Internet applications along with mobile and wireless devices so all information can be shared in real time). And, as the title implies, the book addresses "CRM in Real Time" as the new differentiator in empowering customer relationships.

CRM in Real Time allows your organization to function like a 24-hour nerve center, instantly alerting individuals to changes in customer demand, competitive analysis, inventory, availability of supplies, and profitability. Today's always-on and always-connected digital customer or client is more than ever before relying on a mobile/wireless world with the Internet as its backbone. With technology at the forefront, it is important to remember the roles of people, process, and technology in a successful CRM initiative.

This book offers the following features and topics:

- A definition of CRM and CRM in Real Time with the Real-Time Enterprise (RTE)

- A description of the people, process, and technology issues that impact CRM

- How-to information for creating your CRM strategy, putting together your CRM value proposition and business case, writing your CRM system specification document, selecting your CRM software vendor, and addressing CRM security risks

- A focus on significant topics such as data integrity, the role of ebusiness, emarketing, eservice, knowledge management, international CRM issues, and the increasing use of CRM in government agencies

- A discussion of the increasing movement of CRM toward Real-Time Enterprise, including a 10-step process for its creation

- A selected listing of top CRM software solutions—all ISM, Inc. award winners

If you are thinking about buying a CRM software package, I invite you to visit the ISM Web site (www.ismguide.com) where we feature extensive, comparative reviews of our CRM award winners beyond what can be practically reproduced in this or any other book. Each of the featured software solutions is evaluated against 217 business functions, technical features, implementation features, real-time criteria, and user-friendliness/support criteria.

Those who have read my previous book, *CRM Automation*, may recognize some similarities in this new effort. In fact, *CRM in Real Time* has been built on the core concepts presented in *CRM Automation*, but these concepts have only laid the foundation for the new work. *CRM in Real Time* has been updated extensively with all-new coverage of such topics as Real-Time Enterprise, CRM user adoption, and CRM in government.

I trust that the readers who are returning for another look at CRM will find new and useful information in this book and pick up where *CRM Automation* left off. Good luck in your CRM efforts.

—Barton J. Goldenberg

Introduction

In my spare time, I like to sail. You may wonder what sailing has to do with customer relationship management (CRM), but I've found definite similarities between the two. The basic precepts of sailing actually reflect my business philosophy: Experience, preparation, and teamwork will keep you on course.

The way in which corporations and organizations deal with customers has changed dramatically since 2002 when I wrote my first book, *CRM Automation*. After spending more than two decades as a consultant, I've watched people, process, and technology in CRM evolve and mature. Industries have grown more sophisticated, companies have expanded globally, technology has become faster and more efficient, and people need information and answers in real time on desktops or via mobile services. And people are using today's tools and technology in record numbers. In 2006, cell phone sales exceeded 1 billion; in 2007, Apple's iPod sales surpassed 100 million units. Clearly, companies today are dealing with customers who are always on and always connected.

Enterprises are learning how to be more responsive to their customers. Consider the following three examples in which technology has enhanced business processes and ultimately improved customer service:

- Wal-Mart and the U.S. Department of Defense mandated that all suppliers add RFID (radio frequency identification) tags to boxes in 2006 to better manage product delivery and distribution. Since RFID tags provide more information than traditional bar codes, the contents of a box or pallet can be easily identified by color, size, style, etc., which improved inventory information, provided better tracking and asset management, and enhanced customer service and responsiveness.

- Cleveland-based KeyCorp, one of the nation's largest bank-based financial services companies with assets of about $92 billion, used its CRM in real time to help the bank achieve its strategic push to integrate financial services nationwide and enable customers to fulfill financial services in real time. In fact, KeyCorp can provide new bank products/functionality 12 to 18 months sooner than most of its competitors and achieve higher Internet

banking penetration into retail banking clients than other financial services companies.

- PepsiCo is now incorporating wireless technologies and next-
generation universal application network (UAN) architectures to
deliver information in real time. UAN, an XML-based Web services architecture, is designed to let software developers write
code so that if one element changes in inventory, that element is
changed across all the enterprise's financial, inventory, distribution, manufacturing, and sales systems.

These three examples demonstrate the ways that leading enterprises in
a range of industry sectors keep on the cutting-edge of technology and
deliver key services in real time. Why have global industry leaders committed millions of dollars to build real-time enterprise (RTE) capabilities?
The RTE value proposition rests on reduced costs, operational excellence,
enhanced productivity, better decision making, customer delight and loyalty, and sustainable competitive leadership.

And keeping enterprises in step with customer reliance on real-time
interaction is part of my mission as a strategic advisor to organizations
that are planning and implementing CRM initiatives. As founder and president of ISM, Inc., I have been guiding companies, nonprofits, and government agencies through the entire CRM process since 1985. When
companies turn to us for help, my team starts with an executive briefing,
then creates a customized CRM strategy and implementation road map,
and finishes by implementing engagement management services.

ISM's Software Laboratory, created in 1990, provides independent and
bias-free reviews of CRM and real-time CRM software, including the
award-winning Top 15 CRM and Real-Time CRM software reviews. These
in-depth analyses of CRM software and the latest business and technology
trends ensure that clients get the right solution based on their unique
needs. Each software program that my firm tests is objectively rated
according to 217 selection criteria, including 103 business functions, 52
technical features, 36 implementation capabilities, 9 real-time criteria,
and 17 user-support features.

CRM in Real Time: Empowering Customer Relationships offers readers
a savvy guide to bridging yesterday's technology with today's innovations
to meet tomorrow's challenges. This book, which picks up where *CRM*

Automation left off, is divided into six parts, each of which tackles CRM in real-time issues from different angles.

Part 1 starts off with an introduction to CRM and lays the foundation for finding the right mix of people, process, and technology. Part 2 moves on to the people issues, focusing on what people need to know about securing executive support, user adoption, and the value of training, communications, customer feedback, and strategic planning. Part 3 deals with process issues to establish order with business process, data integrity, and ebusiness. Part 4 concentrates on the technology issues: business application trends, key technology innovations, and the wireless world, including advice on selecting software for CRM initiatives. Part 5 explains the critical issues that are involved in building a solid CRM system, from the 10 steps to effective implementation and creating a business case to outsourcing and security risks. And finally, Part 6 focuses on the future, with brief chapters on selected issues including 10 steps to creating an RTE to Web 2.0 and the digital client. At the end of the book, a collection of appendixes offers examples of the sales process, process flow, a CRM system RFP, software solutions, service providers, and even a glossary of terms.

Today, it is no longer an option to optimize your customer relationships. Given the more knowledgeable and less loyal customer base, particularly the Net generation, no organization can risk securing anything less than outstanding customer relationships. That means having up-to-the-minute customer knowledge and providing support from anywhere anytime—this defines CRM's future with real-time CRM solutions.

In the U.S., there are currently 75 million Generation Y (less than 23 years old) digital clients and 750 million worldwide; by the year 2015, Gen Yers will account for 45 percent of the world's population. Members of Gen Y have known only digital technology their entire lives and expect always-on, always-connected access to the Internet in their digital devices; they are and will continue to become our digital clients long into the future.

For this book, I have tried to show why CRM in real time is the key to the future success of all organizations. But like sailing, sometimes it's not just working together that wins the race—it's working together the right way.

PART 1

An
Introduction
to CRM

Chapter 1

A CRM Primer

Customer Relationship Management (CRM) is a phrase that was coined in the mid-1990s and heavily promoted at the end of that decade. Providing a concise definition of CRM is challenging due to its continuing rapid evolution, but here is a place to start:

> Customer Relationship Management (CRM) is a business approach that integrates people, process, and technology to maximize relationships with customers. CRM increasingly leverages the Internet to provide seamless coordination among all customer-facing functions.

As the Internet and mobile and wireless technologies take CRM into real time, organizations can function like a 24-hour nerve center, instantly alerting individuals to changes in customer demand, competitive analysis, inventory, availability of supplies, and profitability. Add to this the new digital customer or client who uses social networking and blogs to "talk" about your company and products, and you have the environment for a new wave of CRM: the Real-Time Enterprise (RTE).

RTE is the process of interconnecting a company's entire operations via internal and Internet applications, along with mobile and wireless devices, to enable all information—and communications—to be shared in real time.

First, let's take a closer look at CRM. There are three primary reasons why organizations choose to automate their sales, marketing, and customer service functions in a CRM system:

- **High cost of direct sales** – Today, the average cost of an onsite sales call is about $379 (according to a 2006 Hoover's study), and the costs of direct selling (from a sales organization to a customer) continue to rise. CRM can help increase sales force productivity while containing or decreasing rising sales costs.

- **Increased global competition** – Business dealings today reach a global marketplace. To compete on a local or foreign level, effective market intelligence is often critical. CRM can help companies monitor and track market developments more effectively.

- **Need for information** – Sales, marketing, and customer service/support are information-intensive activities. Success depends on two key components: implementing an effective marketing mix strategy (product, place, price, and promotion) and understanding/addressing the marketing mix strategy of your competitors. CRM can help collect, compile, and disseminate needed information about the market, especially for your customers.

Key CRM Benefits

The systematic use of CRM applications has been well-established to provide many benefits to organizations that want to automate their sales, marketing, and customer service functions. The most compelling benefits of a successful CRM implementation include the following examples:

- **Better sales/marketing information** – Customer names, customer background, customer needs, and competitive positioning are some of the data types collected as a result of implementing a CRM system.

- **Improved productivity** – Effectively targeting market identification, reducing the number of cold leads, providing accurate on-the-spot quotations, accessing inventory availability quickly, and entering orders directly from the field help to shorten the sales cycle.

- **Enhanced customer care** – More time is available to spend with customers due to a sales department's reduced administrative workload, an ability to monitor customer service levels, and the ability to highlight existing or potential customer service problems and react more quickly to customer needs.

Improved customer retention/loyalty has become an increasingly important objective for most organizations, and an area that is directly related to the benefits of CRM previously discussed. According to Antony Young and Lucy Aitken, authors of *Profitable Marketing Communications: A Guide to Marketing Return on Investments*, corporations in the U.S. lose about one-half of their customers during a five-year period. It has been shown that the longer a customer is retained, the greater the profitability for the retained customer. An effective CRM system will help a company retain more customers over time.

For those who like hard numbers, ISM, Inc. and the Insight Technology Group have conducted studies of CRM implementations, confirming that the following levels of benefit can be achieved:

- **A minimum 10 percent per annum increase in gross sales revenue per sales representative during the first three years of the system** – This gain occurs because field personnel improve their efficiency (more "batting time" to call on customers and implement strategy) and their effectiveness (improved quality of their sales calls in that field because personnel are more knowledgeable about their customers).

- **A minimum 5 percent decrease in general and administrative cost of sales during the first three years** – This takes place because field personnel (and the company) have no need to send costly literature and information in a shotgun approach to existing and potential customers. Instead, field personnel (and the company) can be selective about sending specific promotional materials to customers.

- **A minimum 5 percent increase in win rates for forecasted sales during the first three years** – This gain results when sales organizations select their opportunities more carefully, drop out of potentially bad opportunities earlier, and concentrate on those opportunities with a high likelihood of closure.

- **A minimum 1 percent margin improvement in the value of a deal over the system's lifetime** – This gain is realized since sales personnel are working closely with a carefully selected group of customers who place as much emphasis on value selling as on discounts, and sales organizations tend to discount less frequently.

- **A minimum 5 percent improvement in the quality rating provided by customers** – This gain is a result of having happier customers who are getting the information they need more quickly, who are receiving better service, and who are building on the relationship marketing approach that sales personnel are now able to offer.

Before deciding whether CRM is right for your organization, you should review all the potential benefits of CRM in detail. From my experience helping companies to automate customer-facing functions in a CRM system, I have learned that senior management needs detailed evidence of measurable benefits to justify what may grow into a large capital investment, plus the investment in time, resources, and staff.

But there is good news: A growing number of tangible and intangible benefits associated with CRM are available, and there are specific ways to measure them. For each of the following measurements of CRM benefits, we have assumed that your company has similar and valid measurement information available today in some format or will be available prior to the start of your CRM project.

Tangible Benefits

I define tangible benefits as those that can be measured in hard numbers. These include increases in the following benefits:

- **Time spent by sales personnel with existing customers** – Consider measuring the number of service calls made per day by sales personnel or the number of hours spent by sales personnel in their interactions with existing customers.

- **The number of new customer prospects pursued by sales representatives** – While most sales representatives like to call on existing customers with whom they have an ongoing relationship, new customers are the key to future growth. Consider measuring the number of new prospects versus existing customers contacted by the sales representative per day, per week, per month, or per quarter.

- **Time spent by sales managers in contacting customers and working with sales representatives on customer issues** – Coaching sales personnel is critical, but managers never seem to have enough time to do it. Consider measuring the number of hours per day that sales managers spend in contact with customers and prospects, and with sales representatives discussing customer issues.

- **Customer service efficiency** – Customer service may be the key differentiator between those companies that lead and those companies that wonder what happened. Consider measuring the turnaround time for customer service issues as well as the number of customer service errors made as a result of misinformation.

- **Timeliness of follow-up correspondence to customers/prospects** – Consider measuring the number of days between the date the customer/prospect was contacted and the date that the customer/prospect follow-up information is sent.

- **Higher close ratios** – CRM helps move prospects efficiently through the sales pipeline. Consider measuring the lift in close ratios that result from CRM tools and techniques.

- **Revenue per month for each sales representative** – This important CRM benefit depends on careful management to ensure that time is saved as a result of automation of the organization's sales, marketing, and customer service functions used productively to deliver more sales. Consider measuring the increase in base revenue generated per month per sales representative.

- **Overall business results** – The sales manager of one company I worked with set up a competition between sales personnel based on their use of the CRM system. The results were overwhelming: Healthy rivalry between personnel led to a significant increase in overall business results (as well as a seven-day cruise for the winning salesperson and his or her spouse). Consider measuring the percent of dollar increase over the budget for the entire sales team each month.

- **Frequency that your company's name is in front of your customers and prospects** – The out-of-sight, out-of-mind syndrome can be quite harmful to your sales efforts. Consider measuring the number of correspondence items sent to customers and prospects by sales and marketing personnel.

- **Customer satisfaction** – Consider using a customer satisfaction survey rating and displaying these ratings in a location for all personnel to review.

- **Better communications within your company** – As more staff spend time in the field with customers and prospects, the need to secure effective communications among personnel continues to grow. Consider measuring the time spent giving and getting information between the field and regional or headquarters offices.

- **Improved "close" rates** – For the percentage of business orders closed, consider measuring the "close" rates of sales reps before and after the implementation of a CRM system.

- **Reduction in "close" time** – For the speed of bringing new business orders to a close, consider measuring the "close" time of sales reps for new business orders before and after the implementation of a CRM system.

Intangible Benefits

I define intangible benefits as those measured using "soft" criteria. Management may prefer the hard numbers, but top-level executives can also appreciate such soft criteria benefits when they are effectively presented. Intangible benefits include the following:

- **Overall smoother functioning within your company** – It can be shocking to learn how much time sales personnel spend on unnecessary administrative matters, or the amount of time a new salesperson spends getting up to speed in a new territory. Consider measuring the time that is spent looking for needed information versus the time that is spent using information and actually doing the job.

- **Increased employee motivation and satisfaction** – This may be difficult to measure, but consider measuring feedback from those employees who use CRM. An alternative is measuring employee-turnover rate for those personnel who use the CRM system.

- **Better trained and more skillful sales, marketing, and customer service personnel** – CRM can provide an excellent training ground for personnel to spend time learning facts and figures about products and services. Consider measuring the ability of sales personnel to access needed facts and figures quickly, including the implementation of required sales and marketing business procedures.

- **Improved use of mobile access devices** – This benefit is important since each of us has a different technological assimilation learning curve that impacts our future use of equipment and technology. Consider measuring the comfort level of field personnel who use mobile devices over time.

- **More up-to-date information and easier access to it** – Up-to-date information and easy access are subjective measurements made by end users. Consider measuring the timeliness of needed information and the ease of accessing this information based on end-user standards.

- **Improved responsiveness to customer and prospect requests** – A sales and marketing manager at a domestic pipe manufacturer used the firm's CRM automation system to "staple" himself to each customer request until it was resolved. Consider measuring the time it takes to respond completely to a customer or prospect request, which may be tied in with customer service.

- **Improved image of your company** – Effectively managing relationships with your customers can play a leading role in building your company's image in the eyes of your customers. Consider measuring the reaction of existing and future buyers to your sales and marketing professionalism.

- **The ability to differentiate your company from the competition** – Many studies have tried to measure the competitive advantage resulting from implementing a CRM system. Consider measuring increased customer loyalty as well as customer perception of your company versus the competition.

- **Support for organizational change(s) within your firm** – I once worked with an airline that had significantly downsized its organization and needed increased support for the remaining sales and marketing personnel. To determine this potential benefit of CRM, consider measuring time spent training new sales and marketing personnel.

- **Improved understanding and better control over expenses** – CRM can assist in this effort, assuming sales, marketing, and customer care expenses are tagged to individual sales personnel and/or accounts. Consider measuring expenses per sales and marketing person and/or per account.

Based on the number of tangible and intangible benefits, the rewards of implementing a CRM system are great. I recall a case where my firm conducted an audit of sales and marketing for a copy machine manufacturer that was designed to measure the impact and potential of a CRM system on sales force productivity.

The audit determined that automating CRM-related activities such as lead tracking, time scheduling, and account profiling resulted in saving an average of one hour per day per salesperson. This equated to an additional 26 days of work time per year for each sales representative. Similar measurements for customer service representatives and top management reflected savings of 30 minutes and 20 minutes per day, respectively.

But saving time isn't the only reward. Generating proposals—an arduous task for sales and marketing departments—becomes far more user-friendly because many proposal components, such as standard proposal paragraphs, online pricing information, and customer information (names, addresses, discounts, etc.) can be automatically incorporated through the CRM system.

The copier manufacturer I mentioned before also incorporated an external, third-party prospect database into its CRM system and supplemented this database with a data entry function that permitted users to enter new prospects from cold calls, telemarketing, and trade shows. The end result was an overall increase of prospects, and many of them were quality prospects that could be sorted and assigned according to predefined criteria.

Perhaps the most dramatic impact of this particular CRM automation project was a 14 percent increase in sales force productivity by the end of the first year of operation, which translated into a healthy bottom-line boost as a result of careful management.

By identifying and analyzing the tangible and intangible benefits of automating your CRM system, your organization will be in a position to determine whether it is the right choice, and you will be better prepared to provide senior management with the requisite business justification.

Challenges to CRM Success

CRM is the No. 1 software application worldwide in terms of software license revenues. In 2006, the global CRM industry (software and services) generated more than $31 billion. While CRM growth slowed to 5 percent in 2004, the industry has since rebounded to an annual 10 percent average growth rate, which is expected to continue through 2010. Factors such as an increased focus toward the growing small- to mid-sized CRM market, increased CRM offerings via the software as a service (SaaS) model, and an increased number of mobile CRM offerings have led to the recovery of the CRM marketplace.

Making sense of today's CRM marketplace has become difficult with an increased emphasis on customer-facing business processes, the growing change in the management impact of CRM, along with all the new software players, new business functional modules, and the new and complex technology alternatives. It's difficult even for companies like ISM, Inc. that have been actively involved in the CRM industry since the mid-1980s.

I continually stress the importance of people, process, and technology integration for a successful CRM initiative. In the past, a disproportionate emphasis on the technology component often proved detrimental to the overall success of the project. Having learned this important lesson, I see organizations face other challenges as they strive to successfully implement a CRM system. Among the most common challenges with CRM are the following:

- **Lack of a sales, marketing, and customer service strategy** – Firms lacking a strategy that incorporates sales, marketing, and customer service often are unable to identify or prioritize areas that could benefit from CRM solutions. Successful CRM initiatives can only be realized when a strategy is in place.

- **Lack of corporate commitment** – CRM requires a corporate commitment from the top. Often this commitment is missing. Successful CRM initiatives require the involvement of sales and marketing personnel, information systems personnel, and external information sources.

- **Internal politics** – Information is power, and key individuals within the firms are often not prepared to share their own information with their colleagues. Successful CRM initiatives require sharing information across the organization; little room exists for those who tend to create and protect their own information power.

- **Lack of proper training** – While the majority of today's managers are computer literate and today's software is increasingly simple to use, proper training of sales and marketing personnel still remains an essential part of CRM success. According to ISM research, those firms that successfully automate sales and marketing functions have claimed that for each $1 spent on computer hardware and software, they have spent between $3 and $15 on training over the life of the project. Training requires a serious commitment within the firm.

- **Lack of know-how** – Firms often may not have the required knowledge to automate their sales, marketing, and customer service functions through a CRM system. In such cases, the use of outside expertise has proven to be a cost-effective way for the firm to learn about CRM.

- **Resistance by system users** – This is one of the most difficult problems associated with CRM initiatives. Those firms that have successfully applied CRM have learned the importance of creating a two-way flow of valuable information between corporate and sales personnel.

Those organizations that have successfully applied CRM have found that all of these challenges can be resolved, and the benefits far outweigh the challenges, making the extra effort worth the time and expense.

Key CRM Components

CRM implementations generally contain up to 11 components. Each component incorporates subcomponents, with each subcomponent equating to specific software modules offered by CRM software vendors.

Ultimately, a CRM automation system is likely to consist of one or more of these components, depending on the organization's prioritized CRM business functional needs. Your CRM system is likely to grow over time to include additional components, including new ones that will emerge as the CRM industry continues to innovate.

One word of caution: It would be unreasonable to expect any initial CRM automation system to include all 11 components since this would be the equivalent of trying to swallow an entire elephant at one time. As you review the following descriptions of the components, ask yourself which ones seem to make the most sense for your company's CRM initiative, and consider the priority order in which you might incorporate them. Here are the following components:

1. Time management

2. Sales/sales management

3. Telemarketing/telesales

4. Customer contact center

5. emarketing

6. Business analytics (executive information)

7. Field service support

8. ebusiness

9. Supply-chain management

10. Multimodal access

11. Data-sharing tools

1. Time Management

This component includes single user and group calendar/scheduling as well as email. Microsoft (MS) Outlook and Lotus Notes have become the calendar/scheduling standards within the CRM software industry. Moreover, bi-directional integration with MS Outlook is also becoming a de facto standard; users can enter a date-specific activity or a contact from within MS-Outlook, and the activity or date is automatically added to the CRM software application and vice versa. In addition to single user and group calendar/scheduling, the time management component also includes the creation and management of task lists as well as email.

2. Sales/Sales Management

This includes the management of contact profiles and history, the management of account information including activities, and order entry. Increasingly, this category includes proposal generators, which permit sales personnel to easily and quickly create a comprehensive and attractive proposal drawing on boilerplate templates, as well as "configurators" that let sales personnel (and increasingly customers) easily and quickly configure products and services based on specific customer needs. Pipeline analysis (forecasting and sales-cycle analysis), sales metrics (win and loss rates), territory alignment and assignment, and roll-up/drill-down reporting functionality are also important considerations.

3. Telemarketing/Telesales

This component includes classical functionality such as call-list assembly, auto-dialing, scripting, call tracking, and order taking. While traditionally this has been an outbound function, telemarketing/telesales handles inbound calls more frequently.

4. Customer Contact Center

Customer service functions, such as incident assignment/escalation/tracking/reporting, problem management/resolution, order management/promising, and warranty/contract management, are included here. Increasingly, customer service and support software includes a Web-based, self-service capability that customers can easily access using a browser. Improvements in customer self-service and support have been significantly enhanced by the use of knowledge management engines, along with the ability to apply the principles of one-to-one customer service. Assisted (interactive chat and Web browsing) and self-service options coincide in the customer contact center environment.

5. emarketing

Marketing continues to receive considerable attention within the CRM software industry. Increased attention continues to be given to Web-centric encyclopedias and knowledge management, to market segmentation complemented by comprehensive campaign management life cycle tools, to lead generation/enhancement/tracking, and increasingly to partner relationship management (offering information links within the differing distribution channel layers). emarketing facilitates one-to-one, permission-based marketing efforts. These marketing subcomponents often depend on customer data received from Web sites, and/or from a data warehouse enhanced by tools such as data-mining engines. Another push for marketing applications results from the 2003 Do Not Call List, which has resulted in companies using more permission-based marketing applications.

6. Business Analytics (Executive Information)

Business analytics include extensive and easy-to-use reporting capabilities. Fixed and ad hoc reports are the norm. To ensure the highest quality of reporting functionality, many CRM software vendors are opting to integrate with leading third-party report writing tools (Crystal Reports, Actuate), which provide comprehensive tools for report writing and graphics. More CRM software vendors are also offering executive dashboards and personalized portals from vendors such as Cognos to help enhance the business intelligence (executive information) component within a CRM system.

7. Field Service Support

Although field service support has not received a great deal of attention in the past, more CRM software vendors acknowledge that this is a large and growing market segment. The field service support component includes work-order dispatching, part order/reservation, preventative maintenance schedules, and real-time information transfer via mobile technologies.

8. ebusiness

This ebusiness component, which is primarily focused on functionality to exchange products/services via the Web, has become more important given the growth of Web-based business-to-business (B2B) and business-to-consumer (B2C) ecommerce applications. It is unlikely that CRM automation software will include every ecommerce component. What has become clear, however, is that CRM software will add a Web-based, front-end interface into commercially available third-party ecommerce engines, which include shopping carts and storefront applications. This front-end interface will support more complex B2B and B2C ebusiness applications that leverage new technological advances in intelligence routing/click stream monitoring, content management/personalization, customer self-service, and cross-selling/up-selling.

9. Supply-Chain Management

As with the ebusiness component, few CRM software packages will offer comprehensive supply-chain management functionality. Rather, CRM software will integrate seamlessly with leading supply-chain management packages such as Teradata, JDA Software, or Commerce Events. This means that companies will have access to the latest eprocurement, logistics management, and B2B exchange applications.

10. Multimodal Access

Customers can now reach your company in a variety of ways: via mail, phone (including the ability to leave messages), fax, email (even sending attachments), and the Web (including chat forums and social networking). This means that your CRM system must support multiple modes of access from your customers, while simultaneously giving the impression that you maintain one holistic view of the customer at all times, regardless of which mode or modes that a customer uses.

11. Data-Sharing Tools

Sales, customer service, and even customers want to know the status of an order and whether a payment has been received. Production line and inventory managers want to know the latest sales forecast. To answer these needs, CRM software vendors opt to build native Enterprise Resource Planning (ERP) hooks into their software, or to seamlessly integrate with ERP systems via third-party "hook" software from companies including IBM and webMethods. Data synchronization, which is important for data sharing, includes mobile data synchronization from multiple field devices (increasingly wireless), as well as enterprise synchronization with multiple databases/application servers.

Many CRM software vendors have built their own data synchronization functionality, although we also see integration with third-party synchronization engines such as Nokia's Intellisync. Unfortunately, no data synchronization standards exist within the CRM industry. Determining the quality of a CRM software vendor's synchronization engine as well as confirming application scalability claims is too often the onus of the buyer. Fortunately, data synchronization testing facilities can now test the scalability of a CRM software vendor's product (Hewlett-Packard's Compaq, Microsoft): Be sure to ask your CRM software vendor to show you its scalability test results if this is germane to your CRM implementation.

Migrating to Web-Based CRM

In the dynamics of the current CRM marketplace, client-server technology is losing to Web-based ecustomer CRM initiatives.

Client-server technology largely supports employee-facing CRM systems aimed at helping internal sales, marketing, and customer service personnel, while the newer ecustomer technologies support customer-facing CRM systems in which customers use Web browsers to access company-specific information and services.

These incongruent technologies are likely to co-exist over the next five years largely because client-server architectures have a large installed client base that has seen the benefits of CRM firsthand. Meanwhile, CRM client-server vendors are adopting a more Web-based, ecustomer centric approach. While many of their CRM automation software packages may not be Web-based from the ground up, they are becoming Web-compatible in order to remain palatable to a large installed user base. Some of these vendors (Onyx, for one) have rewritten their software to be entirely Web-based. For the most part, the installed base trusts its CRM client-server vendors and will work with them as they move toward a Web-based, ecustomer-centric approach. This trust keeps the client-server lifecycle alive despite its increasingly dated outlook.

Web-based, ecustomer CRM vendors are now building a customer base of their own. These vendors offer very impressive software. In fact, Web-based software arguably offers the precise functionality and features—including customer self-service, click-stream analysis, and content management—that today's customers want. This is why business is booming for suppliers such as Salesforce.com, NetSuite, BroadVision, KANA, Infor CRM Epiphany, and Vignette, all of which are aggressively promoting this new and exciting class of CRM automation software.

It's likely that both approaches will co-exist for at least five years, at which point the client-server life cycle will ultimately give way to Web-based, ecustomer solutions. As succeeding generations of Web-using customers grow to maturity, the CRM industry's movement toward a 100 percent Web-based world is unstoppable.

Getting to CRM Success

The customers I have worked with over the years claim a success rate for their CRM initiatives that is well above 70 percent today, and this level of success is confirmed by a number of recent studies by InfoTrends, CRMGuru.com, and other analysts. It has become clear that when properly implemented, CRM delivers bountiful and measurable benefits.

A Mini Case Study

One leading American telecommunications manufacturer decided to implement a global CRM initiative for about 4,500 employees worldwide. When the project was completed, the vice president of sales and marketing (the sponsor of the CRM initiative) was asked whether the initiative was a success. He put his thumb up and said, "Yes," and explained that he now had a comprehensive customer profile of his key accounts that was available to customer-facing personnel. When the firm's CIO was asked the same question, he put his thumb down and said, "No." He explained that the CRM system was supposed to have integrated several dozen internal legacy and external information sources and that this had not happened due to integration complexity.

In the majority of implementations that I've been involved with, the client company has set clear and measurable baselines and objective metrics prior to implementation, then used these metrics to accurately gauge the success or failure of the system. This requires discipline, but, according to management guru Peter Drucker, "If you can't measure it, you can't manage it."

Making Your Case

A CRM business case, including a strong value proposition, is the most appropriate vehicle to drive CRM success. An effective CRM business case will do the following three steps:

1. Set baseline metrics for business functions that will be automated (how much time per week a sales rep spends creating difficult reports, and the number of customer service calls that are successfully resolved during the initial customer call).

2. Set objective metrics or "success criteria" for each of the proposed business functional areas that will be impacted by the system (reps will save X hours per week by not having to create difficult reports since the system will automatically deliver needed reports to the rep; the resolution of customer service issues during the initial call will increase by X percent because the system provides customer service personnel with needed information at the touch of a button).

3. Measure and report on the accomplishment of each objective on a regular basis (preferably quarterly and not less than every six months) to the top management team responsible for the ultimate success of the CRM initiative.

While this simple three-step approach seems logical, it's surprising how few companies get this measurement right as part of their CRM initiative, or how few companies create a CRM business case that incorporates these measurements along with return on investment (ROI) information.

The industry weathered an economic slowdown in the early part of this decade and is now migrating from client-server architectures to Web-based, ecustomer offerings. New players will enter the industry; more consolidations will undoubtedly follow. More companies will set and measure CRM-related metrics in support of their CRM business cases.

If you feel that Chapter 1 has created a sound argument for implementing a CRM system, read on. In the chapters that follow, I will cover topics ranging from how to create a CRM implementation blueprint to a description of the latest business, technical, and CRM industry trends—including the move to a real-time, Web-based environment. This will provide insight into how companies have achieved their specific goals via the CRM value proposition and prepare you to drive your own successful CRM initiative and, most importantly, assist you with the adoption of RTE processes and technology within your organization.

Chapter 2

CRM: The Right Mix of People, Process, and Technology

The success of any CRM implementation relies on the seamless integration of three crucial components: the people, process, and technology used to "touch the customer" from any point in an organization.

This critical mix must be adjusted to help customers no matter where, when, or how they communicate with the organization. While each of these components presents its own set of challenges, how well a business is able to integrate all three is paramount to successfully implementing CRM in real time.

Of the three, the "people" component (company staff) can present the greatest challenge given the sensitivity of users to change. CRM systems, which support and automate the customer processes, almost always require changes in the way users do their day-to-day jobs. Users who do not understand the point of these changes, who have not participated in forming them, or who have not been given a solid background and training will understandably be resistant. Gaining user support early on will be an important factor in the ultimate success of your CRM initiative, so be sure to address the people issues from the outset.

My firm considers the "process" component of CRM to be the most delicate of the issues because the inappropriate use of automation will only speed up errant processes. While many organizations have well-established customer-facing business processes (i.e., those processes that directly interface with the customer during the purchase, payment, and usage of the company's products and services), a CRM system may require tweeking or overhauling their processes.

Companies pursuing a CRM initiative often try to correct their customer-facing process deficiencies not by agreeing internally on how users would like a process to be done, but rather by purchasing CRM software that contains one or more business processes that have been pre-built by the CRM vendor and then forcing the "not-built-here" process on system users. This can be dangerous.

All too often, the "technology" component of a CRM initiative is given a disproportionate emphasis, sometimes to the detriment of the overall project. (Of course, a hyper-focus on technology is somewhat understandable given the ever-growing number of innovative technology solutions.) There are two critical concerns related to your CRM initiative: the need to deal with software vendors and the challenge of staying on top of technology trends. On the upside, the Internet, which has revolutionized company-customer relationships, is an extremely useful technological tool (consider it the primary one) for achieving your CRM goals.

Proactively managing and integrating the people, process, and technology components of a CRM initiative will help you ensure "the mix is right" through all phases of the project. The following list provides a generic model for understanding how the people, process, and technology mix will change for key CRM implementation activities. To understand how the component mix applies to each, check out the following:

Key CRM implementation activities	Most relevant components
Determining business requirements	People and some process
Setting up the project management team	People and some process
Integrating legacy and other needed systems	Technology
Customizing the CRM software	People, process, and technology
CRM system pilot	People and technology
CRM system roll-out	People and technology
CRM system support	People and some process
Growing your CRM system	People, process, and technology

Let's look at a few of the CRM implementation activities in this list to better understand the dynamics of getting the mix right for your business. First, to determine business requirements, you should apply a structured process to ensure that user needs are properly identified and prioritized. But most of the work in determining business requirements will involve people issues, namely, working with your potential users to think through their existing and future needs and to help manage their expectations as to how your CRM initiative is likely to impact those needs. Technology plays a minor role at best in determining business requirements.

Similarly, the people component plays a critical role when you are assembling your CRM project management team; for instance, you will need to agree on who will be responsible for which CRM implementation activities. In determining the optimal way to set up the project management team and subteams, the business process for CRM is also important. Again, technology will have a limited role here.

Yet, when the company is ready to begin integrating legacy and other needed systems, technology becomes critical. The selection of an appropriate Enterprise Application Architecture (EAA) and agreement on appropriate frameworks or the use of middleware toolsets, to name just a couple of technical considerations, will greatly impact the effectiveness and efficiency of systems integration. People may insist that their systems need to be integrated first (and there should be a process for determining which systems to integrate and in which order), but overall, technology drives this activity.

As a final example, when performing CRM software customization, all three components play critical roles. People are critical for ultimately judging how well the customizations meet their needs as well as for commenting on how the workflow impacts the overall user friendliness of the system. Process is important for driving workflow development (which, in turn, gets built by technology). Technology is key for developing, modifying, and deleting screens and for navigating between screens. Clearly, all three components have their places—it's all about getting the mix right.

CRM on a Healthy Track

The following five key trends are behind the current strong growth of the CRM industry:

1. Most companies that purchase and apply CRM understand that an effective mix of people (50 percent), process (30 percent), and technology (20 percent) is the key driver of successful CRM implementations. These companies are achieving success by putting customer-facing processes in order, then enticing personnel (internal, partners, customers) to buy into the enhanced processes, and, finally, by applying CRM technology in support of these enhanced processes.

2. Almost all companies that have undertaken a CRM initiative can now write a solid CRM Business Case in support of their initiative, including a strong value proposition based on enhanced

productivity, lower costs, superior employee morale, better customer knowledge, increased customer satisfaction, improved customer loyalty and retention, or some combination of these factors. Executives and top management teams understand it's not a technology game. They know now that they must incorporate structure and measurement. They're demanding business cases that deliver strong metrics. By setting baseline metrics (where we are today) and target metrics (where we intend to be tomorrow), and measuring these goals on a quarterly basis, companies are proving the value of CRM.

3. Technologies are increasingly driving down costs and rectifying early CRM implementation problems. For example, software based on Microsoft's new .NET platform offers a cost-effective way to integrate CRM applications with other relevant internal (e.g., enterprise resource planning, or ERP, legacy) or external (e.g., supply-chain management, third-party information) applications. Perhaps in response to Microsoft's CRM entrance, mid-market CRM suppliers have developed specialties, especially niches such as manufacturing; this is good news for end users. Meanwhile, better business analytics tools are driving stronger CRM implementations; mobile technologies are enabling cost-effective access to needed information from a variety of devices at any time; and elearning platforms are providing cost-effective, lifelong training at all levels. Furthermore, ecustomer self-service applications are driving down the cost of servicing growing numbers of online customers.

4. The cost of implementations has decreased by as much as 50 percent, based on CRM implementations that ISM has monitored since 2002. Driven by a competitive marketplace, CRM software vendors are increasingly implementing their own software to avoid the risk of CRM failures. Moreover, external implementers are doing a better job of delivering projects on time and on budget. All indications suggest that implementation costs will continue to drop as user-friendly application development toolkits, based on open standards, become the norm.

5. Success is driving success. Increasingly, case studies of successful CRM implementations are being published in trade publications,

through general media, and online. According to CRMGuru.com's "Blueprint for CRM Success," 67 percent of CRM implementations succeed with an average or above-average performance mark as established by the company; this same study demonstrates that once-common failures of CRM are now both predictable and preventable.

What is the reason for all this good news for CRM? Companies are getting the formula for successful implementation right. It has become clear that by following a proven CRM strategy and implementation methodology, companies are steering their way to CRM success.

Within the next five years, we can expect more vendor consolidation along with an increase in vertical market offerings. During this period, ISM forecasts that the CRM industry will achieve a healthy 10 to 15 percent annual revenue growth rate. CRM buyers will have an increasingly rich and varied selection of outstanding software vendor alternatives. The number of successful CRM implementations will rise significantly, and CRM will take the leadership role in driving the emergence of the Real-Time Enterprise (RTE) with CRM in real time.

PART 2

People
Issues

Chapter 3

Understanding the People Component

As I explained in Chapter 2, mastering the people component of any CRM implementation is often the most difficult challenge for any organization, given the sensitivity of users to change. The following are some examples in which the people component derailed or had an adverse impact on CRM initiatives.

Telecom Example

An international telecommunications company launched a global CRM initiative a few years ago that included the formation of a "superuser group" consisting of 12 to 15 representatives from sales, marketing, customer service, ebusiness, and other customer-facing functions. This group, which was formed at the outset of the initiative, was responsible for providing user needs input throughout the implementation.

Senior management had doubts about the company's ability to meet the initiative's deadlines and made the decision not to communicate or actively promote the initiative to potential internal and external users until the implementation neared completion. As with virtually all of the complex initiatives involving people and technology, a number of minor glitches emerged early on. While the glitches were eventually resolved, the company's internal rumor mill elevated them to the level of major problems, even system killers. By the time the company was ready to invite internal and external users for training on the CRM application, nearly half of the users said they knew little about the initiative, and from what little they did know about it, they were not interested in participating. Many staff members declined to accept the training that was offered. The initiative struggled along for four more months, but in the end, the company pulled the plug on the project and absorbed a loss of more than $800,000.

Lesson learned: Launch a full-fledged communications program about your CRM initiative from Day One and ensure that key personnel and users understand how the new system will impact their day-to-day work, and then update them regularly on how the implementation is progressing.

Service Industry Example

A leading service organization launched a global CRM initiative a few years ago and formed a core team consisting of senior managers from technical, business, and training functions. Business users were not involved from the outset because the business manager felt he could speak on their behalf. This turned out to be a mistake. It was evident early on that the business manager was out of touch with the needs of business users and perhaps even saw these users as a threat to his next promotion. He refused to collaborate closely with users and, after a year and an investment of more than $10 million, the organization put the CRM initiative on hold until a reorganization (which included replacing the manager) could take place.

Lesson learned: Don't be afraid to let users drive the system's specifications and implementation.

Publishing Example

An international publishing company established a superuser group to help launch its CRM initiative. This group remained active and engaged throughout the implementation; the group helped to select the CRM software vendor, reviewed software screen customizations, and took on training roles during the system launch in many cases. The company also launched a comprehensive communications program that included issuing a weekly memo that updated potential internal and external users on the status of the initiative, created an intranet site, and scheduled Q&A sessions at key company meetings (including the annual company meeting, regional sales meetings, and customer service get-togethers). When the time came for CRM applications training, an internal argument ensued between users and the training coordinator about which users would get trained first: Almost all users wanted to take part in the first training session. This CRM initiative ended up delivering an average productivity gain of 22 person days per user in the first year alone.

Lesson learned: Get users involved early on and help them to manage their own change.

Chapter 4

Executive Support: The Single Most Important CRM Success Factor

Over the years, my firm has provided CRM strategic advice to dozens of best-in-class organizations in the private, nonprofit, and government sectors. For organizations that have succeeded in their CRM initiatives, executive support stands out as the single most important ingredient for success.

Let's examine why executive support is so critical in the following examples from three levels.

Weak Executive Support

At an international pharmaceutical company, the executive team failed to understand that the successful CRM mix consists of 50 percent people, 30 percent process, and 20 percent technology. Instead, this executive team pushed the CRM technology component onto its personnel without taking into account important process and people readiness issues. The CRM initiative did not succeed.

At a global agricultural firm, the executive team believed that CRM was a simple extension of its back-office ERP (enterprise resource planning) system, and the team was convinced that its ERP technology would be well-accepted by its customer-facing personnel and ecustomers. Middle management disagreed, although sensitive that ERP systems were fine for back-office personnel but almost always inappropriate for front-office personnel and customers. The executive team retaliated by pulling the plug on the CRM initiative.

Mediocre Executive Support

At a global financial services organization, the executives talked the CRM talk but failed to clearly demonstrate their commitment to the initiative. For example, when they should have encouraged their direct reports to take the time to actively participate in the CRM initiative, the executives always seemed to have other, more pressing matters to address. This CRM initiative stumbled along.

At a large government agency, CRM was properly positioned to help drive the executives' revised strategic direction and to help deliver key customer self-support initiatives that were at the heart of the strategy. Yet, as the agency's strategic direction became difficult to implement, executive support for the CRM initiative diminished. While CRM still has a significant impact at the customer self-support level, the initiative is no longer seen as strategic and has moved off the executives' radar screen.

Strong Executive Support

At a biotech company, the president introduced the CRM concept to her executive management team by hiring my firm to present a CRM briefing for the executives. In addition to clearly defining what CRM is, the briefing highlighted CRM's value proposition as it applied specifically to the biotech industry. The president also organized a "learning journey" that became a mandatory two-day field trip for the executive team. One by one, executive team members began to see the light about CRM's value. Over time, they became the chief proponents of the CRM initiative. Their CRM initiative came in on budget and ahead of time.

At a well-known appliance manufacturer, market conditions (competitive products, Chinese imports, and major shifts within the traditional distribution channel) began to erode its impressive market share. The executive team, led by the president and the executive vice president of sales and marketing, created a strategy to counter these market conditions that included reinforcing its brand image and creating the most innovative products, but most importantly, involving the customer/consumer each step of the way. The president and executive vice president personally met with dozens of customers to better understand their needs. Several of these customers were invited to join this appliance manufacturer's CRM business requirements team. When it came time to roll out the company's new CRM initiative, internal as well as external support for the CRM initiative was strong. The initiative has been a success, and the company has gained back market share.

Lessons Learned

By implementing these five lessons, you will not only secure executive support, but you will strengthen it over time:

1. Once you have executive support, nurture it well.

2. To gain executive support, link your CRM initiative to the strategic direction of the organization, and be sure you have a solid CRM business case, complete with metrics that are measured quarterly over the life of the CRM initiative.

3. Help executives find the right CRM mix (50 percent people, 30 percent process, and 20 percent technology).

4. Help executives position CRM properly into the organization, paying particular attention to people issues that inevitably drive the success of the CRM initiative.

5. Executives can initiate the CRM vision, but their direct reports must take on the CRM charge.

Chapter 5

Securing Executive Alignment for Your CRM Initiative

One of the best practices we discussed at a recent *CRM Magazine* destinationCRM conference was the need to get the people, process, and technology mix right for a CRM initiative. The general consensus among speakers and attendees was that many organizations are now spending time to ensure that their customer-facing business processes are enhanced before applying a CRM initiative to support these business processes. We also reviewed technical options now available from existing and emerging CRM vendor camps. This was the good news.

The not-so-good news was on the people side. Two specific issues were raised: How can user adoption rates be increased and how can executive alignment be secured? In Chapter 7, Tips for Improving User Adoption, I cover what companies are doing to improve user adoption rates (ensuring the 3X factor, simplifying the software application, and additional training), so let me concentrate now on what an organization can do to secure executive alignment for its CRM initiative, using customer examples.

Camp 1: "Did I Say I Was Behind the CRM Initiative?"

This camp starts out with the executive team solidly aligned behind its organization's CRM initiative, but then, the team seems to forget its commitment. Typically, one executive steps out in front and leads the CRM charge, and the remaining executives line up behind the leader. Unfortunately, the leader then gets too busy or loses interest and abandons ship. Because alignment was not properly established at the outset, the CRM initiative often comes to sudden halt.

Camp 2: "I'm Behind the Initiative—I Swear It!"

This camp also starts out with the executive team solidly lined up behind its organization's CRM initiative. Typically, a group of executives agrees to lead the CRM initiative, and one of them signs up as an executive sponsor. The spirit among this executive team remains strong during the first few months. Then, as the CRM initiative hits people issues (push back from direct reports to executive team members), process issues ("How can we possibly automate this lousy forecasting process?"), or technical issues (costly integration), the executive sponsor recalibrates expectations, and they are realigned with the executive team. This realignment often happens multiple times, which delays the initiative. But, in the end, executive alignment is achieved, and the project is guided to success.

Camp 3: "Let Me Drive Executive Team Support for the CRM Initiative"

This camp also starts out with the executive team solidly behind its organization's CRM initiative, and then, an executive sponsor quickly emerges from the team. This executive sponsor never lets go of the CRM initiative. The executive sponsor schedules time to discuss the CRM initiative at every executive team meeting. The executive sponsor consistently gets the word out to the troops: "CRM full-steam ahead!" The executive sponsor finds time to work closely with multiple sponsors from customer-facing functions such as sales, marketing, and customer service. The executive sponsor oversees the initiative's implementation plan and drives CRM success.

Lessons Learned

Be sure not to take CRM alignment or buy-in for granted. While executive personalities can and do play a key role in driving initial alignment, so does good planning. Take time to bring your executives together at the outset of your CRM initiative and define what CRM is (your goal: get buy-in on one definition), why the organization should undertake the initiative (identify the pain points), and what the likely payback will be from investing in CRM.

During this kick-off meeting, talk in business terms. Link the CRM initiative as tightly as you can to your organization's business direction. If possible, keep technology out of the meeting. Encourage questions, and be prepared to answer them well. One final thought: Many organizations engage a CRM leading authority to facilitate the meeting; this helps drive executive alignment and improves the likelihood that your CRM initiative gets off on the right foot.

Chapter 6

Executives Take Charge

As we approach 30 years of CRM, executives are increasingly driving CRM to new heights. Here's why:

Executives firmly understand the secret for driving a successful CRM initiative. It's about securing people buy-in (50 percent of success), enhancing customer-facing business processes (30 percent of the initiative's success), and then applying technology to support the enhanced processes (20 percent of success). Despite honorable CRM vendor sales intentions, their big realization is that 80 percent of a CRM initiative's success has nothing to do with technology.

During a recent group sit-down with a consumer package goods customer, I was impressed when the executive vice president for sales and marketing informed the participants in the group that the key value proposition for their CRM initiative resulted from the implementation of their new, multistage sales forecasting process. This new process, which was designed by users and then configured into their CRM software, forces the company to drop the leads early on from the pipeline that do not pass stringent qualification gates, allowing their sales force to focus attention on the most promising leads.

Executives demand valuable business insight. While vendors and industry pundits are busy creating new CRM categories (SaaS, or software as a service), executives remain focused on their basic need for powerful yet easy-to-generate CRM business reports and easy-to-use analytical tools. These reports and tools, which have made great advances over the past few years, help executives to better understand business performance. More importantly, they also help executives coach their subordinates more effectively.

During my visit with a biotech customer, the president confirmed that he was about to pull the plug on the company's CRM initiative since he wasn't seeing promised payback. I asked what the benefit had been of the CRM initiative's two new reports—close ratios and churn analysis—that he said he needed to run his business better. He informed me that IT didn't have time yet to produce these reports. I asked that he give the IT department time to complete the two reports and that he give me an opportunity to coach him on how to use these reports for valuable business insight. I visited the president again for the coaching session, which his direct reports also attended. The session went well, and all participants gained considerable insight into what drove the close ratio and what triggered churn. While the president now claims that I saved the firm's CRM initiative, I reminded him that he was the one who demanded valuable business insight from its CRM initiative and rightly so.

Executives gear up for the ecustomer challenge. During a visit with the president of a manufacturing company, we reviewed this customer's greatest business challenges over the next 18-month period. Topping the list was how to address the new demands of his increasingly difficult distribution channel: He noted that plumbers in this case now had PCs and had become eplumbers. The eplumbers now had instant online access to product pricing from Chinese importers, Lowe's, Home Depot, and the competition. Moreover, eplumbers—armed with valuable pricing information—were quite adept at playing one vendor against the other. "Ecustomer loyalty doesn't seem to exist," he said. "It's a whole new ballgame."

Rather than be intimidated by the new ecustomer challenge, the president initiated an aggressive ebusiness site that offers eplumbers a full array of online services including inventory status, order entry, order status, credit card payment, self-servicing, and individualized plumber portals containing relevant product and market information. Of importance was the fact that eplumbers played a key role in helping to identify desired functionality. And while the jury is still out on the impact of this new ebusiness site, the latest eplumbers online surveys confirm a significant uptick in eplumber satisfaction.

Here's to executives taking charge.

Chapter 7

Tips for Improving User Adoption

You think you've done it right. You spent the money, time, and effort to secure and configure state-of-the-art CRM software. You took the time to incorporate valuable customer-facing business processes into your CRM application. You integrated your CRM application with relevant back-office and ecustomer systems, and you completed what you thought was excellent CRM application training.

After the system was launched, usage grew for three straight weeks; high-fives abounded. But then, you noticed a few user-adoption early warning signals: less daily updating by users, incomplete customer profiles, and few report requests. Since you're proactive, you quickly polled users online to determine the problem. Users confirmed that the system works just fine; it's just not relevant for their day-to-day efforts. One person even said, "The value-add just isn't there." You've realized your worst dreams: Your CRM initiative has entered the "user-adoption" triangle and is sinking fast.

Sound far-fetched? I hear it all the time from even the best-run organizations. Based on my experience of providing CRM strategic guidance to organizations worldwide, the following are my top two suggestions for securing high user adoption.

Ensure the 3X Factor

I introduced the 3X factor in 1986 by saying that to drive maximum user adoption for your CRM initiative, the following needs to happen: For every one piece of information that you request users to put into the system, the system must deliver at least three pieces of valuable information to the user. Deliver less than the 3X factor and chances are that your CRM initiative won't succeed. Deliver 3X or more, and you're well on your way to success. What constitutes valuable information? Take the time to ask your users; they'll let you know.

One of the best ways to realize the 3X factor is to deliver comprehensive customer profiles in the first iteration of your CRM system. One of our clients, a leading financial services company, locked on three different types of customer profiles: the internal broker profile, the external independent broker profile, and the ultimate customer profile. To specify profile requirements, this company facilitated a brainstorming session among customer-facing personnel to identify and then prioritize what information each profile needed. Not surprisingly, the prioritized list of profile requirements included information coming from multiple systems including back-office financial, customer service, marketing, and analytical systems.

As each user enters one piece of information into the customer profile (a new sales opportunity, update on a customer service incident, customer response to a marketing campaign, a credit warning), all other users (on a need-to-know basis) have instant access to enhanced customer profiles from multiple system users, which is what ensures the 3X factor. Sound simple enough? Ensuring the 3X factor often spells the difference between high versus low user adoption rates.

Get Your Communications and Training Right

Too often, companies think communications happens at the launch of their CRM initiative and training happens just before the launch of the CRM system. Nothing could be farther from the truth. Successful CRM initiatives include a communications plan that describes which users/influencers will receive what types of information about the CRM initiative, when, and in what format. This means you need to take time to think through where user hesitancy and even resistance is most likely to play out and then proactively turn this around.

We were proud of our manufacturing client when it presented us with a communications and training profile for each CRM system user. Next to the user name were two columns: The first described what communications would be going to that user when (industry case studies, the value proposition "what's in it for them," and how to connect with strategically placed "CRM champions" throughout the organization). The second column described the time when the user would receive training in one or more of these areas: computer literacy training, business process training,

CRM application training, remedial training, and/or new user training. In effect, each user had a "communications and training schedule" tailored to his or her specific needs. By getting communications and training right, this manufacturer proudly touts a 98 percent user adoption rate 12 months after the system was launched.

At the end of the day, high user adoption results because users find value in your CRM processes and system.

Chapter 8

CRM Project Communications

Integrating a CRM system brings with it myriad questions from users that require careful thought and analysis. So it is to your advantage to create communication-and-feedback mechanisms to deliver information about the vision, objectives, planning, and development of a CRM system. Users as well as nonusers will have questions and concerns, so you need to be proactive in planning for the needs of those in the organization who will be impacted by the CRM initiative. I recommend preparing a well thought-out CRM project communications effort to improve the long-term success for your CRM system. Internal marketing translates to your ability to build and maintain interest within your company for your CRM project over its entire life cycle.

Effective internal marketing consists of the following five initiatives.

1. Announce CRM Efforts Internally

The launch of your CRM initiative should involve great pride and care. Many people in your company will be curious about your initiative. So, you should expect people to start asking questions such as:

- Will I be included in the initiative?

- Who has been selected to participate in the initiative and what were the selection criteria?

- How many people are included in the initiative?

- How long will the initiative last?

- How quickly will the initiative spread to members outside the initial user group?

- What will persons participating in the user group need to do?

47

- Will those participating in the initiative get personal computers (PCs) or other access devices from the company?

- Will additional people be brought in to support the initiative, or will the initiative eventually decrease the number of jobs within the company?

- Will my job change as a result of the initiative?

Prepare your answers carefully to each of these types of questions, because you want to make sure that the appropriate messages are exchanged within your company so your initiative starts off healthy.

To illustrate the importance of internal communications, I completed a software selection road map for a U.S. manufacturer of industrial pipes. In this case, the CRM project leader was overly secretive about the project, and this created some misunderstandings among personnel associated with the project. As a result, several people decided not to continue participating in the ongoing project.

2. Create a "Superuser" Group

Businesses must ensure that a project leader (responsible for coordinating all aspects of project design and implementation) supports the initiative. Additionally, there should be a "project champion," who will be the highest executive willing to promote your system in the organization and prevent bureaucratic obstacles from getting in the way of your success. Your initiative should also be supported by a superuser group (members from sales, sales management, marketing, customer service, and top management) to represent the voice of the user. Your superuser group should include representative individuals who are leaders among the best in their respective job functions and have a strong knowledge of computers.

The superuser group is responsible for participating in meetings (from brainstorming sessions and questionnaire processes to possible field/corporate visits), in your business process enhancement work, during the software selection phase, and throughout the specification/design/implementation stages of your CRM initiative. The time that the superuser group needs to devote to the CRM initiative depends on several factors (e.g., length of CRM initiative, responsibilities of members of the superusers group, etc.), although allotting about five working days during the first three months of the project is reasonable. After the initial three months, the level of participation usually decreases considerably.

Your project leader may be a member of the superuser group, or you may decide to appoint another individual to this role. In addition to your project leader and the superuser group, you also may want to include at least one member of your company's IT department in the project team. You also may want to include a member from the finance or production departments (or others) who may play a significant role in designing and/or influencing the final project's outcome. If your company sells products through distribution channels, you may consider adding a channel representative to the superuser group.

In one success story, a leading U.S. publisher was in the process of automating its 500-plus global sales force. The project leader selected his superuser group and carefully monitored the team during the project initiation, design, and implementation. The value of this successful superuser group paid for itself many times over when project disputes and disagreements, which are normal occurrences in every CRM project, were quickly resolved, and the project moved forward with few interruptions.

3. Manage Communications

Once your CRM efforts have been announced in the company and your project leader and superuser group has been selected, your next internal marketing effort should be focused on communicating with members of the CRM initiative on an ongoing and effective basis.

At this stage, begin open and constructive communications among the project champion, project leader, superuser group, IT department, and any consultants or vendors you may be working with on the outside. You may consider asking some key customers to be in the communication channel as well.

Remember that people within the company will talk about the CRM project, so you will want to send a continuous stream of information to build ongoing internal support and enthusiasm about the project, while keeping all parties up-to-date. Watch for any signs of an internal rumor mill funneling inaccurate information within the company, as this can limit participation and hinder the long-term success of the project. Consider the following forums for CRM project communications:

- Web page or a section on the company intranet

- Internal newsletters or periodicals

- Articles in specific departmental communications

- Presentations at company special events

- CRM project status presentations at departmental management meetings

- Regular email updates

- Letters from executive sponsors of the CRM initiative

- Townhall meetings on CRM issues

Managing your communications effectively can be important if the project will be implemented in more than one region or country. In this case, keep potential superusers within regions or countries informed about your current CRM efforts. This can ultimately pave the way for a smoother transition as you expand the system from one set of users to the next.

In one overseas project, managing communications translated into setting up quarterly review meetings with designated personnel from 12 European countries. The benefit of these meetings was clear: The project was rolled out across Europe with minimum difficulty and maximum country participation.

4. Keep Champions Involved

Initial support from senior management for CRM projects tends to be quite high. The key is to secure a project champion early. Once you have selected your project champion, you should request assistance from this individual on an as-needed basis, and keep him or her briefed every month for at least the first six months of the project and then quarterly thereafter. Briefings should be short and confined to one page of written bullet points (include progress and setbacks), and try to follow up with face-to-face meetings at least every quarter to maintain progress on the CRM initiative.

Other issues and priorities can quickly attract the attention of senior management; be firm about holding your briefings on a regular basis. Otherwise, you run the risk of losing your project champion to another more aggressive initiative within the company. The lack of senior management support is a sure way to bring a project to a premature end. In my experience, one company's project champion lost interest in the initiative and failed to provide bureaucratic support when it was needed. As a result, the initiative ended within three months.

If possible, let your project champion see the emerging CRM system as it evolves. Of course, make sure the system works prior to any senior management preview. Senior managers talk with other senior managers on a regular basis, and good news can travel quickly at this level, which, in turn, can add potential support to your CRM efforts.

5. Maintain a Long-Term View

Lastly, maintain a long-term systems view during your CRM project initiative, and be prepared to survive the project's growing pains. Overcoming a failure or two during your project often strengthens your resolve and demonstrates to senior management that the project has needed user commitment.

I have been involved in many CRM projects that have hit snags, and management's first reaction is to get excited rather than to take the time to address and resolve the situation. I have found that maintaining a long-term systems view will help diffuse most of these situations.

Also remember that your current CRM initiative is likely to be part of a larger, more comprehensive corporate information system offering in the future. Your ability to maintain this long-term systems view and to deliver a system that is flexible and adaptable is key to the long-term success of your CRM in real-time initiative.

If you take the time to address these five key CRM project communication issues, the chances of your project's success will improve significantly. After all, people create CRM systems, and people use these systems. So, you need to remain highly sensitive to the strengths and weaknesses of users and work diplomatically within the boundaries set by these individuals.

Chapter 9

CRM Strategy Foundation

Companies often embark upon a CRM initiative without having a clear vision of where they want to go and how they intend to get there. Needless to say, these companies are the ones that end up reporting that their CRM implementation results are below user expectations. Is this any surprise?

Few companies take time to properly set up a CRM vision and use a structured methodology to create and realize their CRM strategy and implementation road map. Not surprisingly, these companies tend to be ones that report implementation results that exceed user expectations.

What follows is a 12-step approach for creating your company's CRM strategy. Your company may already have accomplished one or more of these steps, so you may not need to implement all of them. Nonetheless, because these steps are designed to fit together like pieces in a puzzle, use these 12 steps as a checklist to ensure that each step has been properly addressed before moving forward with your CRM in real-time initiative.

Step 1: Prepare an Executive CRM Vision

Gaining the support of the top management team is critical to drive the CRM initiative. One way to accomplish this is to spend between 30 and 60 minutes with each of the business leaders of customer-facing departments, the chief executive officer (CEO), and other executives such as the chief information officer (CIO) and/or chief financial officer (CFO) to discuss their CRM visions.

For example, one of the world's leading pharmaceutical companies had a contract with my firm to formulate its CRM vision. I first met with the CEO who clearly had given some thought to what CRM would mean for his company. Regardless of how a customer contacted the company, he wanted them to receive outstanding service, and he was sure that CRM would provide the tools to make this happen. When asked how he thought ebusiness fit into his CRM vision, the CEO felt uncomfortable; this was troubling. The vast majority of the company's customers were computer literate, and certain customer segments were already demanding efunc-tionality (customer self-service, emarketing, and eprocurement).

Next, I met with the business leaders of each of the firm's customer-facing departments. To my surprise, each of these seven executives had a differ-ent view of what CRM was and what its primary objective would be for the company. One executive said CRM was actually sales force automation (SFA), another said CRM was a cost-cutting tool set, and another said CRM would help identify product weaknesses and make recommenda-tions to internal research and development (R&D) personnel. Still, another said CRM would tie together sales and customer service efforts once and for all. But not one of them came up with a definition that was anything close to what the CEO envisioned.

After formulating a CRM vision statement based on input received from all of the interviewees, we helped arrange a CRM vision meeting with the CEO, business leaders of customer-facing departments, and other executives including the CIO and the CFO. The objective of this session was to describe the wide range of CRM visions that had surfaced in our various interviews and agree to a unified CRM vision.

After considerable discussion, the group finally agreed to the following CRM vision:

> Our goal is to provide customers and partners with a coherent, easy-to-use, error-free way to enhance the customer experi-ence. In order to meet this goal, we must implement excep-tional customer-facing processes and provide customer-facing personnel with CRM tools (e.g., feedback mechanisms, cus-tomer knowledge databases, information repositories) that will help enhance job performance and drive cost efficiencies. Regardless of the media channel, we will fully understand the value and satisfy the needs of each customer, ultimately driv-ing customer delight, loyalty, service differentiation, and long-term profitability.

While the definition is perhaps still a bit too long, the company at last shared a view of why CRM would be implemented. The significance of this CRM vision was reinforced when the top management team published its vision statement and distributed it to all company personnel.

Step 2: Determine "Burning" Business Issues

Burning business issues are those that impact the current day-to-day business operations. These issues may concern product or service problems (frequent back orders), competitiveness (the competition offers better service), personnel issues (hiring freezes), marketing or customer service frustrations (having trouble identifying high-value customers), or information-sharing dilemmas (the customer was connected to a different department each of the seven times he or she called since departments did not share customer information).

To uncover these burning business issues, set up additional 30- to 60-minute interviews with the same business leaders of customer-facing departments as well as the CEO and other executives interviewed in Step 1 (the interviews in Steps 1 and 2 can be combined, if time permits). Write an Interim Burning Issues Report that summarizes and groups the current interview findings by business function areas, whether sales, marketing, or customer service. Next, build user support for the CRM initiative by sharing the Interim Burning Issues Report with the next level of customer-facing departmental personnel to get their feedback. Do the findings address these burning issues? Are there additional issues that need to be added? Once needed alterations have been made, the Interim Burning Issues Report now becomes the "final" version.

Successful CRM strategies acknowledge that, while the long-term objective may be the realization of the CRM vision, users are not likely to support the initiative unless these burning issues are addressed along the way. Burning issues have an impact on the day-to-day lives of potential CRM system users, and this is where users feel they need the most help. Respect these feelings. In fact, burning issues need to be addressed early on to build strong support.

To better understand this point, consider an average CRM initiative that typically has three to five phases, and each of these phases are usually completed three to six months apart; each phase implements up to five business functions. A reasonable CRM strategy would look similar to the following example:

	Phase 1	Phase 2	Phase 3	Phase 4
Burning Issues Emphasis	80 percent	60 percent	40 percent	20 percent
CRM Vision Emphasis	20 percent	40 percent	60 percent	80 percent

As this example demonstrates, the first phase of implementing the initiative would involve placing 80 percent of the emphasis on addressing the burning issues and 20 percent on achieving the company's agreed-on CRM vision. The second phase of the initiative, which was implemented six months after the first phase was completed, would provide 60 percent of the emphasis on the burning issues and 40 percent on the CRM vision. In the third phase, the emphasis would be divided between 40 percent on the burning issues and 60 percent on the vision. The fourth phase would reflect 20 percent on the burning issues and 80 percent on the vision. In other words, ensure your strategic CRM vision by accomplishing meaningful, tactical business goals along the way.

Step 3: Identify CRM Technology Opportunities/Challenges

Successful CRM in real time occurs when people, process, and technology are carefully mixed throughout the CRM initiative. I have found that the success of a CRM initiative depends on the following formula: People account for at least 50 percent, process accounts for at least 30 percent, and technology accounts for about 20 percent. So why identify CRM technology opportunities as a separate step when formulating CRM strategy?

CRM technology will offer new business opportunities that may not always be apparent at first. For example, sophisticated CRM technology allowed Amazon.com to create an entirely new business model compared to the traditional bookstore model. CRM technology also has let Cisco Systems offer self-service to its customers, which has saved the firm hundreds of millions of dollars since 1999. It has also enhanced the customer satisfaction ratings among more than 80 percent of its customers who have opted to use the company's self-service capability over alternative options such as telephone support.

In Step 3, review current CRM technology trends and schedule a meeting with the business leaders of customer-facing units (invite the CEO and other executives, if possible, to discuss these trends). Be prepared: The purpose of the meeting is to identify CRM technology opportunities and to have customer-facing personnel determine whether these trends would have a small, moderate, or large impact on their businesses. During this meeting, discuss any key technology issues that are relevant to your company and whether skeletons in the closet exist that could impact your initiative, or simply identify any ongoing technology projects that need to be carefully integrated with your CRM initiative. Document the results of the meeting.

Steps 1, 2, and 3 of CRM strategy formulation—creating a CRM vision, determining burning business issues, and identifying CRM technology opportunities/issues—need to be carefully coordinated to ensure that the CRM strategy formulation starts off on the right foot. While an agreed-upon vision is critical, it needs to be balanced with pragmatic burning business issues. Unless CRM technology trends are known, their potential impact may never be realized in the vision or as a way to address burning business issues. Take time to stop after Step 3 has been completed to ensure that each of the first three steps has been accomplished and that these steps have been carefully integrated.

Step 4: Determine Key People Issues

Step 4 identifies the people issues that are likely to impact your initiative. The issues, which tend to emerge from the interviews held in Steps 1 and 2, include skepticism arising from past failed CRM efforts, lack of training for other IT systems, and a corporate culture that does not promote information sharing across customer-facing departments.

Once identified, the CRM strategy should include recommendations about the steps needed to overcome each of the people issues. For example, they may include a comprehensive communications program to overcome initial skepticism, a detailed training program to address the need for multiple types of training (e.g., computer literacy training, CRM application software training, remedial training, and remote training), or a revised information-sharing approach that actively encourages people to share information across customer-facing departments.

Step 5: Develop a Long-Term Technical Architecture Plan

You will need to review what technology the company currently has in place and what technology will be needed over time to address the company's CRM vision and burning business issues. Many options are available to determine an appropriate long-term technical architecture plan, including conducting one or more technical architecture "grease-board" sessions that result in an emerging technical road map. Then, you will need to research potential technical tools (e.g., enterprise application integration, or EAI, tools) that may be useful for you to accomplish your emerging technical architecture plan. Be sure to write up the findings, including any recommendations.

Step 6: Identify Business Process Issues

For each customer-facing business area, document key business processes and highlight the primary steps in each of them. Assess each process in terms of ownership, goals, measures, interfaces, procedures, integrity, and how each fits with the vision. Then, conduct cross-functional business process meetings to identify process interfaces and shared process areas. Be sure to report on the findings.

For each customer-facing business area, outline the business process steps and key interfaces. At the same time, obtain a general sense of the key business drivers as well as the similarities and differences between the processes. For example, are the sales processes opportunity-driven or account-driven? Is customer service primarily inbound and incident driven, or is it inbound and outbound? As you work with key representatives from each business area, identify any major issues relevant to ownership, goals, measures, interfaces, procedure, integrity, and fit with the CRM vision. During this step, evaluate the metrics associated with evaluating key processes.

This step is designed to understand the similarities and differences between different customer-facing processes, so the impact on the CRM strategy can be assessed. I have found that highly complex processes with significant issues are inherently more difficult to change than simpler processes.

Step 7: Determine Customer Desires and Impact on Customers

All too often, companies undertaking CRM initiatives proceed without feedback from their customers in the initial stages. Companies may feel that they know what their customers need. Most companies also set the rules about how a customer is expected to interface with the company. The danger of creating a CRM initiative without input from customers seems obvious. What if the customers don't see the value in the CRM business functions being proposed? What if they wouldn't use the CRM functionality offered to them?

Executives of one global biotechnology company were convinced that ebusiness was a tremendous value, and the firm made it one of its top priorities to create a new CRM initiative. Management was convinced that these buyers were researchers and were computer literate, and they would welcome the opportunity to gather information, buy, and service themselves electronically. The company was surprised by the turn of events. When the company held three focus groups for three different customer segments, the management learned that customer desire to move from the current service state to an ebusiness mode was weak at best. In one focus group, a participant said that if she could no longer call her friends at the company's customer service department by phone, she would take her business elsewhere.

To avoid creating an inward-facing CRM initiative, several steps can be taken. First, review existing customer information within the business/functional areas. Second, work with business leaders of customer-facing departments to determine the most appropriate way to find needed customer information in an emerging CRM business functional prioritization (prioritizing CRM business functions in the new CRM system to be implemented). Third, work with your customers to understand their CRM needs. Focus groups, customer questionnaires, and customer service interviews are effective ways to gather customer input. Finally, write up your findings.

The bottom line is to take time gathering valuable customer input, preferably from the outset of your initiative and not as a last-minute sanity check.

Step 8: Determine CRM Impact on Competitive Alternatives

A company can also become overly proud of its CRM strategy and can assume that its existing and potential customers are eagerly awaiting its rollout. In reality, these customers may already be using the CRM system of a competitor. Unless the company's CRM system is substantially better than that of the competition, customers may not be willing to adopt your CRM strategy, since it may require a customer to abandon a CRM system they like. To ensure that customers accept and adopt your CRM strategy, take time to perform a competitive CRM analysis and find out what is already out there. Make sure your offering is as good or better than the competition's. If not, return to Step 1 in this 12-step methodology.

Step 9: Provide CRM Program Observations and Recommendations

This step prepares and delivers a CRM program observations document based on the CRM vision, identified burning business issues, and customer input, as well as taking people, process, and technology issues into account. These observations and recommendations also are presented to the business leaders of customer-facing departments, the CEO, and other executives, as appropriate for comment and approval.

Step 10: Create a CRM Road Map

Once CRM program observations and recommendations have been approved (Step 9), the company is ready to create a CRM road map, which is a critical step in pulling together several inputs that will have an impact on the overall success of the company's CRM in real-time initiative. These inputs include a number of key points: corporate strategic business initiatives, IT initiatives, other business initiatives, CRM prerequisites, and the functionality of your evolving CRM strategy. Chart out these inputs on a three- to five-year quarterly log, while making sure to identify dependencies between all relevant initiatives. In addition to helping ensure the initiative's success, the CRM road map serves another critical purpose: It requires all key CRM initiative participants to sit in the same room during a series of two-hour meetings (usually between three and five of them) where they can discuss how the CRM initiative fits into all other corporate initiatives.

Step 11: Recommend a CRM Program Management Approach

This step offers suggestions on implementing the recommended CRM strategy and resulting road map. It often takes into account project management office (PMO) recommendations, including organization design and job descriptions, as well as PMO policies and procedures.

Step 12: Prepare the CRM Program Business Case

The business case is the document that most companies use to approve the CRM investment. Chapter 25, Creating a CRM Business Case, details the steps involved, so these steps are only briefly mentioned here:

- Executive summary (includes an overview of what happens when, to whom, and at what cost)

- Financials (includes specific value proposition and return on investment [ROI] information)

- Key risks and mitigating factors

- Operational/organizational impact

- Appendices (details the basis of the value proposition)

The 12-step CRM strategy formulation is illustrated in Figure 9.1. Think of the 12 steps as a checklist of requirements to create a successful CRM strategy formulation and implementation road map.

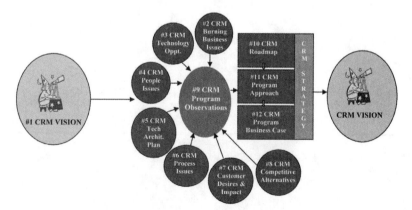

Figure 9.1   Twelve-step CRM strategy formulation

Chapter 10

Putting the "Customer" Back into CRM

Total CRM software spending will continue to grow at an annual growth rate of nearly 12 percent through 2011, according to research from the Gartner Group. My firm's studies put this figure closer to 15 percent. What factors account for this continued, impressive growth? Simply, CRM software vendors, under heavy pressure to help their customers succeed, have started to put the "customer" back into their CRM offerings.

Two examples come to mind of CRM vendors leading the way with innovations worth investigating.

Let's start with Siebel (www.siebel.com), a leading CRM software vendor (now owned by Oracle) that has played a key role in propelling the CRM industry, especially since the mid-1990s. Following the dot-com crash, sales dropped and Siebel took a big hit much like many other CRM vendors. The company came under fire for its implementation processes that were long and considered too costly. As a result, Siebel began to work more closely with its implementation partners and directly with its customers. Even one of my firm's global footwear and apparel customers worked closely with Siebel to incorporate customers' specific needs into a future version of Siebel's CRM suite that was targeted toward the footwear and apparel industry.

Siebel also began to install more of its CRM solutions for customers, directly attributing the success of the implementation to its focus on the customer level. Siebel's emphasis on putting the customer back into CRM may be paying off as Siebel sales have turned around and are on the upswing.

FirstWave (www.firstwave.com), another CRM software vendor, has also conscientiously gone back to the basics. FirstWave, formerly Brock Control Systems, has been around since the early 1980s and has weathered many industry shifts. A few years ago, the firm announced an impressive suite of flexible and scalable CRM modules based on a powerful XML-native framework, while revising its strategy to focus on assisting its CRM customers at all phases of the software purchase. This means the firm helped customers define their CRM requirements, identify metrics for their CRM business case, get buy-in from key stakeholders, and ensure that customers are well-trained and using the system to its fullest potential. In other words, by putting the customer's needs first, FirstWave ensured that its CRM offering is being "bought by the customer" versus "sold by the vendor." The success of this new customer-centric strategy not only attracted customers such as Citizens Bank to FirstWave's customer intimate approach, but it also positioned FirstWave as one of a handful of profitable public CRM vendors.

These two software vendors have demonstrated the value of focusing on the customer as part of the CRM equation. Their success reflects a new wave propelling CRM's consistent growth. This wave of customer focus will also ensure that CRM remains the driver behind the emerging business model explored further in Chapter 32, The Evolving Real-Time Enterprise, which turns the company's entire operations into an interconnected 24-hour nerve center.

Chapter 11

The Necessity of Training

The combination of training, an effective help desk, and a comprehensive systems administration play key roles in ensuring that CRM system users are happy and determine the long-term success for the system. But let's take a closer look at each of these areas.

Training

Based on actual customer data that I have compiled for more than two decades, I have concluded that for every $1 spent on CRM automation technology (e.g., hardware, software, communications equipment), $1.50 should be budgeted for training costs over the life of the project (typically five years). In other words, if you have $1 million in technology costs, you can allocate $1.5 million for training costs, which can be spread over five years (or about $300,000 per year). A greater percentage of this funding needs to be allocated to the first year of the project for application training. Over the years, other consulting firms like the Gartner Group have published a cost ratio of up to $15 of training for every $1 of equipment. While the latter ratio may be high, the message is the same: Never underestimate the importance of training for your project's overall success.

Training can take many different formats. The most common include the following.

Initial User Training

If you purchase off-the-shelf software, initial user training is often included or can be negotiated into the overall price of the software. This training may consist of sessions held at your facilities, at the vendor's facilities, or at a third-party site. Some vendors, especially those that provide Web-based software applications, are now offering online training using collaboration tools and services that run on your in-house or outsourced

Learning Management Systems (LMS). If your company has developed the software in-house, you will need to arrange this training on your own since you have developed the software. There are several CRM training companies, such as the Atlanta-based TRG, Inc., that create and implement CRM training for in-house CRM system developments.

Initial user training sessions usually last between one and two days, although sessions may be longer depending on the complexity of the system. Typically, between eight and 12 user participants attend these sessions. Ideally, the instructor-to-student ratio should be one to four, so keep the number of participants to fewer than 15 per session for the best results.

These sessions should include hands-on training, so participants should have equipment for system access (PCs or handheld devices) assigned to them, with printers and Internet access. This way, as the instructor explains a function or feature, participants can immediately perform the same function or feature on their PCs. It may also be useful to have a teaching script prepared to ensure that the training supports your company's way of conducting business.

The initial user training should provide users with an overview of the system by providing "a day in the life ..." training, then go into individual system functions and features. After each section of the training, be sure that participants take a hands-on test to show that they have understood how to use that section effectively. Participants can use a computer-aided training program, which automatically scores the user's test results. Each participant also should receive a set of User Documentation guidelines on the CRM system during this training session.

Train the Trainer

Use this type of training when your company prefers to do its own instruction or in cases where there are so many system users that it becomes unrealistic to train them all at once. This session is designed for internal trainers to learn how to use the system and teach others as well. This session should follow the same format for initial user training, but each trainer should also be provided with a training manual for required user training.

Training the trainer has some advantages and disadvantages. The key advantage is having an internally controllable, cost-effective means to train a large number of company personnel. The key disadvantage is being dependent on your in-company trainers; if these individuals get busy with other assignments, this may delay the training of users on your CRM system.

Systems Administrator Training

If a vendor sold the software to your firm, this type of training takes place with the vendor and your assigned systems administrator(s). This individual(s) will be performing day-to-day system maintenance such as assigning passwords, customizing screens, and updating databases. Even if the software was built in-house, which happens about 30 percent of the time and usually because the company's IT department feels that developing its own software will better address in-company system requirements, it is still critical that your systems administrator receives proper training.

This training typically takes between three and five days to complete, but two weeks is possible. Again, the training should be hands-on with one instructor for every three participants. Each systems administrator should receive comprehensive system documentation during this session.

Remedial Training

Individuals who are trained on the system and who use the system soon after are likely to retain much of their training. However, even the most seasoned learner can benefit from periodic remedial training updates, particularly if there are new systems releases that include new functions and features. Remedial training sessions should be scheduled within six months after the system has been implemented and at least once a year thereafter. Again, supplemental training can be channeled via elearning and Internet/Web-based online training. Ask your vendor what capabilities are available.

Regardless of the training format(s) you choose, your company should take training seriously. I have seen more than one CRM system fail because of insufficient training. When my firm helped one company with its training, the company did not have PCs set up, the software had not been loaded, no printers were available, and no modems were installed for proper training. This company's CRM system was in trouble from the start.

Help Desk

Every system user should have a comprehensive help function in the CRM software, which may or may not include system User Documentation online. A help desk should also be set up to support your CRM system. Users often contact the help desk by phone, although more companies are implementing a help desk that offers multimodal access via email or intranet.

The help desk fulfills several important needs, including a single phone number to dial when the user encounters a problem. This implies that the help desk should be staffed with properly trained personnel and supported by a system that features proper logging and tracking of call-in questions. In smaller companies, the help desk may be integrated with the systems administrator function. In larger companies, the staff is usually trained to support CRM applications, or the individuals are trained to support more than one application within the company.

A successful help desk requires strict business procedures to handle incoming questions. For example, each question that is received needs to be logged in so that there is a record of the types of incoming questions. When a caller's question cannot be answered on the spot (often called first-line or first-tier assistance), the help desk should route the question to the appropriate individual within your company (second-line or second-tier assistance), such as the systems administrator, then track the question until the query has been resolved. In the worst-case scenario, the question may require changes to the software code (third-line or third-tier assistance), which may mean that the help desk routes the question to the systems administrator, to the IT department, or even to outside software vendors (especially if third-party software packages are being used).

Regardless of the type of question received and its routing procedure, the question needs to be logged into the help-desk system once the caller's question has been resolved. A summary of how long the Q&A process took to resolve as well as the solution to the question should be captured in the knowledgebase for re-use by future CRM system users. Reports generated from this information are used to improve help desk functioning as well as to prioritize training needs or system alterations and enhancements.

Systems Administration

In most companies, a systems administrator is required to manage the CRM system. The responsibilities of the systems administrator include the following:

- Ensure that the systems data is kept up-to-date

- Back up the system files and data on a regular basis

- Provide new users with an ID and initial password

- Make changes to screens and pull-down menus

- Deliver new software releases and updates to the users

- Create and/or report on system usage statistics (how many uploads/downloads/synchronizations are being made, how often, and with what success ratio)

- Report on any problems that may be occurring with the system

- Write new systems reports and implement other technically related systems tasks (workflow routines)

A good systems administrator works closely with the help desk and the external software vendor(s) or internal IT department, while maintaining a close working relationship with system users. As a rule, once the initial systems integration and training are completed, most CRM systems require a half-time systems administrator for up to 100 users. For more than 100 users, one or more systems administrators may be needed, though this will depend on the capabilities of the help desk, the number of users, and the complexity of the system.

Be sure to staff your systems administration function with qualified individuals. Customer-facing representatives or executives in the field who use the system rely on a properly working system with up-to-date, accurate information.

Finally, be sure that you address the need for comprehensive training, an effective help desk, and systems administration functions up front. Case after case has shown that these items can be the deciding factors in rolling out a successful CRM in real-time initiative.

Chapter 12

Ensuring Consistent Customer Service

A knowledgeable friend once asked whether CRM was a new business approach or simply a repackaging of old concepts. This question is actually worth closer examination since I have been in the CRM industry for more than two decades.

I see CRM as a new business approach resulting from two complementary factors. First, CRM lets customers conduct business with a company the way the customer wants; this is new and quite important to many customers. Second, CRM offers new technology tools to make this happen. For this new approach to work, consistent customer service is needed across multiple channels.

When consistent customer service across channels is properly implemented, customers can reach your company any way they desire. Increasingly, customers opt to use multiple contact channels that include voice, leaving a message on voice mail, fax, regular mail, email, Web chat, collaboration, assisted browsing, and customer self-service, such as FAQs or knowledgebase queries. Equally as important, once customers have contacted your company, they expect your frontline agents/reps to be knowledgeable about them regardless of how the customer may have contacted you in the past.

So when the customer in real time tells you: "I am phoning you today about the email I sent to you earlier this week, which was in response to last week's Web chat session that resulted from the letter that I sent you via regular mail last month," that customer expects your company's agents/reps to know about all the contacts that they have had with your company. They also expect your agents/reps to be ready to help them accurately in real time. This is where CRM in real time steps in. How you realize consistent customer service is your concern, not theirs.

Moreover, achieving consistent customer service is indeed a concern for most companies: It may be technically complex and costly, might require rethinking existing customer-facing processes, and may require extensive retraining of your agents/reps who may be initially resistant to change. But those companies that successfully realize consistent customer service will be the winners in today's increasingly competitive marketplace where competition is but one click away. In the old days, we had only switch-based telephony in customer service centers. In the early 2000s, Internet Protocol (IP) Telephony was developed that allowed customer service centers to receive data such as emails and Web chat over their IP Telephone Network. This led to service centers being renamed "customer contact centers" since customers could contact the service center in multiple modes.

Service Today

Technology tools that help companies realize consistent customer service were first offered in 1998 (e.g., Quintus' eContact offering). While no shortage exists today of technology-driven options to ensure consistent customer service across channels, few, if any, standards are driving this area of CRM. The result? Consistent customer service technology is still finding its way.

To a large extent, consistent customer service has been delegated to customer service centers (now more commonly known as customer contact centers). Most often, existing call centers become Web-enabled to expand contact channels for Web chat, email, and possibly other Web-based interactions in addition to voice calls. Or, an ebusiness department that installed Web and email functionality (i.e., some portion of available CRM offerings) may now want to link to a call or customer contact center. (The terms customer contact center and customer call center are not synonymous; customer contact centers are IP telephony-based, whereas customer call centers are telephony-based.)

Here's how CRM software works to deliver consistent customer service across channels. Suppose three customers need help. Customer A makes contact via a voice call on a toll-free 800 number; Customer B comes in via an email; and Customer C arrives via Web chat. Today's technology lines up the requests from each of these customers in a common queue. Assuming the customer service agent is trained to handle multichannel requests, the agent then begins to interact with Customers A, B, and C in whatever order the requests are listed in the queue (some companies send all email requests to one agent, all Web chat requests to another agent, and so forth). Automated email and Web chat responses let the agent respond to more than one customer at a time. All customer interactions are recorded and placed into the customer's contact file. Reporting tools are used to monitor customer service efficiencies consistently and highlight areas that may need improvement.

Most companies that now offer consistent customer service face a similar dilemma: Do we continue to build an offering using the organization's existing telephony infrastructure, or do we move to the emerging IP network alternative?

Benefits of Consistent Customer Service

Customers who take the time to contact a company expect to be serviced quickly and efficiently. A customer who is visiting your Web site may need help in real time. If a customer sends you an email, he or she expects a quick response. If the customer registers a complaint, he or she wants a confirmation that you are in the process of resolving that complaint. Other customers may feel their complaints will not be heard or resolved properly, so they do not even bother to contact the company; they simply move over to the competition. This partially explains why U.S. corporations now lose half their customers in five years, according to Antony Young, co-author of the 2007 book *Profitable Marketing Communications: A Guide to Marketing Return on Investments*. The impact of losing customers can be significant: In an industry landmark study by Frederick Reichheld (*The Loyalty Effect*, 1996), he found that if a company loses one customer each day who spends $100 per week, the loss in sales per year can total $1,900,000.

As companies increasingly supplement their service capability with electronic capabilities (email and Web offerings), the situation remains equally problematic. For example, Jupiter Media Metrix found that 65 percent of all companies offering email service do not respond to a customer's email within 24 hours.

On the flip side, consistent customer service across channels appears to deliver real benefits. Customers who are engaged quickly and efficiently regardless of the channel used tend to be more loyal to a company, which drives long-term customer retention and profitability. From the company perspective, an increased opportunity to cross-sell and up-sell exists. By training an agent to handle multiple channels, companies are seeing a reduction in agent frustrations and turnover, two serious problems that can trigger up to a 50 percent annual turnover rate for a company. Companies also reduce their costs: A 2005 Giga study concluded that Internet-based customer self-service reduces call center operating costs by 95 percent.

Yet, 54 percent of customers who used a toll-free telephone-based call center still choose to speak with an operator. These types of calls cost a company an average of $12 per inquiry, compared to $6 per email inquiry (which represents 9 percent of customers) and $.50 per inquiry for customers who use Web-site self-service (37 percent of customers). For those interested in customer service benchmarking information, take a look at the work by Purdue University's Center for Customer Excellence, which has been performing customer service industry benchmarking studies for more than a decade. In short, consistent customer service across channels can result in sufficient existing and potential benefits.

Leading Vendors Offering Consistent Customer Service Products

Here are a few of the leading software solutions for some or all aspects of consistent customer service:

- IPCC by Cisco (www.cisco.com)
- Avaya (www.avaya.com)
- Syntellect (www.syntellect.com)
- Aspect (www.aspect.com)
- Genesys by Alcatel-Lucent (www.genesyslab.com)
- Clarify by Amdocs (www.amdocs.com)
- KANA (www.kana.com)
- eGain (www.egain.com)
- Firepond (www.firepond.com)
- Trilogy (www.trilogy.com)

Key Challenges to Consistent Customer Service

If your company would like to benefit from consistent customer service across channels, here are the questions you will want to answer:

- Has your company taken time to understand what customer service methods your customers prefer? While reviewing current customer service statistics has value, it is also necessary to provide incentives for target customers to participate in focus groups. These focus groups are designed to obtain additional, valuable information concerning consistent customer service requirements.

- Has your company created a clear vision that articulates a consistent customer service strategy?

- Has this vision and strategy been communicated effectively to internal customer-facing personnel as well as to external customers?

- Do the current customer-facing processes support consistent customer service across channels, or do your processes need to be adjusted or even re-invented?

- How will your company train customer service agents effectively to think outside silos (e.g., I am responsible for phone inquiries while you handle email inquiries) and to want to participate in your multichannel support efforts?

- Will your current telephone network (Public Switched Telephone Network, or PSTN, which is the international telephone system based on copper wires carrying analog voice data) allow for consistent customer service across channels, or should you be implementing emerging IP network technology that is capable of effectively integrating voice and data information?

This last question is important yet complex. Today's customer service technology is in a transitional phase, and the IP network initiative is already transforming how customer service centers are now being set up. Many customer service centers today currently have two networks: an IT network on which their computer and their data operates, and a telephone network that Alcatel-Lucent, Siemens, Nortel, or others provide, which has all call routing functionality on it and which tends to be proprietary. Many middleware vendors now offer CTI integration between these two separate networks, but the middleware solutions are not cheap and may take considerable time.

This is where companies including Cisco's IP network product offering come into play. Cisco suggests that two networks are unnecessary and that the hardware switch-oriented nature of a PSTN goes against the trend of the emerging switchless data world. Cisco provides a solution that supports a company's telephone as well as data network needs within the customer service environment. In February 2001, Cisco changed the game by launching its IPCC (Internet Protocol Contact Center), which was designed as a seamless transition for customers from traditional PSTN applications to new world integrated IP applications (e.g., unified messaging, integrated Web collaboration, instant messaging, and chat). Cisco now has stiff competition in the IP telephony space from Avaya, Nortel, Siemens, 3Com, and others that offer their own IP network solutions.

Several issues should be considered as they relate to the IP network alternative:

- A large installed base of customer service centers currently run their customer services over a PSTN. Despite technical shortcomings of PSTN telephone switching equipment (e.g., the inability to support multimedia customer interactions such as voice, chat, email, browser-sharing, call-me-now, etc.), the large installed base of customer service centers may be reluctant (for financial reasons) to dispose of their telephone-switching equipment and to replace it with an IP network. Vendors who currently sell PSTN products are not necessarily promoting this transition.

- Using current PSTN technology, a customer service supervisor can monitor customer voice calls but cannot monitor integrated voice and emails in real time. Using an IP network, simultaneous monitoring is feasible.

- By moving to an IP network, a company incurs a one- or two-minute network carrier charge at most (2 cents per minute) while the call is passed over to the IP network. Compare this to a PSTN call where the company incurs these 2 cents per minute carrier charges during the entire voice call until the calling party hangs up. The net result is potentially significant cost savings per customer call.

- In the IP world, queuing doesn't exist, so when a packet, or piece of a message transmitted over a packet-switching network, is sent in an IP network, it goes across the wire, and it looks for an IP address. When it finds the address, it expects to be consumed. But what if that IP packet is voice? How do you queue voice?

Until recently, there wasn't a way to queue voice packets on an IP network, which is what most customer service centers need to provide consistent customer service across multiple channels. With its acquisition of Geotel in the early 1990s, Cisco was among the first to offer integrated voice recognition (IVR) and queuing functionality within the IP network. IVR has since become the standard feature in most customer contact centers.

New technologies continue to emerge that are designed to provide consistent customer service across channels. While these may be impressive, companies must not underestimate the importance of implementing processes that support consistent customer service. Moreover, companies must not downplay the importance of ensuring that in-company personnel and external customers feel comfortable and agreeable with the changes that consistent customer service inevitably brings.

CRM is a new business approach that lets customers conduct business with a company the way the customer desires, that offers new technology tools to make this happen, and that consistent customer service across channels has arisen as a result of those two factors.

Looking at the emerging trend of consistent customer service across channels, my biggest concern would be that this initiative is too driven by customer service or customer contact center personnel. Line management, whether sales reps, sales managers, marketing personnel, or top management, needs a complete customer picture as much as customer service personnel. While customer service is a key component of CRM, the time is right to ensure that consistent customer service across channels is based on the inputs related to CRM's remaining four components: sales, marketing, business intelligence, and business as well as customer input. For example, sales personnel may want to view a comprehensive customer profile that includes a list and summary details of personal visits to that customer, or letters (snail mail) sent from that customer as much as voice or Web transactions with that customer. My firm's research suggests that few customer service systems now actually support this type of integration. In this regard, the CRM industry still has a way to go.

Using Service to Win Big

A company can differentiate its products (or services) from competitors in the short term, but all products become commodities in the long term. Why? Product excellence can eventually be copied. Competitive products offered with excellent customer servicing, however, has become the most effective combination to differentiate products and services over the long term.

As a result, CRM and the new customer service capabilities that it offers to an increasingly sophisticated and demanding customer base are becoming integral to companies using this product/customer service excellence strategy.

For example, one well-known global footwear and sports apparel manufacturer actively listened to its customers and to the marketplace. The company knew that its products were perceived to be among the very best, but the firm's executives also realized that they needed to improve their relationships with retailer distribution-channel partners. So the company's top management team made CRM a key to its long-term differentiation strategy, especially the service components of CRM.

The manufacturer launched significant self-service capabilities for smaller retailers. These small retailers are now electronically linked to the company: They place orders, confirm stock availability, make payments, and lock in delivery dates, all online.

For mid-sized retailers, the company opted to create multiple retailer segments, to build comprehensive customer profiles for each retailer segment, and to customize service for each retail segment. For example, in one segment, the manufacturer now uses wireless handheld devices to take stock, to automatically generate replenishment orders, and to confirm dependable product delivery dates in real time.

For the large retailers, the company created an impressive key account program. Each retailer account team accessed a common account profile, performed common account planning, and delivered and monitored negotiated service levels on a daily basis. This service-team approach helped this manufacturer sustain its market leadership position within the industry.

Another example is a financial services company specializing in student loans. Despite its size (meaning that its student loan rates are competitive at best) and its lack of brand recognition, executives at the lender decided that the future of the company depended on its ability to "outservice" the competition. So the firm turned to CRM to provide comprehensive customer profiles, to analyze windows of opportunity from leading borrowers, to implement aggressive direct marketing campaigns, and to link university financial aid offices, parents, and students to the company's full suite of online student loan services. Fortunately, using CRM as a service differentiator is proving to be the winning card: Although its loan portfolio doesn't compare with lenders such as Sallie Mae, Citibank, or Wells Fargo, this lender is taking market share away from these big players.

Whether it's faster or more accurate service, or cost-effective self-service, companies are increasingly complementing their long-term commodity products with award-winning CRM services as the most effective way to achieve differentiation and survival. How well has your company integrated CRM services into your long-term business strategy?

Service as the Differentiator

As previously noted, although an organization can differentiate its products and services from competitive offerings in the short term, all products become commodities in the long run. And this is why the combination of competitive products and services tied in with excellent customer support has become the one successful way to differentiate organizations from each other.

In a world of increased competition, organizations are often turning their support to achieve long-term differentiation for their products and services. Customers often see as much or more value in the support that an organization offers as a part of its products and services than in the actual products and services provided. Best-in-class support organizations confirm that the optimal way to master support is to achieve success initially from within the organization, and then expand these efforts outward through the distribution channel and to their customers.

Achieving Long-Term Differentiation Via Services

Once again, while an organization can differentiate its products and services from those of the competition in the short term, all products become commodities in the long term. Why? Because an organization's products and services may have an advantage over the competition one moment, but this advantage may be reversed the next moment. What this means is that competitive products and services, tied together with excellent customer support, has become the most effective combination to differentiate an organization's products and services in the long term. Here is an example:

A global apparel manufacturer concentrated on the teenager segment. As an active listener to its customers and to the marketplace, the company knew that its products were perceived to be among the very best; it also knew that it needed to improve its relationships continuously with employees as well as with its retailer distribution channel. So the company's top management team decided to make support capabilities a key component of their long-term differentiation strategy. For example, the company launched a service management strategy for employers where personalized portals will offer employees direct access to all types of company support functions ranging from the IT help desk to new job postings.

Mastering Support Capabilities

While support capabilities are eventually offered to an organization's external customers, best-in-class support organizations confirm that the optimal way to perfect the process is to first practice and support capabilities internally.

For example, internal support capabilities may include IT services such as help desk support, asset management, hardware support, mobile computing support, or network and systems management support. The idea behind mastering support capabilities from within demonstrates to employees several ways to achieve superior support capabilities using real-life situations. This will also let employees understand the value of receiving the superior support that all customers ultimately crave. Based on this experience, when the time comes to extend support capabilities to external customers, happy internal customers enjoy the effort of driving support excellence.

Mastering support capabilities in this way is how the city of Des Moines, Iowa, successfully built its well-documented Citizen Response

System in 2002. Des Moines tried to be one of the best-run cities in the country and wanted to automate the way it received, managed, responded to, and resolved requests from its 200,000 residents. The city had already implemented the HEAT Service & Support software solution from FrontRange Solutions to assist its internal IT help desk in managing calls and providing problem resolution for its computer and network systems users. After examining possible solutions, the city's process improvement team decided to leverage its internal support experience and use HEAT as the most appropriate and logical extension for its external Citizen Response System initiative (see Chapter 31, CRM in Government, for more about the Des Moines CRM initiative).

Achieving the Right Mix of Support Capabilities

What support capabilities are needed? While this formula will differ for each company, here are some essential components for internal support illustrated by the internal IT help desk and for external support by the external customer support center.

IT Help Desk

Since adopting distributed computing, IT departments have been faced with an increasingly difficult task of managing the support of IT services. Ebusiness created additional pressures on IT departments to provide services such as access to Internet-based applications 24/7. This amplified the need for a well-designed IT help-desk strategy that included effective processes (problem resolution), appropriate levels of technology (remote support tools), and a comprehensive data architecture. If an IT help desk is not implemented properly, this can prevent the benefits of applying process enhancement and automation from being realized, but more importantly, this can cause potential damage to the IT department's reputation.

Customer Support Center

While commonalities with IT help desks exist, customer support centers tend to capture customer data into applications that enable more focused customer service and an increased emphasis on first-interaction

resolution. Customer support centers also use this customer data to identify and realize cross-sell and up-sell opportunities, determine future
marketing activities, and offer more personalized interactions. A critical
factor in the success of a customer support center is the company's ability
to employ "customer-sensitive" personnel, train them well, and integrate
the best tools and processes to help personnel deliver the "optimal customer experience" each and every time.

Here then are some common and unique service capabilities that a
company will want to consider in support of long-term differentiation.
Common functions for the IT help desk and the customer support center
include the following:

- Log problem calls/emails

- Assign one owner to each problem

- Resolve any escalating problems, as needed

- Track problems until they are resolved

- Build a resolution knowledgebase for internal personnel and
  external customers

- Identify problem trends and recommend proactive corrections
  (product modification or enhanced training)

Unique functions for the IT help desk include the following:

- Support and track configuration changes, track IT inventory, and
  manage the company's IT assets

- Create and implement meaningful service-level agreements

- Develop and use management reports for evaluating vendor
  equipment, improve service-level agreements, and proactively
  service IT-related customer issues

Unique functions for the customer support center include the following:

- Dispatch and field servicing

- Cross-sell and up-sell

- Manage opportunities

- Determine appropriate marketing activities (permission-based marketing)

- Promote personalized interactions via personalized portals

Customer Support Futures

Several customer support trends have already had an impact on internal and external support capabilities and are likely to continue. This can also have an impact on an organization's ability to achieve long-term differentiation for its products and services.

- **Unrelenting customer demand** – As customers experience more support options, they are less tolerant of long calls, long waiting times, inaccurate answers to questions, poorly trained support agents, and lack of access to their own information to resolve their own issues. Unless addressed with urgency, this is likely to lead to frustration and customers taking their business elsewhere. In fact, a 2004 Gartner Group study predicted that 75 percent of companies will continue to fall below customer expectations for customer support excellence through 2008, and the result will be average turnover of 100 percent of the customer base every five years.

- **New revenue opportunities** – While unrelenting customer demand may negatively impact a company's customer base and resulting revenues, it also provides an opportunity to generate new revenues. The percentage of support centers with agents who are actively cross-selling and up-selling is less than 5 percent today. The same 2004 Gartner study predicted that by the end of 2008, 40 percent of all support centers will have a significant impact on an enterprise's revenue stream. This large potential implies that many new support needs to include specialized training, holistic customer profiles, available cross-sell and up-sell information.

- **Cost reduction pressures** – A 2005 Giga study found that a support center pays $12 for a nontechnical call and between $12 and $18 for a technical call.

- **More self-service** – Demand for self-service has and will continue to grow exponentially for several reasons, especially since the Net generation prefers to take charge and resolve their own needs online, and the Net generation isn't going away. Whereas 3 percent of the American workforce currently works in support centers, a 2005 Gartner Group study forecasts that by 2010, there will be around 5 percent of the American workforce working in support centers despite high support center attrition rates that currently run between 15 percent and 30 percent annually.

Another important reason is the cost reduction pressures previously mentioned. Organizations want—and even encourage—customers to use self-service options to get answers to repetitive-type questions, which lets support centers concentrate on exceptions and more relevant customer experience issues as well as maximize support center efficiencies.

Both of these reasons imply the need for increasingly sophisticated esupport tools to provide customer advice and problem resolution (e.g., integrated phone/email/Web tools, knowledge management systems, remote support capabilities that resolve issues over a LAN or WAN or via phone lines or a modem). In fact, Gartner has found that about 70 percent of all support centers have now implemented Web-based support applications.

Perhaps more importantly, these two reasons imply the need for well-designed, proactive programs that encourage and facilitate internal and external customers to follow more self-service options:

- **Demand for real-time customer service** – Thanks to the Web, customers now expect real-time information and even real-time support. Yet, few organizations today are using customer support capabilities cost-effectively, and even fewer are offering such capabilities in real time. This implies a potential need to create real-time enterprises that offer an integrated customer support framework with complete real-time views of the customer support issues across all customer-facing channels.

- **Growth in integrated CRM applications** – All of these factors point to a final important trend: the need for tighter integration across sales, marketing, and customer support applications. This results from cross-selling and up-selling becoming more of a company's support capabilities, online marketing and sales becoming more intertwined, and sales and customer support needing to work together in real time.

Why Support Matters

A 2005 study sponsored by staffing firm Kelly Services and Purdue University's Center for Customer-Driven Quality concluded the following:

- 92 percent of U.S. consumers form their image of a company based on their experience using a support center.

- 63 percent of consumers will stop using a company's products or services based on a negative support center experience.

- 86 percent of those calling to express dissatisfaction with a product or service were more likely to stop using the company if their experience with the customer support agent was negative.

Simply stated, support capabilities aimed at addressing the needs of internal and external customers have become a more critical component in three ways: by ensuring higher levels of quality service, by building and sustaining optimal customer relationships, and by creating long-term customer satisfaction and loyalty.

PART 3

Process
Issues

Chapter 13

Realizing Effective Process Change

The process component of CRM is considered the most delicate because any inappropriate automation of CRM business processes will eventually lead to errors in CRM implementation and to the creation of inappropriate processes in the organization. While most companies have customer-facing business processes in place (those that directly interface with the customer during the purchase, payment, and usage of the company's products and services), these business processes often need to be updated or replaced.

For effective process change, a company must first examine how existing customer-facing business processes work. Then, the company needs to redesign or replace deficient processes with new ones, created and/or agreed upon internally. In other words, while it's not wrong from an educational perspective to look at built-in processes within a CRM software package, new processes are easier to implement when the processes are internally driven. Companies implementing a CRM initiative often correct their own customer-facing process deficiencies by purchasing CRM software that contains one or more business processes prebuilt by the CRM vendor and forcing the process on system users instead.

When reviewing your customer-facing business processes, use a structured approach. For example, does each customer-facing business process have clear ownership, goals, and measures? Does each process have proper departmental interfaces that ensure needed customer information flows across multiple departments? Does each process have documented procedures? Does each process have integrity in which the process gets implemented the same regardless of who implements it and where?

Following are a few examples to underscore the impact of implementing new CRM processes on an organization's operations.

A Consumer Goods Example

In 2007, one of our global consumer goods customers embarked upon a CRM initiative that included the creation and automation of a "key account" management process, yet the company encountered problems right out of the gate. Rather than mapping an appropriate key account management process, the organization decided to look for a CRM software vendor who incorporated a key account management process within its software, and the firm found a vendor who offered a generic key account management capability. The consumer goods company purchased the software and trained its personnel on how to use the software's key account management process.

During the software training, however, those users became increasingly uncomfortable with the depth and value of the software's key account management capabilities. The users-in-training felt the software's key account management process failed to address key internal issues, such as the criteria for choosing a key account, guidelines for determining which personnel join a key account management team, and policies for customizing service level agreements for each key account. After much debate, the organization put the CRM initiative on hold, created its own key account management process internally—with full backing from potential users—and produced a revised request for proposal (RFP) based on the internally generated process specification.

This organization discovered that the following steps were needed to maximize the effectiveness of customer-facing processes: Rely first on internally generated processes (preferably with customer participation), document and train on new or modified processes, and then look into CRM software tools to help make the customer-facing processes work more efficiently.

A Global Life Sciences Company

In 2006, one of our global life sciences customers decided to revamp its lead management business process before implementing an overarching CRM initiative. Why? Prior to the new process, sales leads would come in from a variety of sources including the company's Web site, trade shows, magazine ads, and word-of-mouth. All leads were quickly screened by the marketing department before they were assigned to field sales personnel based on ZIP code and/or area of specialization. However, two kinks emerged in this approach: First, the marketing department did not have sufficient time to qualify leads during busy periods, and second, the department was hesitant to send out unqualified leads to field sales personnel. The result? Leads often remained in the marketing department until they could be qualified, which translated into delays of days or even weeks when the lead was often cold; second, the field sales personnel were often overwhelmed by the number of leads from marketing and had trouble knowing which ones to pursue first.

To correct the situation, the company gathered the sales, marketing, and top management together to create an ideal customer leads process. Leads were designated as "A" (ultrahot), "B" (hot), "C" (warm), and "D" (cold). Designations were made based on a number of agreed-upon weighted criteria (e.g., contact method, product interest, and type of application). The new lead-management process was accepted and promoted effectively throughout the company. Next, all marketing and sales personnel received training on the new process. Lastly, the new process was automated using CRM software workflow tools. Today, lead screening is automated, and sales reps are sent prioritized leads immediately after the company receives the lead.

As a result, the company changed its lead close from 10 percent to 15 percent, which translated into millions of dollars of new and ongoing business.

A Global Manufacturing Example

Meanwhile, a global manufacturing company proposed to streamline its sales process using CRM software and mapped the existing sales process via a Visio flowchart, which can be found in Appendix A at the end of the book. This flowchart illustrates the mapping of a global manufacturing company's existing sales process, which is one of the essential steps for successful CRM implementation.

By mapping the sales process, this manufacturing company determined that the process currently had seven steps and took an average of six months to close a sale. The vice president of sales suggested that using CRM could cut the sales close process by two months (from six to four months). During the process, however, the company also learned that delays in the sales process were not necessarily the result of delays in the sales department. Instead, they were often a result of inefficiencies in other departmental processes that impacted the sales process. For example, to complete the fourth step of the sales process (the work scope and definition step), sales personnel depended on receiving timely drawing (takeoffs) and preliminary pricing, which almost always arrived late. To complete the fifth step of the sales process (the proposal submittal step), sales personnel depended on the corporate and legal departments to approve the bid, which were also routinely late. In other words, decreasing the sales process from six to four months depended as much on streamlining how other departments conducted their processes and interfaced with the sales process as it did on helping sales personnel to sell more efficiently.

In this case, it's clear CRM software can only do so much: It won't create or replace a business process, fix an ineffective or broken process, create or maintain customer relationships, make decisions, or produce products and services. So, take time to review customer-facing processes in detail and make the necessary corrections before implementing your CRM in real-time initiative.

Chapter 14

Understanding Business Process Review

CRM software solutions may promise an "ideal" customer relationship process via instantaneous sharing of detailed customer information across multiple interfaces. But this ideal is not always optimal or even feasible. CRM acts as an enabler for your business processes (e.g., sales, marketing, and customer service), and for the more total holistic, integrated customer process. So, the success of any organization's CRM initiative depends on the functionality of existing or future business processes.

All organizations have business processes, even though many may claim a lack of process. Processes are those natural business activities that produce value, serve customers, and generate income. Indeed, all organizations have business processes, though they may not all be documented, fully understood, or extremely functional.

CRM applications don't replace business processes or fix an ineffective process; they also don't create or maintain relationships or produce a product or service. In fact, automating an ineffective process can be costly and lead to a CRM system not working, but it also diverts key personnel time and financial resources.

Instead, CRM provides the opportunity to enhance existing processes as well as create new, more integrated customer-centric processes. To maximize the value of these opportunities, you need to understand the key business processes that lead to the purchase, payment, and use of your company's products and services, with a special emphasis on the processes targeted for automation. And you need to build this understanding from a company and customer perspective.

The following are a number of areas to consider when reviewing and potentially modifying business processes. Because my firm has helped many organizations with business process assessments, the information presented here should help your efforts, whether you perform the CRM business process evaluation in-house or seek external assistance.

A multistep procedure has proven to be highly effective in identifying gaps in existing business processes and determining corrective action(s) needed before or during CRM implementation. Two basic approaches to this procedure depend on the perceived state of readiness of your organization.

In the abbreviated business process review, the company's business process functionality is initially assessed. In this assessment, a limited number of days are typically spent with key process owners in direct interviews and meetings to get an overview of current business processes and to make preliminary recommendations for business process enhancement.

A full business process review is typically used in the following circumstances:

- The findings of the CRM business process assessment previously described warrant a more in-depth evaluation or redesign of business processes.

- Current business processes are dysfunctional enough to warrant obtaining a detailed process review and recommendations report before beginning a CRM system design and implementation process. This approach may be needed if you plan a significant process redesign in conjunction with the implementation of CRM.

Regardless of the depth of assessment chosen, it's imperative to do the following:

- Create a visual model of key processes

- Develop an understanding of business process needs from the perspective of customer-interfacing personnel and customers

- Identify gaps in process functions

- Determine the necessary actions to position your business processes for effective CRM implementation

In determining functionality, the following key questions are important to ask about the business process elements that are evaluated:

- **Ownership** – Is there clear responsibility, authority, and accountability for the success of the process invested within a functional group or groups?

- **Integrity** – Is the process consistent across time and within all units that use the process within the organization?

- **Interfaces** – Are critical interfaces between groups (internal), partners (external), and with customers understood and functional?

- **Procedures** – Have the key process steps been documented and agreed upon by process owners and customer-interfacing personnel?

- **Metrics** – Are performance standards and measures routinely used to determine the process' success from a company and customer viewpoint?

Each of these elements should be evaluated for individual business processes and the total set of processes targeted for a CRM initiative. Not all elements will have the same level of functionality. For example, the sales process within your organization may have exceptionally clear and authoritative ownership, but the interfaces between sales and marketing or customer service may be highly dysfunctional. The more dysfunctional elements create gaps that must be corrected before or during the CRM implementation.

Ten Steps to Process Review

The following is a brief description of my firm's 10-step business process review procedure. These steps provide general guidelines for the activities that need to take place for a better understanding of the current and desired business processes related to CRM.

Step 1: Meet with the Client to Plan an Initial Schedule

Meet with key client representatives to determine strategy, direction, and a list of possible participants in the business process project, and outline a tentative schedule for engagement with the client staff.

Step 2: Research Background Materials

Review client background material for "as-is" business processes including existing process flow documents and start researching the possible relevant industry best practices.

Step 3: Interview Client Representatives About Current State Processes

Set up interviews/meetings with process knowledgeable client personnel to determine "as-is" or current processes, and note any potential quick wins and other ideas that could impact the "to-be," or future process work.

Step 4: Draft "As-Is" Processes and Make Best-in-Class Comparison

Based on the data collected in Step 3, map the as-is process flows. If best-in-class has been determined, compare client as-is processes to industry benchmarks.

Step 5: Collect Feedback on "As-Is" Process Flows

Send process flows and documentation to participants with a list of ideas that may have been culled from the research conducted on their behalf. Participants provide feedback and relevant updates are based on the feedback.

Step 6: Hold Workshops to Review Feedback

Meet with client participants to discuss "aha" moments and other insights from the core team's review of the as-is workflows; incorporate other feedback from the participants. Missing elements or clarifications should be collected and discussed.

Step 7: Hold a Business Process Improvement Workshop

Set up a workshop to develop ideas for process improvement and develop preliminary "to-be" process flows. Outcomes of this workshop typically include the following:

- Process goals and objectives

- Process assumptions

- Proposed process metrics

- Other process issues and considerations

- Activities and efforts involved in the work flow

Step 8: Draft "To-Be" Process Flows

Develop Level 1 and Level 2 process flows. Level 1 represents the highest level of the process steps and notes additional processes that are called from the key process; Level 2 provides process details for each key activity/step in the first level's process flow. Process flows document high-level activities, decisions, and flow of information including the interfaces to functions, individuals, and systems (CRM system). Consider the sample flows that follow.

This workshop, which can last from two-and-a-half to four hours, will provide a time to vet, change, or modify ideas and suggestions that have alternative impacts. The result will be an agreed upon set of "to-be" process flows and a list of key actions needed to produce the final set of recommendations and projects to fulfill the vision.

Step 9: Provide Process Flows to Client for Vetting

Send the process flows and supporting documentation to the project leader for distribution to business process improvement participants. Participants will provide feedback on the process flows and make them available to make relevant changes.

Step 10: Provide Recommendations

Present observations and recommendations for process improvement projects and chart out the next steps. The recommended projects are prioritized, based on relevant criteria that might include the following:

- Urgency (what is needed for the first phase of implementation)

- Potential impact (revenue enhancement, cost reduction, efficiency improvement)

- Available resources (personnel identified for additional process work)

An example of a Level 1 process flow is included in Appendix B at the end of the book. This figure represents an example of an ISM Level 1 process flow for a hypothetical company, XYZ, Inc. Level 1 is the highest level of the process steps for a CRM implementation and refers to additional processes that are called from the key process.

Chapter 15

Why Business Processes Must Precede Technology

While I was on vacation in 2006 in Milano Marittima, a small seashore town on the Adriatic Sea, I watched Italy win the World Cup. I was impressed by how well Italy and France played, but more importantly, I was struck by how structured their plays were. Like well-oiled machines, the Italians and French had created many different plays and had practiced them time and time again until they became second nature to the players. If only organizations implemented CRM in a similar manner.

The right way to implement a CRM initiative is to first determine what business functions you want your initiative to address (sales, marketing, customer service, ecustomer, business analytics, or some combination of these), then prioritize these functions (remember to bite off only what you can chew since successful CRM initiatives get rolled out in multiple iterations), determine how well your current business processes support prioritized business functions, enhance business processes as appropriate, and, finally, apply technology to optimize your well-oiled business processes.

Unfortunately, too many organizations depend on CRM software vendors to supply needed business processes. This is backwards logic; let me explain. Some CRM software vendors build valuable process capabilities into their software (Onyx's software builds Miller Heiman Blue Sheets directly into the software). But many software vendors are not sufficiently business-process savvy to know which specific business processes to offer in their software. They default by building in generic processes along with a business process/workflow engine. This helps to customize their generic processes to varying degrees, which may or may not fit your organization's way of doing business, or they offer vertical, industry-specific software that builds in relevant industry-specific business processes to varying degrees that again may or may not fit well with what you need. But neither of these two options is optimal.

Here's a third option that is being practiced by best-in-class organizations worldwide. You document your key "as-is" business processes (using "swim-lane" techniques, which is a type of process flow diagram that depicts what or who is working on a particular subset of a process) and note where they fall short. Then, you review best-practice business processes (more of these can now be purchased from external sources) that help address your noted shortfalls, and you agree to move your "as-is" business processes to "to-be" business processes that feel right for the way your organization conducts its business. With your "to-be" business processes in place then, and only then, can you go out to CRM software vendors to determine how well their built-in business processes and/or business process/workflow engine matches your specific business process needs.

If this match is a reasonably good one (read "80-plus percent fit"), you compromise a bit and move forward by purchasing the CRM software. If this match is not a good one, you then need to critically examine whether the software vendor's business process/workflow tool capability (or a more powerful third-party, vendor-compatible business process/workflow tools) can be used to customize their software to meet your specific "to-be" process needs.

We have and will continue to perform this third option for several of our customers with favorable results. For example, a global footwear and apparel manufacturer said that continuous business-process improvements have now become a part of its DNA.

This brings me back to Italy's recent World Cup victory. Knowing the plays was a part of the Italian team's DNA. The players then executed these plays with excellence. In your organization, think of your processes as the plays and your CRM software as the players. Get your plays right, then choose and train your best players.

Chapter 16

The Importance of Data Integrity

Data cleansing/data management is a core component of every successful CRM program, and it should be developed at the outset. Data integrity consists of two processes: data cleansing and data management. It should also include ways to document current data inventory, develop data standards, cleanse existing data, and develop processes to maintain, change, and enhance the quality of your data. The justification for data integrity is critical as illustrated in the following:

- Quality data is a strategic asset that will impact the success of your CRM system.

- The quality and accuracy of data (i.e., customer, market, competitor, product, and supplier data) in the CRM system will impact a consistent, error-free way to enhance the customer experience.

- Data inventory is important to determine the source, location, flow, and extent of existing data to understand which data may be used for the CRM system.

- Data cleansing is critical to eliminate any data duplication. For example, eliminating duplicate customer entries will reduce marketing costs by preventing duplicate marketing mailings, faxes, and emails.

- Data cleansing tools (such as the Business Objects products) cleanse, standardize, and consolidate customer-centric data anywhere that data is touched, stored, or moved. The tool helps to consolidate multiple identities of the same customer across several legacy systems data sources to create a single customer view.

- Data-cleansing tools can be integrated into an enterprise application architecture. Several data-cleansing tool vendors already have application program interfaces (APIs) developed for CRM and ERP (enterprise resource planning that includes back-office systems) applications. Depending on the company's enterprise technical architecture, these APIs should be relatively easy to implement. The data-cleansing tools follow business rules that proactively maintain data quality.

- An ongoing plan to maintain data cleanliness and integrity (parsing, correcting, and matching data) can help prevent data degradation over time.

- Quality data can help deliver more accurate reports to customer-facing personnel and customers.

- Costs (associated with poor data quality) can sometimes be reduced, including redundancy costs (storing same data in more than one database) and infrastructure costs (costs of hardware used for data storage).

Lessons Learned

Cleansing/managing CRM data seems quite logical. To some, it may even sound easy. For those who have gone through the effort, cleansing/managing data is an ongoing and sometimes elusive effort within each CRM initiative. Here are a few examples that may be helpful along with a case study.

In 2006, a global telecommunications company was having data integrity issues. The company had 36 different data sources, ranging from Oracle back-office databases to myriad incompatible legacy systems that contained bits and pieces of customer information. While the CIO was convinced that all 36 data sources needed to be integrated into the emerging CRM data warehouse, the vice president of marketing and sales (who was paying for the CRM initiative) disagreed. He thought the number of data sources could be limited to 15. This issue turned into quite a debate, and in the end, the CIO won.

But conditions deteriorated as the cost and time needed to integrate each of the 36 databases continued to grow. The fundamental question of cost versus benefit was at hand for bringing existing data into the emerging CRM system. And after many months of delays and excuses, the IT department, which concluded that it had underestimated the complexity of cleaning the data and bringing it across to the new CRM system, agreed with the vice president of marketing and sales and limited the number of integrated data sources to 15.

Lesson learned: Carefully determine the cost/benefit of integrating data before starting any integration.

During one of my firm's assignments with a global postal service, I also applied this "lesson learned." For the postal service, the CRM program manager felt that more than 150 data sources needed to be integrated. To address the cost/benefit issue early, I suggested that the CRM program manager approach each data source owner, inform the owner about the cost to integrate the proposed data, collect this money up front, and then start the integration process. The CRM program manager followed my advice. In the end, only eight data-source owners were prepared to pay the required money, and the remaining 142 data sources declined. While the company saved millions of dollars, the company's loss for not having needed data was minimal, since system users were given incentives to collect missing data just before the system was launched.

Lesson learned: Consider that it may be less expensive and less time consuming to recreate or re-enter data than it is to integrate all supposedly needed data sources.

A Case Study

In 2006, a leading global biotechnology company wanted help to facilitate the specification and implementation of its global CRM initiative. While the company had global customers, each of the company's geographical locations often kept its own customer records in data formats that were frequently incompatible globally. Some of the company subsidiaries, faced with bad quality data, decided to use the CRM system initiative as a reason to discard their old data and avoid importing any records.

The U.S. subsidiary, which was rich in valuable/historical data, had to import large amounts of data. In fact, the U.S. entity imported more than 250,000 records from three sources: marketing, sales reps, and its SAP back-office financial application. According to the company's CRM project manager, "The potential for importing duplicate records was quite high, and detecting and de-duping was quite challenging. We tried to map as many contacts in the CRM system to the contacts currently held in SAP. This mapping process was also extremely time consuming."

Following are some of the lessons learned (remember that these are specific to this biotech company's unique situation).

1. Understand the Data Integrity Requirements and Process

- Data integrity (including cleansing and management) is a big job and often one that is the least understood except for those who are closely involved with it. Be prepared to spend time repeating data integrity explanations to many people and why it is needed.

Recommendation: Those who will make decisions need to be involved from the beginning of the data integrity process; otherwise, they must learn to trust recommendations from the data team members.

2. Start Early

- This company started its data integrity process in 4Q 2006. After roughly one year, this company still has a lot to do; the data integration process is still incomplete.

Recommendation: Create one administrative system to track all data integrity tasks and subtasks so all team members can share and view the process. The company used Microsoft (MS) Project and the Informatica Data Explorer product to manage the data migration process. MS Project was useful in general managing the project, while the Informatica product was useful at the hands-on level, such as mapping data from one data source to another and setting up the migration of legacy data for use in the new CRM system.

3. Work to Secure a Cohesive Data Integrity Team

- The skills set that was needed for this biotech company included the following:

  - One programmer with SQL (structured language query) knowledge

- An Informatica Data Explorer product expert to set the data in the right format for non-technical people to use

- One dedicated person to manage the project

- An expert in the specific type of internal data to qualify what is good, clean data. This company tried to use external services to clean the data, but the firm ended up spending an unreasonable amount of time explaining and training the outside service. For some companies, data cleansing/data integrity is far too complex for outsiders to understand or implement. Consider data-cleansing tools in addition to personnel.

- Team continuity is critical to success. This company lost three data integrity team members because they were needed on other company projects. This caused delays in completing the data integrity/data cleansing since this process requires transferring complex knowledge, which may be too technical for others to effectively use in such a short time.

- Skilled, detail-oriented personnel are needed. One company programmer left the team because he could not handle the detail required to successfully implement these data integrity procedures.

- All team members should receive software training on the selected CRM software package before starting to implement data integrity efforts. Without the knowledge of the selected CRM package, data integrity team members may have difficulties envisioning how the data flow and connect to each other. This company also saw value in having a project leader who was skilled in computer programming or with reasonable computer knowledge. This helped with understanding what could be done when cleaning up and exporting/importing data.

Recommendation: The project planning must include efforts to create and secure a cohesive data integrity team through team continuity, skilled, detailed-oriented personnel, and team members receiving the appropriate CRM software package training.

4. Communications

- Meet weekly with the data integrity team members. Complement this weekly meeting with a daily walk-around to all team members. This prevents a data integrity team member or programmer from starting to work on a data integrity assignment without a clear vision.

- Manage user expectations. For example, the sales reps from this company gave the data integrity team its data. The reps didn't understand one important factor: While the reps' data may have been clean, data from other departments might not be. When combining data, the de-duplication process can be extensive and time-consuming. This company found that it was valuable to share the naming conventions used in the data integrity process with the system users during their initial training. They also outsourced the de-duplication process to a third-party vendor.

Recommendation: Communications should be a key element of the data integrity process. Regular meetings and the management of user expectations are crucial factors for its success.

5. Project Management

- Ensure that you have strong project management skills and a data project manager who budgets 90 percent of project time to managing data-related projects instead of participating in the actual cleansing process. A project manager who gets caught up in trying to do too much data cleansing and importing may lose sight of the overall goal. Usually, it takes only 10 percent of hands-on data cleansing to understand likely issues and problems. If these issues and problems are not apparent, the roles of the data project manager and the CRM project manager should be given to different people.

- Define all data elements object by object, then transfer the responsibility for securing needed data elements to those who "own" and use the data. The definition of data elements, which should be consistent with data dictionary rules, should be done at the outset of the data integrity project.

- Ensure that the data project manager keeps complete records on the status of data. Otherwise, it can become an administrative nightmare to sort out which data has been imported, cleansed, and quality controlled.

Recommendations: Make sure that the principles of project management are included in the data integrity process, such as having a data project manager with strong project management skills, defining all the data elements, and having complete records on the status of data.

6. Integration with Other Systems

- Warning: Do not try to over-integrate. This biotech firm that was used as an example integrated products, literature, and sales orders at too premature of a pace. It became too big of a job for the biotech firm to handle as the premature rate of integration led to numerous instances of insufficient and inadequate data that were available for the staff at crucial moments.

Recommendation: Focus on the most useful/needed data integration. For this company, it was sales orders. Other integrations can wait or can be done manually until a stable system and an educated system user-base have been established.

7. Technical Issues

- Test and ensure the quality control of imported data every time a data import is completed. Import small amounts of data to test the import integrity process before ramping up the import procedure.

- Hire competent consultants who have experience in importing data. For example, the consultant for this company did not know that importing ZIP codes beginning with "0" would create a problem, leading to some ZIP codes not being imported and an incomplete ZIP code database. As a result, the company had to spend the money again to import the data correctly.

Recommendation: Be sure to keep a checklist of technical requirements that must be met when selecting a consultant for a project.

8. Data Integrity

- Assign the data integrity process to one or more individuals in
  the company. Ensure that each person receives proper incentives to care about data quality. Many people use data but few
  pay much attention to its quality.

- Data integrity implies long-term planning. List the tasks needed
  to clean and keep data clean. Define how you intend to identify
  "bad" records and how you intend to clean such records, even if
  this means cleaning the records manually. Create an internal
  data-cleansing group dedicated to cleansing the data records
  individually, if this is required. This company created a data entry
  group, which was responsible for many of these tasks. The
  biggest problem was asking them to work on data cleansing
  while simultaneously maintaining their regular workload.

- As we have seen, data integrity boils down to the resources and
  the dedication among data integrity team members. If the data
  integrity project is planned carefully and executed properly, you
  can maintain the team's long-term dedication as well as guarantee the success of your CRM initiative.

Recommendation: Make sure that your company provides sufficient
resources and instills dedication among data integrity team members for
the project to succeed.

Building a Data Quality Strategy

The case study we reviewed illustrates two of the most important
aspects of a CRM program: Prepare and keep CRM data clean, and ensure
that you have a proper data quality strategy as your CRM in real-time initiative moves forward.

Here are the key steps for building a data quality strategy:

- Purchase toolsets and integrate them into the enterprise applications where customer data is used.

- Review and check management data for quality on a regular basis.

- Understand the company's customer-facing employee information needs.

- Provide a unified view of customers by setting up a master enterprise data architecture.

- Launch a data quality program to maintain a high-quality data standard.

- Set up a data quality audit task force of employees who use customer data at different levels in your organization.

- Do not underestimate the time and effort it will take for appropriate data cleansing. My firm has found that it is inefficient to cleanse and migrate all the legacy data in a company's systems to the new CRM system all at once. Instead, the company should first determine which legacy data is essential for the new CRM system to function, and then cleanse this legacy data. Afterward, this legacy data should then be migrated to the new CRM system. Additional legacy data can be cleansed and added to the CRM system when appropriate.

- Provide naming conventions that are consistent with the consistent local use of terms. For example, be consistent: Use the complete word, or use abbreviations for a particular word (e.g., "Street" versus "St." and "Avenue" versus "Ave.").

- Implement integrated automated data-management tools for accurate address and ZIP codes. These tools also contain business logic to ensure that the data follows naming conventions, including product names.

- Secure an executive commitment to the initiative to make sure that data quality is supported.

Chapter 17

CRM and the E-volution of Ebusiness

Electronic business, better known as ebusiness, is not a new concept in the business world. The electronic commerce portion of ebusiness has been around since the late 1960s, but the growth of the World Wide Web has led to an explosion in technologies that facilitate the processes involved in building individualized relationships with customers before, during, and after goods and services are purchased.

As we continue to discuss ebusiness, eservice, and emarketing, we'll make observations on their status along with key applications and infrastructure issues, and what lies ahead of all areas of ebusiness e-volution.

Quite possibly because of the rapid development of technologies, processes, and models underlying ebusiness, myriad definitions of ebusiness exist. So we will use the following definition as defined by TechWeb's TechEncyclopedia:

> **e-business:** (Electronic-BUSINESS) Doing business online. The term is often used synonymously with e-commerce, but e-business is more of an umbrella term for having a presence on the Web. An e-business site may be very comprehensive and offer more than just selling of products and services. For example, it may feature a general search facility or the ability to track shipments or have threaded discussions. In such cases, e-commerce is the order-processing component of the site.

Ecommerce is essentially the exchange process (buying, selling, and collaborating) between internal and external business partners as well as end customers across electronic platforms (intranets, extranets, and the Internet/Web). It is also a component of an overall ebusiness strategy.

Many companies that have made business and financial investments in ebusiness have proven that online business can be very profitable. Ebusiness involves more than just letting customers view a few Web pages about company information; it's the ability to extend the enterprise to customers. In the past, this would have required major investments in custom software on customer computers, which is an unlikely proposition.

Keep in mind that ebusiness is only one piece of the puzzle; it is a component of the overall CRM framework. Other CRM components, including sales and marketing and call centers, are required to provide the full customer experience in real time (the ability to service all the customer's requests and needs within one system) depending upon the type of organization that implements ebusiness.

Unlike brick-and-mortar operations, ebusiness isn't constrained by space, time, or type of currency. Today, goods can be ordered, purchased, and shipped globally (subject to weather conditions) at any time. Ebusiness is inherently shifting more power to customers, producers, and distributors because of the direct connections between entities in the exchange process. In some cases, the need for intermediaries is eliminated. See Figure 17.1, which illustrates the ebusiness and ecommerce links between businesses of all sizes via customer and business portals. Ebusiness is conducting business online, and ecommerce is the exchange

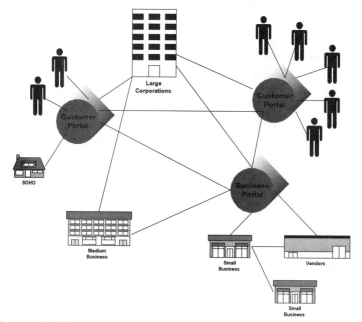

*Figure 17.1   Ebusiness and ecommerce links between businesses of all
sizes via customer and business portals*

process between internal/external business partners across electronic platforms.

Ebusiness reflects the changing roles in the producer-customer relationship where the consumer takes a more active role in the way the producer is doing business. An example would be the feedback mechanisms that are provided to consumers via ebusiness that allow more feedback and more immediate response and measurement/analysis of that feedback. In this way, ebusiness is bringing customers closer to the actual producers of products and services.

Ebusiness and CRM involve more than just purchasing and installing software. It means that organizations have to conduct business and leverage technology in a different way. To maintain a competitive industry position, management must realize that the business rules are being rewritten. The vast majority of the Global 2000 companies have significant ebusiness components to their overall business.

Supply-chain management is another area of ebusiness. Electronic links among and between suppliers, distributors, resellers, and retailers are being incorporated more into the ebusiness framework. These various entities, using Web-related technologies and architecture, are taking advantage of opportunities to exchange information, products, and payments to expedite the transaction process. For example, suppliers that use CRM software applications to automate sales, marketing, and customer service functions are also using ebusiness via the Web to share information about customers, competitors, shipping/delivery, inventory, and financials with members of the supply chain. In other words, ebusiness invites communication and cooperation with supply-chain members that can increase the business effectiveness of the channels. This also fosters interdependencies that force supply-chain members to mutually consider strategies, knowledgebase, and business structures/processes.

Ebusiness technology is still evolving. Electronic data interchange (EDI) had been the leading platform for conducting ebusiness before the rapid expansion in Web technology. EDI was generally used by large companies with substantial financial resources to buy their own proprietary infrastructure for the interchange of information about payments, deliveries, and inventory. EDI provides secure data communications between organizations with the translation of data between disparate computing systems. EDI requires significant investments in computers (hardware and software), third-party service providers and telecommunications (dedicated data lines and value-added networks, or VANs), regular maintenance, and training. Web technologies, such as the emerging industry standard XML (extensible markup language), provide EDI functionality at a lower overall cost.

Web technologies also provide reach and accessibility of ebusiness to small businesses and consumers who do not have the resources to implement EDI. XML, EDI, and Web technology are being integrated and used concurrently, an integration that is also fueling the expansion of ebusiness.

Business-to-business (B2B) ecommerce far outpaces that of business-to-consumer (B2C) in volume of generated revenue. Sales, technical support, customer service, and public relations are the main reasons cited by 70 percent of Fortune 500 companies that have or are building ebusiness structures, according to a 2005 study by ISM.

Key Applications

Ebusiness is being used to augment or replace existing models of transaction and interaction with customers. For example, in B2C ecommerce, Barnes and Noble bookstores are using ebusiness to evolve from brick-and-mortar retail outlets to click-and-mortar, where customers can order from an online store as well as retail outlets. The focus of most ebusiness efforts has been related to the following business functions:

- Sales of products and services (including payments)

- Product development (gathering customer feedback)

- Customer self-service (FAQs, online tutorials, chat/discussion groups, and automated email response)

- Post-sales support (order status, billing, and technical support)

Works is an example of a company that is using ebusiness processes and systems. This B2B company is another Web-based business that changes the online purchasing paradigm much like Amazon.com has done. By forming a "Web-centric" company, Works is able to transcend the traditional geographic constraints of brick-and-mortar operations. Works has developed a supply-chain, workflow-enabled software suite that allows companies to order business products online and manage both online and offline expenditures from indirect goods and services.

The range of benefits can be derived from application of ebusiness including the following:

- Enhanced customer service

- Market expansion

- Cost reduction

- Customer retention/loyalty

- Streamlining the sales cycle

Ebusiness provides many opportunities for companies to grow their business. But given the brief history of ebusiness using Web technologies, several issues associated with the implementation and use of ebusiness continues to be the top challenges. These include the following:

- Resistance to organizational change

- Business process redesign and systems integration hurdles

- Lack of ebusiness expertise

- Difficulties in matching technology to business needs

- Security concerns

Ebusiness Infrastructure

Since ebusiness potentially opens the corporate information technology infrastructure to millions of users, several important points should be considered when designing and implementing an ebusiness system. The information technologies infrastructure must be designed from the ground up to handle this environment, and it must do the following:

- Be massively scalable.

- Provide consistent service quality with low administrative overhead to let companies take advantage of new business opportunities.

- Offer 24/7/365 availability while providing security and transaction integrity.

- Integrate tightly and leverage existing business systems.

- Handle hundreds of applications and new services that can be transformed in Web-time that translates into the following: four months = 1 Web year. (The 4 months = 1 year is a concept that is widely used in the Silicon Valley, where this concept was developed in 2005 based on their good knowledge of the Web.)

- Support the complexity of integrating B2B and B2C trading.

All business functions from the front office (sales, marketing, and customer service) to the back office (accounting, manufacturing, and logistics/distribution/delivery) will continue to be automated, primarily via software that is built on or takes advantage of Web technologies. The closing of sales, payment, and delivery of the product will also be done electronically, especially those created in digital media (music, books, videos, reports, financials, etc.). Potential customers will be able to participate in their own "lead qualification" process by filling out an online form or survey, the results of which are analyzed by ebusiness software and then fed back to the potential customer in real time (wherever applicable).

Ebusiness will be enhanced by two factors: customer self-service and eservice applications that enable customers to find information about products/services with or without help from actual customer service agents. Customer expectations will definitely increase regarding the availability of information about their respective purchases via ecommerce. If a product or service is not offered through ebusiness, customers will ask why because they expect rapid results from ebusiness. This applies for B2B as well as B2C transactions. Customers will also expect that any organization with CRM systems will capture all transaction-based, permission-based, and observation-based knowledge. The customers will also expect that enterprises will make this information available, if appropriate within privacy guidelines, to any "customer touch-points," so that a company presents a unified voice to the customer.

Ebusiness is blurring the lines that once divided business departments and functions in manufacturing, marketing, sales, and distribution. Advances in the development of XML and other Web-centric languages, architectures, and systems will heighten the movement of data across the

Web. But the integration of people, process, and technology remains the key to success for ebusiness and CRM.

Eservices and CRM

One-to-one marketing, launched in the late 1980s, emphasizes the individualized marketing relationships with customers. One-to-one customer service, launched in the late 1990s, emphasizes the individualized customer service. While the two initiatives increasingly work hand-in-hand, one-to-one customer service has taken on increased significance as a result of new and powerful Web-based tools. Let's examine why.

Customer service and support is an important and undisputed part of the CRM picture. The rapid growth of ebusiness verified the need to provide customer access to presales or post-sales information across multiple interaction points or channels. Driven by advances in Web technology and customer demand for unassisted and assisted customer support, CRM vendors are offering various Web-based customer service options across multiple contact channels to supplement the phone support that has been offered via call centers in many cases. The customer interaction center, also referred to as the customer contact center by some organizations, is a component of the overall eservice area that integrates customer self-service, interactive support, and multimedia portal management to provide that access to customer data.

Eservice products, which attempt to integrate all customer interactions into one coherent string of communications, can include the following:

- Self-service via FAQs

- Self-service via a knowledgebase, which can be searched using different query methods, including natural language query

- Email management and response

- Interactive Web-text chat with a live agent, including a "call me now" option

- Real-time voice chat via the Web connection (voice over IP or VoIP)

- Virtual agent, artificial intelligence "bot," or an assistant that processes natural language queries and presents responses from a knowledgebase

At least an estimated 78 percent of all customer contacts and inquiries will be conducted through the Internet, according to findings from ICMI in 2007. Dynamic self-help customer service solutions have risen from seven percent in 2000 to more than 50 percent in 2007. These statistics clearly indicate that the eservice component of CRM is growing rapidly. My firm forecasts that self-help will account for 80 percent of all solutions in North America by 2010.

Companies with a Web presence that may be planning to sell or interact with customers online are advised to consider eservice options. Vendors with these solutions typically provide Web-based customer self-service (with assisted service) for consistent help instead of the standard call center staffed by live agents. This approach can increase customer satisfaction and build customer-switching costs (the cost for a customer to switch all his/her account numbers from one vendor to another). I have also found that many organizations experience an average 20 percent to 25 percent increase in Web-based conversion rates (actual closed sales) by simply adding real-time interaction capabilities, such as chat and callback features, on their Web sites.

Reducing costs is one potential benefit of implementing eservice. Based on a 2005 Forrester study of 46 companies offering CRM, 54 percent of customers who call a toll-free call center choose to speak with an operator, which costs a company an average of $33 per inquiry. This compares with $9.99 per inquiry for the 9 percent who use email and $1.17 per inquiry for those who follow self-service on a site.

Eservice Providers

Understanding why eservice is important is just the first step. The next step is finding out who provides these solutions.

Eservice products primarily come from the following two main areas:

- **CRM vendors** – These offer specific functionality focused on the eservice capabilities previously reviewed. Many vendors that once provided interactive text chat, email management, or FAQs have rounded out their offerings to include multiple interaction channels. Some vendors concentrate on eservice as a point solution that are typically easier to install than large frameworks with higher risks during implementation. Companies such as KANA, eGain, Divine, Inc., Chordiant, LivePerson, Autonomy, and ATG offer eservice solutions.

- **Call center vendors** – This group is trying to reposition itself as an eservice vendor, which means that the group must have full call center functionality including Interactive Voice Response (IVR) and Computer Telephony Integration (CTI), in addition to connectivity to PBX/switches, VoIP, email management, self-service, media blending, skills-based routing, interactive text chat, assisted browsing, and preferably workforce management. Call center vendors that have moved into the eservice space include Syntellect and Genesys, as well as the more traditional call center hardware providers such as Alcatel-Lucent (Avaya) and Cisco. Amdocs, Ltd. (Clarify) has been affiliated with the CRM space for some time.

More companies today are using eservice solutions as (or along with) CRM applications to capture customer information to forge better relationships. For example, a travel services company in Florida in 2006 implemented CosmoCom technology for customer interaction via the Web. The information gathered was then integrated with a leading CRM application, using a standard SQL database. Since the eservice was implemented, the number of toll-free calls for customer service has been drastically reduced.

When evaluating eservice applications, look for solutions that include the following elements:

- An option for personalized self-service.

- A way for end users to escalate to assisted service and seamlessly transfer information across communication channels (VoIP, Web chat, email, Web forms, CTI, or voice integration).

- Accommodation for more than one account or "tenant" on a system server.

- The option to queue all types of customer/agent interaction (voice, call-me-now, email, and Web chat) and provide media blending with integrated skills-based (sending the call to the person who has the right skill set) and load-balancing capabilities (hiring the optimal number of personnel based on call/query patterns determined over time).

- Consolidation of the organization's knowledgebase and intellectual capital, made available throughout the enterprise; this could be accomplished by providing COM (Component Object Model) and CORBA (Common Object Request Broker Architecture) objects that can be called from CRM and ebusiness frameworks including IONA, BEA, and IBM WebSphere.

- Learning through cumulative customer feedback and development of solutions to let the enterprise provide proactive service to users; the ability to transfer customer history from your platform to other systems provides a good competitive advantage.

- Ability for enterprises to deploy eservice technology rapidly without large integration/implementation efforts; companies are spending time implementing CRM, ERP, and MRP (materials requirements planning) to ebusiness, and they do not have time to integrate point solutions.

- Scaling of costs effectively as an organization's service needs to grow.

- Seamless integration between technologies using architectures such as COM/COM+ wrappers, C++, EJB wrappers, XML, ODBC, AJAX, JAVA, and native tools.

- Ability to handle multiple sessions concurrently, regardless of the contact method used to reach the contact center (phone, interactive text, or email).

- Strong work-flow functionality.

- Dynamic self-service and custom Web page presentation through inference technology (e.g., case-based reasoning, search agents, and fuzzy logic searches).

- Ability to be purchased on a pay-per-usage basis or a licensed per-seat basis.

Since customer self-service has become such an important part of customer service and support options for CRM systems, certain items should be considered when evaluating customer self-service. Let's investigate these in more detail.

Ecustomer Traits

Web-based CRM architecture lets more customers have access to your company's products and services. Needless to say, all customers and particularly ecustomers have become savvy buyers. Ecustomers know how to get to the competition quickly. They expect you to offer them faster channels to purchase products or services, lower prices, improved quality, or a combination. They expect quick and comprehensive answers to all their questions. They want to be able to contact you at one moment via phone and the next moment via the Web, and they expect you to have one holistic profile of them regardless of how they make contact. More ecustomers are requesting personalized entry and services, all within a secure environment, and they look to you for "communities of interest" to meet other buyers with similar traits.

Given the increasing demands from ecustomers, Web-based customer self-service is on the rise and has already become critical in attracting and retaining your customers' loyalty.

Cisco: A Case Study

Cisco is a good example of a company effectively using Web-based customer self-service. It integrates complete customer service and support functions through Web-based applications across the following areas: customer call centers, Web self-service tools, field service management systems, and problem resolution technologies.

A number of Web-based service and learning tools provide the customer with complete support, service, and training. When the customer is unable to answer service questions online, integrated click-to-talk tools provide immediate access to live agents who see what steps the customer has taken and leverage existing customer information to help resolve the issue. The agent can take direct control of the customer's browser and show the customer where the information can be found online.

This initiative, which Cisco calls New World Customer Care, has delivered some impressive results for Cisco including the following:

- Realized savings of more than $330 million by avoiding headcount growth and limiting the infrastructure required to support that growth.

- Improved customer satisfaction (from 3.4 to 4.3 out of 5).

- 82 percent of orders are placed online.

- 83 percent of support questions are answered through Web self-service tools.

- Re-deployed more than 1,000 engineers and 600 customer service representatives to its higher value-add core businesses.

- Now offer 12,000-plus customers worldwide access to online support tools.

- Customer purchasing efficiency has increased by 20 percent through online ordering.

- Reduced delivery times by up to five days domestically and seven-plus days internationally.

- Cut order error rates to less than 1 percent.

- Kept headcount growth to 1,600 despite the fact that customer service and technical support call centers have more than doubled in size since 1995.

When implemented successfully, Web-based customer self-service gives customers the capability to access needed information and perform service functions their way. This includes the following:

- Incident assignment, escalation, tracking, and reporting

- Problem management and resolution

- Order management

- Warranty and contract management

Knowledge management engines, which help companies learn from each customer service incident, further enhance the ability for customers to conduct their own self-service.

Recommendations

If you are considering Web-based customer self-service for your firm, consider learning about the leading eservice vendors that offer Web-based customer self-service options. Some companies that provide customer self-service solutions are outsourcers, such as PeopleSupport, SupportSoft, and ATG. Many others exist; this is just a sampling.

Understand that the key risks of implementing a customer self-service solution include the following challenges:

- Potential customer dissatisfaction, even loss of customers, resulting from frustration of having to use an inefficient self-service offering

- Customers feeling the customer service function has been dehumanized

- Customers objecting to having insufficient responses to their questions

- Overlooking the need to tightly integrate your customer self-service system with other components of your CRM system (sales and marketing) to ensure closed-loop servicing

- Customer displeasure of up-selling or cross-selling during a customer service

- Failure to train customer service personnel to field questions properly online

- Failure to provide alternative servicing options to customers when the self-service system is not working

However, understand the key rewards of using self-service include the following:

- Enable customers to do business "their way"

- Let customers track and configure products 24/7 online

- Increase the ability to up-sell and cross-sell customers during customer service

- Increase customer satisfaction/loyalty rating when customers get what they need faster, at a lower price, and/or with better quality

- Place emphasis on maximizing customer satisfaction rather than the effectiveness of the company's customer service staff

- Lower service costs by reducing customer support and IT staff expenses (20 percent per year savings is being achieved by best-in-class companies today)

- Allow customer support representatives and IT staff to be re-deployed to other revenue-generating activities

Outstanding customer service will be the key differentiator that distinguishes leading companies from the others. Eservice and customer self-service are particularly engaging because the solutions today can help organizations achieve outstanding customer service. For those who want to expand their research beyond this brief overview, focus on the people and process issues that will be integral to the success of the system, no matter which technology you ultimately decide upon.

Knowledge Management and CRM

Nowadays, knowledge management (KM) technology helps companies to capture, organize, manipulate, and share explicit and implicit data. This software is used to automate specific customer service processes, which is why it's important to understand how KM works from the process perspective first.

In CRM implementations, KM adds the ability to learn from each customer interaction. In CRM, information can be turned into actionable knowledge that can be useful to employees for customer profiling and personalization, or to the actual customer for self-servicing. Over the past few years, KM technology developments have propelled the use of customer self-service, which enhances customer retention rates while lowering customer service costs.

Driving the impressive growth of customer self-service is KM software capabilities. International Data Corp. (IDC) reports that two market segments constitute KM solutions: KM access and KM infrastructure. According to various IDC Webcasts in 2006, enhanced KM software will further drive the self-service functionality within customer contact centers.

KM software focuses primarily on the following areas: expressing knowledge, storing knowledge, sharing knowledge, refining knowledge, and retaining knowledge. Moreover, KM technologies allow for multiple data access and retrieval methodologies including keyword search, natural language queries, case-based reasoning, decision-tree reasoning, and expert-based reasoning. KM technology narrows a user's search progressively to an answer that is currently held within a knowledgebase.

For example, a knowledgebase can be used to respond to online user queries. If the user querying the knowledgebase determines that the response is inappropriate, this knowledge goes into the knowledgebase, and it then searches for a more appropriate response. This automated process continues until a response to the user query has been found. In some cases, the process may even involve human interaction if an appropriate response cannot be found within the knowledgebase. In turn, this solution then gets added to the knowledgebase (subject to verification).

Customers appreciate getting answers to inquiries quickly and correctly. This helps build customer satisfaction, and it ultimately increases loyalty over the long term. The same customers will gravitate to the companies that offer a customer contact center that incorporates enhanced KM tools to facilitate self-service.

The pros of using a KM system include the following:

- Available 24/7/365

- Quick response to customer queries

- Flexible use based on sophistication of user

- Scalable

The cons of using the system include the following:

- Possible inaccuracies/errors in response(s) to customer queries

- An organization may have a limited number of customer contacts

- Tendency to require serious process re-engineering

Vendors that provide KM solutions or a KM component within CRM-related offerings include KANA (purchased Broadbase), Ask.com, RightNow, Knova, and ATG.

Companies implementing eservice aspects of CRM realize that the knowledgebase should be accessible via multiple communication channels, whether through Web chat and email, or phone, fax, and mail. One of the key benefits of a centralized knowledgebase is the ability to hold a single, integrated dialog with a customer regardless of his or her preferred communication channel. If implemented correctly, a knowledgebase enables every contact center agent (or customer) to be as up-to-date and informed as the best agent, because the knowledge is automatically available to any agent who uses the system.

A growing number of companies are using KM tools. For example, Nike.com has a search engine that lets customers easily search for comprehensive product/service information, which helps Nike to cut internal costs associated with live agents responding to basic phone and email inquiries. In another example, Eddie Bauer has integrated a knowledgebase into its contact center that provides users with self-service options including a library search of FAQs (including natural language query) and interactive chat.

Cisco Systems uses KANA technology for its Cisco Connection Online (CCO) service, a global support organization that integrates with Cisco's global call center. Currently, about 80 percent of Cisco customers' self-service inquiries are resolved using the CCO, which eliminates responding to an estimated 75,000 phone calls per month.

When looking for a KM solution, consider the following:

- Speed

- Flexibility of usage

- Open data model

- Accuracy

- Multiple hardware platforms and operating system environments

Here are the initial steps to get started on developing a knowledge-based contact center:

- Analyze the quality and quantity of interactions with customers across different access methods

- Compare the interaction costs across the different access methods

- Analyze the available resources and infrastructure to support a knowledgebased contact center

One important development is having an impact on the future of knowledge-based contact centers: the emergence of contact center KM analytic tools that provide powerful customer reports (supplying information on which customers are contacting you when and about what) as well as internal efficiency reports (how effective is your knowledgebase and which areas need to be enhanced), and the emergence of truly multilingual contact centers.

As you investigate KM as a component of your CRM implementation, refer to your requirements analysis to determine real needs and how KM might be applied to filling those needs. And remember that it's important to extend your enterprise to your customers and let your customers conduct business with you in the ways they prefer.

Emarketing and CRM

About 26 years ago, some marketing professors at the Wharton School at the University of Pennsylvania made the landmark statement that the marketing profession was half-science and half-art. The scientific part consisted of gathering valuable marketplace information about customer needs, customer satisfaction, and competitors; the artistic part consisted of applying this information to create marketing mixes to ensure that the right product/service was delivered to the right segments, and that the product/service was distributed, priced, and promoted to entice segment buyers. At the time, thought prevailed that no one right way existed to segment a market and that the two greatest tools a marketing person could be born with are a nose to smell and a belly to feel shifts in the marketplace.

Has technology changed this way of thinking? Absolutely. Starting in the mid-1990s, several CRM software companies began to offer basic marketing automation functionality. This included helping companies create marketing encyclopedias as repositories for valuable marketing information, managing key events such as a trade show, and managing basic marketing campaigns. Customer profiling, assisted by predictive modeling tools, also began to emerge.

In the late-1990s, emarketing vendors that were taking advantage of the booming Internet and building on the work of marketing automation vendors extended marketing functional capabilities. In fact, today's emarketing can be defined as an expanding set of automation tools to help companies identify their most valuable prospects and customers, to convert and grow them, and to keep their loyalty for life. The expanding set of tools includes the following:

- Targeted Web marketing (Web banner advertising)

- Permission-based email direct marketing (special promotions)

- Online customer behavior analysis (click-stream monitoring)

- Lead acquisition, distribution, and management for sales reps as well as for distribution channel partners

- Customer profiling and segmentation

- Integrated campaign management and measurements

- Customer engagement tools (reward-based surveys)

- Customer personalization tools

- Customer-driven services (collateral fulfillment, event management and execution, inquiry processing, direct mail requests, and placement of orders)

A number of leading emarketing vendors serve today's market. Here are three and their key strengths:

- Unica – Customer analytics and campaign management

- Aprimo – Campaign management and analytics

- KANA – Customer interaction platform and many of the above functions

Many of these players have been in an aggressive acquisition mode (e.g., Aprimo acquired the enterprise marketing solutions business unit of DoubleClick Inc. in 2005; Unica bought MarketingCentral in 2007). These acquisitions are a way to compete within the more established CRM space by offering comprehensive Web-based CRM offerings rather than one or more "best-in-class" emarketing "point" solutions. Today's emarketing vendors are focusing attention on integrating data from operational CRM systems, such as sales, marketing, customer service, and executives, as well as back-office ERP software packages, such as Oracle, SAP, PeopleSoft, and others to create more universal customer profiles and increase the effectiveness of marketing efforts.

At the core of an emarketing system is an effective knowledgebase that continuously learns from its users. It serves as a repository for the structured and unstructured data, drawn from various systems, and it is critical to the execution of emarketing functions. Some emarketing vendors have written their own knowledgebases, whereas other emarketing vendors opt to integrate third-party, best-in-class knowledgebase solutions.

Emarketing systems are red-hot for good reasons. For example, a 2004 Forrester Research finding stated that emarketing, when properly implemented, can reduce costs for the production and delivery of promotional materials from $.50 to $1 (per unit) for a single catalog mailing to $.10 for a highly personalized email campaign. Emarketing can help out in three ways: It can speed up marketing campaigns, especially for email direct marketing, allow you to test a marketing campaign before incurring large costs, and provide higher campaign response rates.

Emarketing can also help out in other ways: It can help to eliminate waste by focusing on the most profitable customer segments, generate more revenues from the existing customer base, help understand the behavior of your customer base, and generate customer loyalty via personalization of services. Many companies are turning to emarketing to help them manage leads via distribution channels as well as to provide headway into other CRM software modules, including customer self-service, cross-selling, and up-selling.

While the future of emarketing appears vibrant, users face challenges ahead that they will eventually need to resolve. These challenges include the following:

- What to offer once the customer gets to your site

- How to create a site environment that makes the visitor stay (site "stickiness")

- How to maintain customer loyalty if competition is just a click away

- How to create a meaningful Internet community for ecustomers

- How to use interactivity to replace the loss of persuasive human interaction

- How to understand a customer's needs beyond inferential click-stream monitoring (predicting and interactively exploring the click paths that visitors take through a Web site, page-by-page and click-by-click)

- How to build trust when customers wonder whether the information they provide will be kept private or used inappropriately

Additional emarketing challenges revolve around integration issues: How are new emarketing tools integrated with existing marketing automation tools (process management tools for campaign workflow, response management, lead management and routing, and event coordination), with other CRM core functions (sales, sales management, customer service, business intelligence, and ebusiness), with regular marketing activities ("click" marketing versus "mortar" marketing), and with classical marketing activities (decisions about which products for which segments at what prices)?

While these challenges can be daunting for some, other companies have successfully implemented emarketing systems and rave about the results. Here is a case in point. In 2005, my firm worked with a leading DSL provider in North America. Prior to implementing the company's emarketing project, the vice president of marketing explained that his company was overwhelmed by the number of hot customer leads from a variety of sources. Yet no system was in place to efficiently send leads to the sales force or to track the leads. Of greater concern, this DSL provider had no way to monitor the work of the distribution channel member, the local phone company responsible for provisioning the customer's DSL line. This DSL provider was often not sure when provisioning had or would take place. Meanwhile, the hot customer leads were inundating the DSL provider with calls and complaints concerning the availability of their

DSL and when it would be installed. Unfortunately, the DSL provider had no way to accurately respond.

After installing an emarketing system, which was eventually linked to the local phone companies, the DSL provider was able to effectively capture, distribute, and track its hot customer leads. These hot customer leads could also receive an exact status of their order over the phone or via their Web site using the self-service options.

As the problems with lead and order fulfillment began to ease, the DSL provider turned to other functions of its emarketing system to find new customers (e.g., permission-based, email direct marketing) and to service these customers (e.g., direct ordering by customers and use of customer self-service built on a knowledgebase to correct DSL line problems). About six months after installing the emarketing system, the vice president of marketing shared some good news: The customer satisfaction rating had risen from less than 60 percent at the start to above 85 percent during the six-month period.

The future of emarketing is bright and may well prove to be the engine growth to CRM and eCRM, particularly as digital marketplaces (many sellers to many buyers) develop. This is an increasingly important role for emarketing that has become a set of tools that will help to segment, attract, and keep customers satisfied (the artistic side), while simultaneously offering a way for sellers to monitor customer behavior and satisfy customer needs (the scientific side). While technology has dramatically altered the way we conduct business today, the basic ideas and premises for marketing remain unaltered.

Customer Touch Programs

If asked, most companies will admit to having a customer touch program. According to one Biotechnology executive in 2007, "We mail our catalog to each customer annually, and our sales force calls on each customer at least twice a year."

Although different ideas abound about what a customer touch program is, I see a customer touch program as a structured process for maximizing sales with a select group of customers. A customer touch program consists of placing groups and individual prospects or customers on customer touch "tracks." The number of tracks, the number of steps per track, and the timing between the steps will depend heavily on the business and types of prospects/customers targeted. For example, one track may be dedicated for new leads generated from a trade show. Following this track, the steps include the following:

Step 1: Within 48 hours after the trade show, send a follow-up email thanking the prospect for visiting your booth.

Step 2: Call prospect within five working days after the end of the trade show.

Step 3: For interested prospects, send a literature package explaining current product/service offerings within 10 working days after the end of the trade show.

Step 4: Follow up with a personal visit within 15 working days after the end of the trade show.

Step 5: For a prospect that orders one of your products/services, send a personal thank-you letter note within five working days after the order has been placed.

Step 6: Add the customer to the "new customer" track.

Equally important, the process for dealing with existing customers may involve a completely different track. The procedure could be organized in the following steps:

Step 1: Mail new product/services information to the customer at least every quarter; stress the importance of ongoing "newness."

Step 2: Call the customer at least once every quarter to reinforce the new products/services mailing.

Step 3: Visit the customer at least once every quarter to maintain a personal relationship.

Step 4: Place the customer on the list to receive your company's monthly email newsletter.

Step 5: Send an annual Seasons Greetings card.

Step 6: Send the customers a copy of recently published articles written by your company or about your company.

Step 7: For key customers, offer each customer a portal where they will find a copy of the company's monthly email newsletter along with email messages, new product information, and other important information for that specific customer.

Step 8: For each customer who has not placed an order for perhaps six months, escalate for the appropriate staff to contact the customer name/profile/order history to sales management.

For a successful customer touch program, my firm recommends that organizations put four building blocks in place:

1. **Effective target group segmentation** – Select relevant criteria for determining target groups, and assign responsibility to an individual to keep segmentation up to date.

2. **Well thought-out messages/collateral** – For each track, determine which messages and collateral will have the biggest impact on the prospect/customer. Create an inventory of messages, and assign an individual to keep messages timely and relevant.

3. **A customer touch process** – Customer touch tracks tend to have some automated as well as some ad-hoc steps. Be certain your customer touch program process is well thought-out and documented. Assign the appropriate personnel to execute the designed tracks.

4. **CRM tools supporting the customer touch process** – A variety of excellent tools are available to help you manage customer touch programs. CRM companies such as Database Systems Corp., can help organize, automate, and monitor customer touch efforts. This includes creating needed customer touch program templates and storing them in an easy-to-access location. Some packages even include recommendations on which type of customer touch programs work best for specific circumstances.

But CRM software tools are often complemented by a number of factors: effective account and contact management processes, outbound email and permission-based marketing functions, reliable customer contact functions, and simple, yet powerful business intelligence capabilities.

Here are the essential elements of a customer touch program action plan that need to be determined:

- Criteria for target groups (determine what characteristics will place them in a group)

- Group codes for designated target groups and enter these into CRM program

- Customer touch tracks as well as customer touch campaigns/processes that should be used for each target group

- Inventory of existing messages/collateral that need to be approved before sending them to target groups and updated as necessary

- Messages that should be used for each customer touch program campaign

- Frequency of messages/visits/other "touch" activities sent to each target group

- Which customer touch program templates need to be created in your CRM system for each campaign; create these templates accordingly

- Objectives and content for prospect/customer surveys that will be used in your campaigns (effective tools to determine initial prospect/customer desires)

- Integration of survey results into customer touch messages as appropriate

- Loading of tracks (set up automated processes) into the CRM system and launch the customer touch program

- Measurement and monitoring of results on a regular basis

- Learning from each customer touch effort and adjust as needed

Although you may think you have a meaningful customer touch program in place, CRM technology tools let these approaches enhance your customer touch program efforts and keep your customers satisfied in real time. Given the growing competitive nature and lack of brand loyalty among customers, why would you want to risk the chance of not reaching customers effectively on a regular basis? Ask these questions: Whose customer touch efforts are catching the ear of prospects and existing customers—yours or a competitor? And who will be the one that prospects/customers remember when they are in the buy mode?

PART 4

Business
**Application
and Technology**
Issues

Chapter 18

CRM Business Application Trends

From 2006 to 2007, a number of new CRM business application trends have made a significant impact among users.

Here are eight major trends that currently affect the business functional evolution of CRM systems with noticeable increases in the following:

1. Consolidation and mergers among CRM vendors

2. CRM focus on the small- to mid-sized business segment

3. Use of business intelligence analytical tools (predictive modeling) in CRM solutions

4. Number of mobile CRM offerings and a move toward real-time CRM

5. CRM offerings via the software as a service (SaaS) model

6. Availability of search engine marketing functionality

7. Availability of Web 2.0-type functionality

8. Implementation of CRM software by CRM vendors

1. Increased Consolidation and Mergers among CRM Vendors

Responding to customer pressure to provide comprehensive applications, CRM vendor consolidation by major players is likely to increase. Some small CRM vendors, particularly those in well-defined niche markets, will survive. Some examples of key CRM acquisitions over the past few years include the following:

- Oracle acquires PeopleSoft (2004) and Siebel (2005)

- CDC Software acquires Pivotal (2004)

- FirstWave acquires Connect-Care (2003)

- Infor acquires SSA Global Technologies (2006)

- M2M Holding acquires Onyx Software (2006)

Oracle's acquisitions of PeopleSoft and Siebel along with the emergence of SaaS will encourage further consolidation among CRM software companies as multimillion-dollar CRM enterprises will view other acquisitions as necessary to survive in an increasingly competitive CRM market. CRM functionality is offered more often as part of a larger suite of products. One example is the announcement that the PeopleSoft and Siebel CRM functionality will be rolled into the Oracle Fusion applications. The significance of these key CRM acquisitions is still yet to be determined. Some of these organizations have already effectively integrated their offerings, such as FirstWave Software, which appears to have effectively integrated Connect-Care software, while others, such as Oracle's acquisition of PeopleSoft and Siebel, have not. However, many are still in the integration phase.

Likely impact: Customers will have more choices in comprehensive CRM software.

2. Increased CRM Focus on the Small- to Mid-Sized Business Segment

More small- and mid-sized businesses (SMB), defined as those companies with less than $500 million in annual revenues, or alternatively, companies employing 20 to 150 people, are adopting CRM systems. For example, in 2004, AMR Research predicted that the SMB market will reach $44.1 billion in CRM sales by 2010, given that only a maximum of 20 percent of SMB companies are using CRM applications. Another study by Access Markets International found that mid-sized businesses are likely to spend more than $1 billion in CRM applications in the U.S. at the end of 2007. In the same study, CRM spending within the mid-market CRM segment is predicted to grow at a compound annual growth rate of 9 percent until at least 2011.

Consequently, the SMB market has become increasingly attractive to CRM software vendors. CRM applications targeting SMBs offer easy-to-implement solutions with an opportunity for a quick ROI. For example, Salesforce.com, RightNow, and NetSuite have targeted the SMB market with Web-based SaaS CRM software for a moderate monthly fee. Siebel has also realigned its technology to aggressively target SMBs with its Siebel CRM OnDemand solution. Microsoft's CRM offering is now targeted solely to SMBs. SAP rolled out a hosted version of its CRM software application for the SMB market in early 2006.

Likely impact: Customers can choose from a range of better CRM software offerings in tune with the needs of small- to mid-sized companies.

3. Increased Use of Business Intelligence Analytical Tools in CRM Solutions

Business intelligence analytical tools, or predictive modeling (techniques from statistics and data mining that process current and historical data to make predictions about future events), now can predict the monetary value and profitability of a particular customer. These predictions can range from profiling customers based on their behavior to segmenting markets and from predicting customer purchases based on past purchase information and psychographic/demographic data to determining cross-selling opportunities. Marketers are discovering that analytics programs are beneficial for tailoring marketing messages without violating privacy and other government regulations. Business intelligence analytics will remain an important part of the corporate agenda as companies find that they face a 10-fold increase in the amount of data generated by their IT systems until 2011. AMR Research forecasted at the beginning of 2007 that analytics applications that year will sell better than other CRM components, including call management, sales force automation, and marketing automation. IDC forecasted that core and predictive analytics will have a compound annual growth rate of 7.7 percent and 8 percent, respectively, between 2007 and 2008.

IDC also predicted that the worldwide analytic applications software market will be worth $11 billion in 2008. Many analysts have also now opted to cover this increasingly important functional area, such as Gartner's Business Activity Monitoring offering. The Gartner Group predicted that by

2012, business intelligence analytics will be an integral part of 85 percent of all business applications. As a result, CRM vendors are integrating analytical tools/functionality directly more often into their CRM offerings. A top example is Unica, which specializes in marketing campaign software with analytical tools for market segmentation, along with SAS, which has an alliance with Siebel and Amdocs to integrate their data mining and statistical tools with the CRM suite from Siebel and Amdocs. Other examples include SAP's mySAP CRM application, PeopleSoft's Customer Behavior Modeling application, and Infor CRM.

Likely impact: Customers will have access to better, faster analysis of what is happening within their businesses, which will allow decision makers to make better-informed decisions.

4. Increased Number of Mobile CRM Offerings and a Move Toward Real-Time CRM

CRM vendors continue to develop and release CRM application modules, especially those that are bundled with or work on a large variety of handheld and/or wireless devices. These include personal digital assistants (PDAs)(with various operating systems) and smartphones that support wireless infrastructure technologies like CDMA (Code Division Multiple Access), GSM (Global System for Multiple communications), TDMA (Time Division Multiple Access), CDPD (Cellular Digital Packet Data), SMS (Short Messaging Services), and packet radio networks. Smartphones use cellular networks—not wireless hotspots—to transfer information, which means the user does not have to go to a Starbucks or hotel lobby to access data in the CRM system. Wireless components are increasingly allowing users to make business decisions in real time, along with creating analytics in real time; all of this points toward the growing direction of real-time CRM. Annual growth in the wireless CRM market is expected to be between 35 and 40 percent through 2008; IDC has identified mobile CRM as a substantial portion of the growth expected for mobile and wireless products/services. I predict that by the end of 2008, all CRM applications will be ready for wireless use. By 2010, VisionGain projects that the mobile CRM market will surpass traditional CRM growth rates, representing 20 percent of total CRM revenues in U.S. mobile solutions. These mobile solutions are more often being adopted by financial services, manufacturing, and professional services industries that need access to real-time information in the field, according to a 2006 Gartner Group report stating that 45 percent of the American workforce is using mobile technology of some kind. The market for mobile CRM products will be considerably larger in the U.S. than in Europe, which has been slower to adopt handheld device solutions for enterprise applications.

For example, Antenna Software (www.antennasoftware.com), known mainly as a wireless-ready field service connector to CRM leaders Siebel Systems, SAP, and Amdocs, offers an AntennaNetwork that integrates CRM, field service, and supply-chain tactics. The software enables service techs to automatically call on manufacturer knowledgebases, break-fix data, and the like via a wireless Web connection, and leverages some of the latest field devices including the Motorola's Accompli. Another example is Salesforce.com's mobile module, which uses the same source code to communicate with PDAs, BlackBerry devices, and mobile phones. This mobile module was introduced when Salesforce.com acquired Sendia in April 2006. By integrating Sendia's application server to the Salesforce.com AppExchange platform, Salesforce.com now sells the AppExchange Mobile package, which provides wireless access for businesses via Salesforce.com and AppExchange applications from mobile devices. PeopleSoft's CRM application is available on laptops and handheld computers without a connection to a corporate network or the Web. Saratoga Systems has released Saratoga CRM Wireless, which offers tight integration with small mobile data devices such as RIM BlackBerry. Siebel, Onyx, Amdocs, and SAP all provide access to their CRM application modules on handheld devices on Microsoft (MS) Windows CE and Palm operating systems.

Sage, which acquired Corum's mobile division in 2006, announced plans to make mobile functionality available for its entire CRM product line. Some CRM companies also offer mobile enterprise applications aimed at vertical industries. For example, the Siebel Pharma Handheld application lets pharmaceutical sales professionals manage physician information, activities, call reports, and the distribution of pharmaceutical samples over a PDA.

Likely impact: Customers will have increasing access to time-sensitive information in the CRM database from handheld and/or wireless devices, giving companies new options for improving customer satisfaction, productivity, and financial performance.

5. Increased CRM Offerings via SaaS

CRM software vendors are offering CRM software solutions more often via the SaaS model, which is also referred to as Application Service Provider (ASP). A 2006 IDC report predicted that many software companies will derive a majority of their revenues from subscription agreements rather than perpetual licenses by 2010. This outlook for the SaaS model contrasts to the late 1990s when a host of startups began offering ASP applications over the Web. Many of these startups went out of business because companies were hesitant to let outside companies run their important applications and because integration tool sets were not sufficiently robust. However, in the past few years, large and small companies have become more comfortable with SaaS. The SaaS model can circumvent traditional problems with the client-server model including high prices, cumbersome deployments, and the inevitable software upgrades. A 2006 Gartner Group report projected that during the next three years, half of the software sold to companies will be paid as a monthly fee, as part of a long-term contract, as a monthly rental fee, or as a pay-per-use basis.

"It is a much more financially reasonable model for customers," according to Joanne Corriea, a market research vice president at the Gartner Group. At the beginning of 2007, market research firm ID predicted that worldwide SaaS sales would exceed $8 billion at the end of 2007, primarily from the demand of SMBs. The SaaS model is also being adopted more often by enterprise companies, especially evident with the 2007 Salesforce.com deals with Dell and Merrill Lynch for a 15,000-seat and a 25,000-seat license, respectively.

Salesforce.com, which offers CRM software on the SaaS model, is earning more than an estimated $450 million in annual sales in 2006. Siebel offers a SaaS CRM software application called Siebel CRM OnDemand, and SAP released a SaaS CRM software application in February 2006. Microsoft announced tentative plans to release a SaaS version of its CRM product in early 2008.

The growth and competition among hosted CRM applications has led many CRM vendors to add additional functionality beyond CRM. For example, Salesforce.com added enhancements to AppExchange, an Internet platform and directory where Salesforce.com customers can select and add additional functionality (offered by Salesforce.com partners) to their Salesforce.com application. Salesforce.com currently has more than 400 certified AppExchange partners who can integrate their applications with the Salesforce.com CRM application on the AppExchange Internet platform. The AppExchange applications include diverse packages for areas such as finance, electronic signatures, document management, project management, credit collections, mobile workforce management, data cleansing, human resources, and many others. NetSuite offers a similar product, the NetFlex Applications Program, to provide additional industry-specific functionality from NetSuite partners to its customers. AppExchange and NetFlex applications also provide a platform for the integration of point solutions, which are integral to certain vertical industries.

Siebel offers a hosted CRM solution with embedded interactive analytics. In addition, three hosted CRM vendors—NetSuite, RightNow, and Salesforce.com—offer mass email functionality. With NetSuite, up to 120,000 emails at a time can be sent for a marketing campaign; RightNow has a partnership with Quiris, Inc. and the Aaronson Group to deliver email marketing; and Salesforce.com has released an integrated offering with Responsys Inc. to let users run Responsys email campaigns from Salesforce.com.

The only drawback of the SaaS model is that the customer "depends" on the provider. In early 2006, Salesforce.com experienced an outage that affected not only its customers, but customers of the Salesforce.com customers as well. This might have meant that invoices were not sent, fulfillment was delayed, and more. Furthermore, if a company decides to sever its relationships with a SaaS provider, the company's data in the SaaS package might be in a database that is incompatible with the company's format, leading to a multitude of problems.

Likely impact: Customers have more comprehensive SaaS CRM software offerings to choose from, along with the option to upgrade to a client-server version of the CRM software. The emergence of the SaaS model will mean more emphasis on business expertise, value-added services, and nurturing on-going relationships with subscriber customers with less emphasis on expensive implementation projects.

6. Increased Availability of Search Engine Marketing Functionality

CRM vendors are now providing options for marketers to generate and manage search engine keyword marketing campaigns with a specific click-through URL address to embed within Google AdWords or a sponsored search on Yahoo! or MSN. For example, Salesforce.com offers a Wizard tool that walks the user through the process of creating a keyword marketing campaign on Google AdWords. In this case, a company will create a paid search ad listing that will appear on Google whenever a Web user conducts the selected keyword(s) search on Google.

For example, a Google search on the keywords "high speed internet" will bring up the paid search listing for www.covad.com, which appears on top of the Google listings and can be set up on Salesforce.com. The user can access built-in analytics to track the daily budget, number of clicks, click-through rate, cost-per-click, total number of opportunities generated, ROI, and total cost for each search engine keyword marketing campaign. Salesforce.com also provides 17 predefined report templates for further analysis of each search engine keyword marketing campaign. NetSuite CRM v. 11.0 offers search engine marketing functionality for Google AdWords and sponsored searches on Yahoo! and MSN with configuration. The NetSuite CRM application automatically tracks keyword clicks from the lead capture phase through each sales process and provides a ROI calculation.

Likely impact: Customers can increase the effectiveness of search engine keyword marketing campaigns that lead to greater marketing efficiency for companies in their Web-based marketing efforts.

7. Increased Availability of Web 2.0-Type Functionality

CRM vendors are now beginning to provide access to what some analysts are calling Web 2.0 functionality. Web 2.0 refers to a perceived second generation of Web-based services that emphasize online collaboration and sharing among users. It is a world where computers and other technology have shifted from a means of one-way static communication to platforms for interaction and community building.

Several CRM vendors are taking the first steps toward offering Web 2.0-type functionality in their CRM applications:

- **Customer feedback** – RightNow CRM 8 offers a feedback feature where organizations can set up Web or email surveys to capture customer feedback in real time. The surveys can be targeted at a specific group or set as general customer feedback. Afterward, customer feedback can be routed by topic to the appropriate company division for an appropriate response. Companies can build in escalation rules to handle negative feedback such as sending the feedback to a specific customer service supervisor.

- **Ecommerce** – NetSuite CRM v. 11.0 can be integrated with eBay's auction site online marketplace. The NetSuite CRM users can list and sell items on eBay and monitor eBay auctions, while automatically creating the customer records and sales orders from completed eBay auctions. NetSuite also offers an ecommerce engine where NetSuite users can create and publish different Web sites from a single NetSuite account. Each Web site can feature its own Web site design, products, and domain name.

- **Open source software** – The community-developed software movement, also known as the open-source community, is based on the approach that companies or communities will make the source code of software available online (the programming that makes a software application work). Qualified persons can contribute their improvements to their applications with the source code for their own or company's use. Salesforce.com has led the open source movement by making its Apex language and development platform of its on-demand applications available to users. Apex is a Java-like programming language and environment used by Salesforce.com developers to create the company's hosted CRM application. With Apex, customers will be able to customize any component in their existing Salesforce.com implementation or build their own Apex code and replace existing Salesforce.com features with ones that are more suitable to their needs. Apex components and applications also can be shared via Salesforce.com's AppExchange platform directory.

Likely impact: Customers have access to more CRM software functionality that enhances the goals of Web 2.0 with greater online collaboration and sharing among users.

8. Increased Implementation of CRM Software by CRM Vendors

CRM vendors are now offering implementation of their CRM software in-house as an incentive to their customers to purchase their CRM software application. Prices for such implementation have dropped as much as 50 percent from 2005 prices as user-friendly application development tool kits based on open standards have become the norm. Nevertheless, implementation costs are still by far the greatest cost in an overall CRM budget. The CRM industry still depends heavily on successful implementations to propel future growth.

In my firm's survey of the 2007 Top 15 CRM vendors, we confirmed this trend. Of the Top 15 SMB CRM companies, 88 percent declared they are doing more of their own implementations now than in 2006, whereas 80 percent of the top 15 enterprise CRM companies are performing more of their own implementations than in 2006. Likewise, 56 percent of all SMB vendors are currently handling 60 percent or more of their own implementations, whereas 80 percent of all enterprise vendors are currently handling 70 percent or more of their own implementations.

CRM vendors are likely to increase their implementation offerings in the future to increase client satisfaction with their CRM applications. According to a 2007 Forrester Research survey, 40 percent of companies surveyed would not recommend their CRM professional service provider to others; this indicates the need for successful implementation of CRM software applications in the marketplace. Pivotal and Onyx offer standardized implementation fixed-fee implementation packages. FirstWave currently provides its customers with offerings from professional service organizations to implement the FirstWave CRM application at customer sites.

Likely impact: Customers now have more appropriate CRM implementation offerings to choose from, thereby increasing the overall potential for successful implementations of CRM applications.

New business application trends are likely to emerge annually. Although it is always difficult to determine which trends will stick and which will pass, I see these eight trends continuing and maturing over time, based on observations by my firm's Software Testing Laboratory, along with market input from customers and leading authorities.

Customers are encouraged to understand these trends and to ask potential vendors about their current and future plans for each of the trends.

Chapter 19

The Technology Component

Given the ever-expanding number of technology offerings and alternatives, the technology component of any CRM implementation can be overwhelming. Two primary issues are related to technology: dealing with CRM software vendors and staying on top of CRM technology trends.

Let's start with CRM software vendors. Today's CRM technology will address most of CRM user requirements. Customers can choose from dozens of competent, financially sound CRM vendors. Nonetheless, can the CRM vendor deliver what it promises? The response to this question is not always evident.

Here are a few examples. In one case, a leading CRM software vendor claimed its software seamlessly integrated with all back-office systems. Once the software had been purchased, the purchasing company realized that the integration was not seamless, and it actually required a fairly expensive ($200,000) piece of enterprise application integration (EAI) middleware to connect it seamlessly to its SAP back-office system.

In another case, a leading CRM software vendor claimed that all CRM system users needed to purchase their customer service base module if users expected to exchange data among the sales, marketing, and customer service functions. Fortunately, the purchasing company found out that this was not necessary since all functions could easily draw and share information from the common database regardless of the base module used. The purchasing company nearly purchased $150,000 of unnecessary software.

In a third case, one of the largest database software vendors claimed that its emerging CRM software offering would contain the most comprehensive CRM functionality in the industry. Quite a few potential buyers actually waited months and months for the promised functionality to arrive. Finally, under pressure from a variety of sides including analysts, the database vendor was forced to admit that it would not be able to offer promised functionality. Soon after, the company opened its emerging yet incomplete CRM software's API (application program interface) to third-party software vendors. One of the lessons learned concerned CRM software vendors: Remember these vendors encounter fierce competition (and analyst/venture capital pressure) that may force them to stretch the truth from time to time. So ask the company to demonstrate its product promises and solutions in real time.

Staying on top of CRM technology trends has become increasingly difficult because of the proliferation of CRM technologies in the marketplace. Rather than trying to keep up with each new technology, companies should track technologies that are most likely to impact the CRM industry's future as well as their own company's CRM efforts (Chapter 20, Key CRM Technology Trends, reviews a few of the latest technology trends). For example, this may include customer self-service applications that are built on top of an effective knowledgebase, emarketing applications (permission-based direct marketing, wireless, and voice recognition capabilities), or the use of major framework tools to consolidate and enhance N-tiered architectures (distributed among three or more separate computers in a distributed network) within a CRM implementation. While we can't learn about every new technology trend that is likely to impact CRM, it's beneficial to keep up-to-date on the big ones.

Chapter 20

Key CRM Technology Trends

Since significant technological changes have taken place in CRM software and industry direction in the past few years, here are 14 major trends that are currently affecting the technical evolution of CRM systems:

1. CRM vendors are moving their architecture from client/server, Web-enabled, and three-tiered architectures to full N-tiered architecture with Web-based applications.

2. XML is playing a major role in all areas of CRM.

3. Ajax now provides SaaS CRM applications with robust customization and connectivity functionality.

4. Wireless components are increasingly common in CRM platforms.

5. More CRM vendors are offering graphical workflow mapping tools.

6. Many vendors are offering Enterprise Application Integration (EAI).

7. CRM vendors are including more portal architecture.

8. Numerous CRM vendors are incorporating business intelligence through ETL (extraction, transformation, and load) software or connecting to data warehouses.

9. CRM vendors are developing process-oriented architectures.

10. Call-center vendors are integrating computer telephony services more often with CRM software support to provide increased customer response and contact management.

11. More Voice over Internet Protocol (VoIP) options are being offered in the CRM marketplace.

12. Enterprise Bus Systems (EBS) connectors are now available on the CRM market.

13. CRM vendors are now offering Service-Oriented Architecture (SOA).

14. Growing hybrid options in licensing CRM are becoming prevalent.

When evaluating a vendor, compare their technical directions against this list. The following list includes a detailed description for each of these CRM technology trends.

1. Client/Server to N-Tiered

Over the last few years, vendors that have driven the growth of the Web have created new architectures to accommodate increased Internet traffic and other demands. Several CRM vendors have embraced new technologies such as N-tiered, Web-centric, XML-enabled, etc., and used this as a marketing message. Many other vendors have remained in the client/server era but have bolted a few Web interfaces onto their product to remain competitive.

Some vendors have adopted 100 percent Web-centric architectures and have totally forgotten about the requirements of users who are occasionally connected. Other vendors still have both products (client/server and N-tiered) and have forced customers to develop in two different architectures; this raises the costs of systems integration and customization. Do a thorough analysis and understand the vendor's architectures before you decide on a new system.

2. XML Playing a Major Role

Leading CRM vendors have not hesitated to add XML functionality to their platforms. But just as many client/server vendors have made Web-enabled applications and took time to re-architect them to Web-centric architecture, the same holds true for XML. XML is flexible since it provides a data standard that can encode the content, semantics, and schemata for a variety of cases. The functionality can be as simple as a document definition or as complex as a stand-alone applet that operates in a disconnected mode. Here are some examples of where XML can be used in real-time CRM:

- **An ordinary document such as a word document or spreadsheet** – Currently, many vendors let users save these types of documents in XML, so the document can be viewed by a variety of devices.

- **A structured record, such as a customer record, appointment record, or purchase order** – The XML architecture allows these items to be contained as individual objects.

- **An object with data and methods, such as the persistent form of a Java object or ActiveX control** – This permits even more information on customers and their transactional history to be contained.

- **A data record, such as the result set of a query, can be saved and viewed later or distributed** – Data warehouses can store these types of XML.

- **Metacontent about a Web site, such as Channel Definition Format (CDF)** – Viewers can become subscribers to a particular organization's site and have their objects updated as changes are made. This architecture works well for partner relationship management applications where information that is shared with partners is held behind the firewall.

- **Graphical presentation, such as an application's user interface** – Using XML at the presentation layer lets clients interface with the CRM application natively with multiple devices such as thick (laptops and workstations), thin (Web browsers and WAP-enabled devices), and bulgy (PDAs and car-stereo systems).

- **Standard schema entities and types** – This would be a standardized format for items such as client records, product descriptions, prices, etc.

- **All links between information and people on the Web** – Contact information can be updated automatically via LDAP (lightweight directory access protocol)-type services.

- **Active exchange of data providing the Real-Time Enterprise (RTE)**

These examples of XML functionality are currently used in many commercially available CRM offerings as well as open source ventures.

3. Ajax Providing SaaS CRM Applications with Robust Customization and Connectivity Functionality

The latest versions of major SaaS CRM applications, such as Salesforce.com and NetSuite, now offer support for Ajax (Asynchronous JavaScript and XML). The intent of Ajax is to make Web pages more responsive by allowing the exchange of small amounts of data with the server behind the scenes, so that the entire Web page does not have to be reloaded each time the user makes a change. So Ajax increases the Web page's interactivity, speed, and usability. Since Ajax is a fairly new approach, some analysts predict that it will be an important technology to make the Web more interactive and popular.

The current version of NetSuite CRM provides enhanced Ajax support. This enhancement lets users dynamically change data without having to regenerate the entire Web page. With this new capability, a sales rep can edit the status of a list of contacts without having to go into each customer record to make these changes. Salesforce.com can be integrated with an Ajax tool kit to help build or link up to sophisticated applications (such as Google Maps) in a timely and efficient manner.

4. Wireless Components

Wireless devices do not automatically communicate with back-end systems, particularly when a variety of products exist—PDAs (with various operating systems), WAP-enabled phones (that do not all follow the same WAP standards), a combination of wireless infrastructure technologies (CDMA, GSM, TDMA, CDPD, SMS, and packet radio networks)—to exchange information with diverse databases and systems including SAP, PeopleSoft, Siebel, Onyx, and Pivotal.

The latest in middleware solutions must be part of your mobile enterprise project if you hope to untangle the myriad front-end and back-end technologies. But other things need to be considered including reduced bandwidth caused by wireless latency and anomalies. Add the nonwireless-friendly network protocol called TCP/IP to this mix, and vendors have plenty of work to do.

While this may seem overwhelming, vendors such as Microsoft, OracleMobile, Sun Microsystems, Palm, Ericsson, AvantGo, Openwave, and MobileAware, among others, are investing large amounts of research and development (R&D) funds to bring wireless application architectures to market. Microsoft's Pocket PC has a module that allows it to function as a mobile phone. Wireless CRM is currently working on Hertz, Symbol Technologies, and BlackBerry-type devices.

When choosing a wireless-enabled product, make sure that the application or interface is user-friendly and responsive. Too many vendors have not mastered the small user interface or wireless technology. Make sure that the vendors also have options for users that are not always in wireless coverage areas.

5. Graphical Workflow Mapping Tools

Graphical workflow tools let users quickly create a business process workflow, and instruct the CRM program to automate the workflow. Most CRM vendors have been slow to develop graphical workflow, business rules, and scripting tools. Although the technology has been there, some CRM vendors, such as Pivotal, and CTI vendors have been developing dynamic graphical tools for years. Over the last year, a movement toward more graphical tools has increased, and we expect that more CRM vendors will begin to release these tools during 2007 and 2008. The better products will have the ability to work in graphical and programming/scripting modes.

6. Enterprise Application Integration

Enterprise Application Integration (EAI) is defined as the use of software and computer systems architectural principles to integrate a set of enterprise computer applications. EAI tools that allow CRM vendors to connect their applications to other applications may be used within a company (e.g., ERP [Enterprise Resource Planning] systems, legacy systems, and ebusiness systems). EAI has continually gained wide recognition since 2004.

EAI has become more important because enterprise computing often traditionally takes the form of islands of automation. This occurs when the value of individual systems are not maximized due to partial or full isolation. If integration is applied without following a structured EAI approach, many point-to-point connections grow up across an organization. Dependencies are added on in an impromptu basis, resulting in a tangled, difficult-to-maintain mess. This is commonly referred to as spaghetti, which is a comparison to "spaghetti code," the programming equivalent.

For example, the number of n-connections needed to have fully meshed point-to-point connections is given by $n(n-1)/2$. So, for 10 applications to be fully integrated point-to-point, $(10)(9)/2$, or 45 point-to-point, connections are needed.

However, EAI is not only about sharing data between applications; it focuses on sharing business data and business process. Attending to EAI involves looking at the system of systems, which involves "large scale inter-disciplinary problems with multiple, heterogeneous, distributed systems that are embedded in networks at multiple levels."

Currently, the best approach to EAI is to use an Enterprise Service Bus (ESB), which connects a number of independent systems together. Although other approaches have been explored, including connecting at the database or user-interface level, generally, the ESB approach has been adopted as the strategic winner. Individual applications can publish messages to the ESB and then subscribe to receive certain messages from the bus (a transmission path where signals are dropped off or picked up at every device attached to the line). Each application only requires one connection, which is to the bus. The message bus approach can be extremely scalable and highly evolvable.

EAI is related to middleware technologies such as message-oriented middleware (MOM) and data representation technologies such as XML. Newer EAI technologies involve the use of Web services as part of service-oriented architecture as a means of integration. EAI tends to be data-centric. In the near future, content integration and business processes will be included.

The results of EAI have been mixed for CRM vendors. Some vendors have actually developed their own EAI offering; others have teamed with EAI vendors such as TIBCO, DataDirect Technologies, BEA, Microsoft BizTalk Server, and Vitria.

Other CRM vendors have chosen to provide native hooks to ERP and other systems, which can create long-term maintenance issues especially if multiple native hooks have been created and each hook needs to be maintained. Other vendors have provided an XML integration tool set. Over the next few years, it is likely that we will see the consolidation of the EAI vendor space, and more CRM vendors will begin providing native interfaces to the leading EAI vendors.

7. Portal Architecture

Portals provide a way to put a customized face onto your company's CRM platform. Several CRM vendors are beginning to get into the portal space led by companies such as BroadVision, Vignette, IONA, BEA, and others.

Personalization, within a portal environment, is available in many different options:

- Customer personalization (MyCompany.com)

- Partner hub personalization

- Sales rep personalization (summary page including forecasts, hot leads, and relevant customer news)

- Management personalization (today's sales, forecast, and customized almost real-time reports)

- Employee personalization, such as 401(k), paycheck information, and company news, an area most CRM vendors are not likely to be involved in

Whatever your requirements, more vendors will be offering some of these features. Many vendors also have the flexibility to customize portals because they have chosen to develop them with enterprise software vendor frameworks and use application server engines via application service vendors.

Within the area of portals, growing interest is mounting regarding the Enterprise Information Portal (EIP). EIPs combine the best features of the consumer portal with a platform to put mission-critical enterprise data, applications, and processes at the fingertips of Web-enabled employees and partners. EIPs, which can be viewed as an enabling platform for information dissemination and collaboration, are important enabling technologies for CRM and every variety (B2B, B2C, and B2E) of ecommerce. EIPs act as a single point of access to internal and external information. Other functions include the following:

- Control of user access to information
- Search across all organizational information sources
- Allowing users to publish and share information
- Enterprise Application Integration (EAI)
- Work-flow business process support and collaboration

8. Business Intelligence

Anyone who followed the stream of press releases from CRM and customer contact companies in 2007 knows that analytic applications vendors are quickly merging with customer intelligence and CRM providers. If companies are not privy to changes in their corporate landscape, they are more likely to be blindsided. The convergence of BI (business intelligence) and the Internet—or esolutions—is the critical next step to supplying company infrastructures with the decision-making capabilities and Web-enabled functions they need to move forward in ebusiness. From a BI standpoint, clients leverage their ERP investment by pulling information from that system into a separate, organized intelligent structure where educated decisions can be made. This information helps them leverage their new Internet site with their existing data warehouse to create the overall infrastructure needed to support and supply BI information for CRM initiatives. Companies must continually gather information about their competitors to stay at the top of their game. Software is used to collect data daily and store it in a data warehouse.

This type of analytic application provides CRM and BI solutions with the following three key capabilities:

1. The ability to quantify the value of the customer contact

2. The ability to set thresholds to trigger rules and events (automate delivery of specific content such as personalized offers and product recommendations)

3. The ability to help qualify customer information

A data warehouse is a large analytical database that can serve as the foundation for BI activities. Data warehousing is a process supported by several underlying enabling technologies, such as data extraction, transformation, and load tools, that is built on popular database engines including Microsoft SQL Server or Oracle that support OLAP (Online Analytical Processing) technology. The data extraction on the surface uses ETL software. Some of the current ETL software includes Cognos, iWay Software, and Informatica.

Data mining can best be described as a BI technology that has various techniques to extract comprehensible, hidden, and useful information from a data population. Data mining makes it possible to discover hidden trends and patterns in large amounts of data. The current technology for this is data analyzers; these can be integrated with your CRM suite, like Oracle's Performance Analyzer that generates data and makes it available for your CRM application. Data analyzer packages can be integrated on the SAP and Salesforce.com CRM products via the SAP NetWeaver and Salesforce.com AppExchange applications. Whichever you choose, this ability to detect trends and make future decisions based on competitive information will leverage your company into greater profits.

9. Process-Oriented Architectures

Process-oriented architectures, such as Siebel's UAN (Universal Application Network), are platforms that function using any programming and compiling tool. This architecture addresses itself more to business processes than a particular technology. It uses XML and HTTP derivative technology to pass information between clients and servers, making the platform underpinnings less critical.

10. Computer Telephony Integration

Computer telephony integration, which can be applied throughout your organization on all platforms, is independent of browser technology. It can be adapted to a Web-based CRM-software and integrated into it through modular technology. As calls are received, the caller is identified and sent to the CRM support solution ("screen pop"), and customer and historical data can be accessed by the responding support representative. The representative can then gather additional information in the Web application and store it in the CRM application. Depending on the technical infrastructure in your organization, it may be necessary to integrate ESBs or other middleware products to facilitate bidirectional communications in this environment; however, the benefits of CTI should be factored into your technical decision-making process.

11. Voice Over Internet Protocol

Voice over Internet Protocol (VoIP) is garnering a lot of attention. Many of the telephony switch providers now include VoIP capabilities, because it reduces long-distance costs (sometimes entirely) and the technology has made great strides in the last 24 months. As customers move to this technology, CRM applications will need to adopt VoIP connections for what has previously been simply known as CTI (Computer Telephony Integration). These systems provide the same abilities, and the development time to market should be short. One question that remains in this area is how quickly customers shift to a VoIP-based system. Often, ACD (Automatic Call Distributor) systems have been implemented at a great cost to the customer, which can sometimes be too large for an organization when talks focus on retiring an entire system. It will happen, but many CRM customers may not see an immediate need to end their use of their older telephony systems for several years to come.

12. Enterprise Bus Systems

Siebel, Oracle, and SAP include connectors (for a price) to these frequently used EBSs that allow a spoke/hub data-access point. Gone are the days of relying on a CRM application to make independent connections to each disparate system across the enterprise. In smaller environments, this may make sense, but when data access points become excessive, EBS starts to make more sense.

13. Service-Oriented Architecture

The topic of SOA has come to the forefront, and it implies the use of portal technologies. Many CRM vendors are also trying this, but it has meant a painful re-fit of the applications that have caused delays in releases. Fortunately, SOA-capable portals are built with the intent of integrating multiple-data systems to provide a one-window view of necessary data, while still allowing legacy systems to perform in their normal capacity with little customization. In fact, the portals need a data retrieval place and somewhere to display/edit it. This means that most of the customizations are done from the portal side to create a totally customized customer experience, but it also eliminates the need for large deployment teams, since a savvy systems administrator with the right skill sets and tools can do much of the configuration.

14. Growing Hybrid Options in Licensing CRM

As the CRM market matures, more flexible licensing options are becoming available for CRM software applications in the marketplace. Here are two major licensing options for CRM software applications:

- **Subscription licensing** – An organization subscribes to the CRM application, and it is accessed via the Internet.

- **Perpetual licensing** – The organization will own the CRM application, but it will reside at a service provider's data center or on-premise.

Some on-premise CRM applications, including C2 CRM v. 8.0 and ExSellence 5.0, are now offered via the subscription-licensing option, whereas a number of partner-hosted CRM applications are offered via the subscription or perpetual-licensing option. Typically, the CRM software vendor's application is not offered as a partner-hosted solution, but rather as a client-server application. However, a significant number of CRM vendors, such as Pivotal and FirstWave, have licensed business partners to host, operate, and maintain their clients' CRM solutions. The CRM vendor business partner will provide access to the CRM application either via the CRM vendor's Web interface or via more standard remote access solutions, such as thin client models from Citrix, Microsoft, New Moon, and others.

Since the CRM application is offered with the option of a subscription or perpetual license, both licensing options provide the CRM vendor's clients with a different pricing model to the on-premise option. Due to partner-hosting of the CRM application, no changes will occur to the client's desktop, server, and database-operating systems. The two partner-hosted licensing options will meet the needs of companies looking for the speed to market as well as those with IT-resource constraints. However, organizations with critical requirements such as advanced integration, specific workflow, and security and Sarbanes-Oxley compliance issues may not find that the on-premise subscription licensing or partner-hosted model will meet their needs.

During the last year, CRM vendors are using technology for development and application that have weathered many changes. We can expect to see more consolidation in technologies and companies. As you consider CRM solutions, pay attention to how tightly integrated the CRM vendor's modules actually are. Some CRM vendors have literally taken years to introduce integrated modules after purchasing a CRM-related technology vendor that had specific CRM technology or functionality. When evaluating CRM technology, focus on the CRM vendor as an entity rather than a specific aspect of the company's product/service offering. The technology may be "hot," but more importantly, the vendor must have the resources and experience to deliver the technology to you based on your CRM system requirements and schedule. Remember that technology accounts for no more than 20 percent of the overall success of a CRM initiative with people accounting for at least 50 percent and processes for at least 30 percent.

Chapter 21

A Wireless World

Mobile CRM users, such as field sales and service personnel, are among the biggest fans and key beneficiaries of wireless technology. All CRM project leaders should recognize this value as well.

The following three key trends are helping to propel CRM initiatives as well as our emerging wireless society living and working in real time:

1. **Hotspots** – Hotspots are public areas where people can access the Internet using devices based on 802.11b, or Wi-Fi (a wireless network standard with a range of about 300 feet from a network's access points), or radio transmitters. Of the estimated 150 million laptops and 14 million PDAs in the U.S., most include the Wi-Fi feature. The availability of hotspots has increased dramatically since 2005. A growing number of U.S. towns and cities now offer free or subsidized Wi-Fi access, including San Francisco; Philadelphia; Raleigh, North Carolina; Anaheim, California; and New Orleans. British Telecom has built a number of citywide Wi-Fi networks in the U.K. in partnership with local government, while the city government of Paris is currently building a free citywide Wi-Fi network in partnership with Alcatel-Lucent. American Airlines and Virgin American are also preparing for hotspot availability in their entire transcontinental fleet of 767s in 2008. Expect additional hotspots in the next few years; the Wi-Fi Alliance states that there currently are 530,000 hotspots in the U.S., 800,000 in Europe, and more than a million in Asia.

2. **Chips ahoy** – Leading computer chip manufacturers, led by Intel, have built wireless radio chips into their processors since 2004. In fact, Intel has already delivered its first family of integrated wireless 802.11b radio chips as part of the Centrino mobile processor architecture. Intel has also committed to

investing $100 million in Wi-Fi companies, and plans to spend triple that amount promoting its Centrino chips. In fact, all of the laptop manufacturers now include Intel Centrino-based chips with built-in Wi-Fi or a Wi-Fi wireless chip in laptops shipped with an AMD mobile processor. The bottom line is that all laptops, even the low cost ones, now have built-in Wi-Fi.

3. **Today, not tomorrow** – As a result of the wireless boom, more hardware and software vendors are investing larger amounts of research and development (R&D) funds to bring wireless architectures and applications to market. These include Amdocs, Antenna, AvantGo, MobileAware, Ericsson, Microsoft, Openwave, OracleMobile, Palm, Siebel, Sun Microsystems, and many more. A 2006 Infonetics Research study found that 60 percent of American companies already use Wi-Fi, and this is likely to exceed 85 percent by 2010. Based on a study by my firm, we project that there will be more than 7 billion wireless computer devices connected to the Internet by 2010.

The impact of wireless technology was apparent to me during a 2007 business trip to Dallas. When I checked into the Marriott Courtyard at the Dallas/Fort Worth airport, I informed the desk receptionist that my computer modem was no longer working and asked whether there was a business center I could use for Internet access. He pointed up to the ceiling at the Wi-Fi hotspot in the hotel lobby.

"Use this," he said. I thanked him, but informed him that I did not have a portable Wi-Fi modem card with me. He said, "Not a problem," and offered me one. "What will all this cost me?" I asked. He surprised me and said, "It's free of charge to our guests."

What does all this mean for the CRM industry? Based on a 2007 survey of CRM software vendors, 90 percent of all CRM software applications now work in a wireless environment. The wireless impact on CRM has already started to change the way customer-facing personnel work: Look for rapid answers to customer questions, fewer delays, instant access to order status and inventory, and real-time intelligence, all of which confirm CRM's driving role behind the real-time enterprise (RTE).

Business in an Instant—Brought to You by Mobile and Wireless

Here's an interesting perspective from my friend Tim Bajarin, president of Creative Strategies, who is the industry's leading authority in the mobile and wireless space:

> About 10 years ago, I had an interesting discussion with Bill Gates while on a visit to Microsoft. At the time, he was touting some new mobile software that Microsoft was about to release and when talking about it, he reiterated that this was part of his vision for "information at your fingertips, anytime and anywhere you happen to be."
>
> In fact, if you have been following Microsoft for any length of time you already know that this mobile mantra has been one of the major drivers for the company as it looks to the future. This is why they have made such a major investment in Windows Mobile software and smart phones and why today this idea of delivering a more robust mobile OS for laptops, tablets and smart phones has become part of their DNA.
>
> As of last year, laptops outsold desktops and by the end of the decade, many analysts believe that laptops will account for 65 percent of all computers sold. Today, smart phones represent only about 7 percent of the 1.1 billion cell phones sold annually, but by 2010, analysts believe that smart phones will account for as much as 22 percent of all cell phones sold each year.
>
> The reason for all of this mobile activity is the fact that we are becoming more and more a mobile society. Business and consumers want their information, email, applications and even entertainment on demand, no matter where they happen to be.
>
> That trend is clearly in the sight of all of the major personal computer, consumer electronics, telephony carriers, and mobile handset makers as they rush to deliver high speed wireless networks and mobile devices of all kinds [that are] capable of delivering business in an instant.
>
> New third generation (3G) and fourth generation (4G) wireless networks (i.e., EVDO, HSDPA, etc.) will soon deliver

wireless connections with speeds well over 4 MBPS. In the future, WiMAX networks will become the wireless workhorse that can deliver high speed wireless connections up to 70 MBPS. And WIFI hotspots are popping up all over the US to make it easier to get connected even if you don't have a cellular modem in your laptop.

As more and more applications get delivered via the Internet cloud, the need for high speed smart wireless devices will increase. No wonder that all of the work behind the scenes is getting business and consumers alike ready for a world where business applications, information and even consumer driven entertainment is delivered as Bill Gates suggested "anytime and anywhere you happen to be."

Chapter 22

CRM Software Selection Tips

When a company decides to find a CRM system to automate the sales, marketing, and customer service processes, this decision may be prompted by the sales force, sales management, marketing, customer service, or other members of the executive staff. While it's not important who initiates the procedure, it is important that executives from sales, marketing, customer service, and other departments work together to ensure that the CRM process integrates different needs across these functions and that sufficient time is allocated to this integration process. While these steps may seem obvious to many, this is not always the case for some companies.

How to Select Software

Several CRM software selection methodologies currently exist to help organizations get the process started. Here is the following 10-step methodology that my firm has developed and implemented with reasonable success at dozens of companies worldwide.

Step 1: Technical Baseline Review

Your technical staff should define the current technical platform and capabilities, including data synchronization, links to ERP (Enterprise Resource Planning) systems, and potential system expansion (the Internet/Web for ebusiness).

Step 2: Customer Visits with the Customer-Facing Personnel

A CRM project team member should talk to a cross section of customer-facing representatives from sales, marketing, customer service, and other partners. Allot anywhere from a half-day to a full day per representative. Observations from the visits will serve as input for the brainstorming session and the needs-analysis questionnaires.

Step 3: Brainstorming Session

Your CRM project team should conduct a structured session with key personnel, including sales representatives, marketing and sales managers, executives, customer service managers, and IT specialists to discuss their perceived CRM business functional needs. Plan on allowing three hours for a group (between 10 and 18 people). These participants are typically chosen as the superusergroup to participate in later CRM audit steps and act as ambassadors for the pending CRM system.

Step 4: Needs-Analysis Questionnaires

A customized needs-analysis questionnaire should be administered to a group of between 30 and 60 potential CRM system users, including participants in the brainstorming session. Three different questionnaire types are typically sent to three different decision-making groups: customer-facing personnel, managers, and executives. While the three questionnaires may ask a few of the same questions, these questionnaires should also ask specifics that focus on the different decision-making responsibilities of these three groups. The questionnaires can confirm and consolidate findings revealed during the field visits and the brainstorming session, as well as encourage respondents to do a preliminary prioritization of the business functional needs, technical features, and user-friendliness issues.

Step 5: Business Process Review

Review and highlight your business processes to address existing business process issues as well as business process requirements (see Chapter 14, Understanding Business Process Review, for more information and suggestions). Recommendations should be defined for a step-by-step approach to implement best-in-class business processes that apply to the CRM system. This way, you can plan properly for short-term as well as long-term business needs of your CRM system.

Step 6: Business Functional Prioritization

Identify your prioritized business functions, based on the results of the field visits, the brainstorming session, the needs-analysis questionnaires, and the business process review. The results can be presented to your management team.

Step 7: Technical Platform Recommendations

In light of your prioritized business functions and the results of your technical platform review, make recommendations for appropriate technical platform alternatives for CRM software, hardware, and communications.

Step 8: CRM Report

The report, which will be presented to your management team for approval, should contain the information needed to formulate your system specifications, including business and technical requirements.

Step 9: Software Selection

If you decide to use external software, consider looking at between three to five software packages that include the CRM functions you have identified. An experienced CRM consultant may be helpful in writing your RFP (Request for Proposal) and reviewing, selecting, and negotiating with your selected CRM vendor.

Step 10: Software Implementation Assistance

Once you have made your software selection, a CRM consultant can help implement your CRM initiative, primarily in the areas of project management and systems assurance. This includes the following points:

- Help select your systems integrator, your training partner, and your approach
- Evaluate project plans
- Participate in weekly operations review meetings

- Assist in implementing specific tasks/project management (training manuals, pilot rules, and performance measurement criteria)

- Help with system assurance/customer satisfaction (ongoing process improvements)

The CRM software selection process should usually be accomplished within 8 to 12 weeks, assuming the prospective company has committed to an aggressive CRM timeframe. Regardless of the methodology you use, be sure to use a structured approach.

Technical Feature Requirements

During the CRM software selection process, your team needs to draft an initial list of technical feature requirements. These features should come directly from discussions with key placeholders who helped develop the CRM system.

Some confusion may arise between the technical features of a CRM system, which facilitate the use of the system, and technical platform issues, which deal with the architecture used to support your CRM system. Decisions concerning technical platform issues most often rest with the company's IT department. Here are the following examples of technical platform issues:

- Will your CRM system have a Net-native (hosted on Web or ASP), Web-centric architecture (browser-based), or is a Web-enabled client/server architecture adequate?

- What operating system environments will be compatible with your CRM system (Active Directory, Microsoft (MS) Windows family of OS products, Novell, UNIX, or Linux)?

- How will your CRM system be accessed (Internet/Web, virtual private networks, handheld devices, or wireless technology)?

- How will your data be synchronized between CRM system components and users (servers, databases, and locations)?

- Does your technical infrastructure and data storage capacity accommodate any additional needs that a CRM solution will present, or would outsourcing your CRM solution to a hosted solution, such as Siebel or Salesforce.com, provide better cost/benefit?

- Does your technical infrastructure promote the integration of your phone system into a CRM solution for managing contacts, call centers, and the help desk?

- Which database(s) will be used for your CRM system, including the number and location of database servers (Oracle, MS-SQL Server, Sybase, and IBM DB2)?

- Are the middleware (Scribe, Tibco, or BEA) components in place to allow integration of back-office or legacy system data into your CRM solution? Do these solutions (or the ones built in-house) accommodate the bidirectional exchange of information?

- Should you move to more advanced data-sharing technologies such as Web services, XML, or SOAP-based technologies to inter-connect your legacy systems?

- Should a data warehouse solution be integrated with your CRM solution? If so, what tools do you need to derive the maximum value from your CRM solution: data transformation (Informatica, Oracle Warehouse Builder, SqlSvr DTS, or Business Objects ETL) and data mining (Cognos or Business Objects/Crystal Reports)?

- With which groupware platforms (Lotus Notes/Domino or MS Outlook/MS Exchange) will your CRM systems need to interface?

- With which ebusiness platforms (BEA, IBM WebSphere, Vignette, or BroadVision) will your CRM systems need to interface?

- What security features are available to protect your CRM system data?

- What interaction with the National Do Not Call Registry will be required in your CRM implementation?

- Will your existing computer hardware support the CRM system? If not, which new hardware will be necessary?

While CRM users should be aware of these issues and provide user input where needed, such as technical integrity across multiple company systems, decisions about technical platform issues remain largely outside the jurisdiction of users.

Here are a few guidelines to define which technical features should be included in the CRM system:

1. Work with your IT department and/or an external consultant to define possible technical features that could be included in your CRM software.

2. Remember that technical features are required in a CRM system to facilitate the eventual implementation of your prioritized business functional requirements. For example, if placing your company price lists online is a prioritized business function, you will want to make sure the software you choose has the appropriate technical features to update price lists easily.

3. Learn about possible technical features by reviewing existing CRM software. Review some of the vast quantity of packaged and hosted CRM software solutions to gain insight into the latest technical features.

My firm worked on one CRM assignment with a publishing company where the project leader had a technical background. During the system specification meeting, he showed us the latest technical features for CRM. While many of the proposed technical features would be valuable to his company's system, others were little more than technical toys. To bring reality to the playing field, we asked the project leader about the top 10 business functional requirements for the proposed system. After getting four out of 10 correct, he began to listen more carefully to user needs.

Ensure that the technical features will assist your CRM system users directly to implement prioritized business functions successfully. While often dazzling, technical features should not be judged on their wizardry, but rather on their business value. Some of the greatest value of technical features is their ability to help users feel comfortable with the system, enable them to access and navigate the system, and help make the system intuitive to their needs.

Writing the CRM System Specs

Once you have completed your CRM system needs analysis, prioritized your business functional requirements, and defined the technical features and user-friendliness/support requirements, you can write a systems specifications document for internal IT personnel or for a qualified short list of external vendors via an RFP.

It's important to remain in charge of the external vendor process, yet provide sufficient information so that external vendors as well as internal IT personnel can customize and deliver a system that fulfills your unique set of CRM needs.

While we aren't suggesting that there's only one best way to write your systems specifications document, we understand that each company has its own set of rules and regulations about writing one. However, here are a few recommendations that I've found to help structure a CRM system specifications document:

- **General conditions section** – List general conditions of significance to your company such as the right to reject, performance conditions, response verification, and conditions.

- **Vendor instructions** – Provide a clear description to the CRM vendor about the purpose of the specifications document, communications regarding the proposal, timetable for the proposal, selection and award process, vendor response deadlines, vendor presentation rules, and contract negotiations.

- **Proposal guidelines/formats** – Specify the format of any proposal (in electronic format), present exceptions to the RFP, list what is needed for vendor contact information, and provide evaluation criteria (product features and operational capability consistent with specified requirements, specialized relevant experience of the firm, completeness in addressing all aspects of the RFP, and financial stability of the vendor).

- **Vendor profile** – Ask the vendor to provide the following background information:

    - Size of the company and whether it is local, national, or international

- Location of the office that will handle your account

- An affirmation that the vendor has a history of providing quality work

- A profile of the vendor's product lines along with the industries served

- A list of elements that differentiate the vendor from other organizations

- The names of at least three clients who can be used as references

- **Business functional requirements** – My firm recommends the following approach (the functions have been selected for exemplary purposes). After most of the business functions that are listed, fill in the ranking space according to five categories:

  - F+ (Functionality fully provided)

  - F (Functionality partially provided, and it can be enhanced to full functionality)

  - D (Functionality does not exist, but it can be provided at no additional cost)

  - DB (Functionality does not exist, but it can be provided at an additional cost)

  - X (Functionality does not exist, and the vendor has no plans to develop any additional options)

For "F" and "D," indicate whether Company X can develop this, or whether vendor support is needed. For "F," "D," and "DB," provide a time estimate for the development. After each business function checked with "F+," "F," "DB," and "D," provide a comprehensive description of the business function now offered in your software package (use additional sheets as needed).

Then, list your business functional requirement, as well as technical features and user-friendliness/support criteria; have the vendors assess how well their software meets your needs. In Appendix C, we've included a list that provides examples of the types of business functions, technical features, and user-friendliness/support criteria that you might expect to find in a CRM system RFP. Remember, your RFP will probably only contain a subset of these criteria, based upon your prioritized list of required functions and features.

Once the vendors have submitted their RFP responses, the next step is to review their responses and to invite between one and three vendors to make presentations at your facilities, which usually takes an average of four to eight hours each. To keep the vendors focused on your company's specific needs, ask the selected vendors to demonstrate the functions and features that they responded to positively in their RFP.

To help ensure a realistic assessment of the software, ask the selected vendors to set up their software on equipment at your site and within a technical environment similar to the one that you are likely to use for the eventual system (e.g., with 10,000-plus user records in the system for a test).

If your IT department will be building your CRM system, your system specifications document would obviously concentrate on the details needed for business functional requirements, technical feature requirements, and user-support requirements.

Take time to carefully write a system specifications document that will be sent to a qualified short-list of external vendors in an RFP or by internal IT personnel. This way, you are likely to improve the chances that the CRM system you receive closely mirrors what you specified.

Questions to Ask CRM Software Providers

The process of selecting the best software vendor for your real-time CRM initiative is not easy. Software vendors come and go, while technological changes often shake the very base on which vendors build their applications. With these potential difficulties in mind, ask each vendor on your short list each of the 12 questions that follow.

But first, here are two observations: If you find that a vendor on your short list is evasive in responding to any of these 12 questions, continue to ask questions now rather than later; also, do not rely on any single answer as the basis for your vendor selection decision. Instead, get the answers to all 12 questions, and then apply business judgment to decide how well the vendor's responses deal with your specific needs.

Question 1: How Long Has the Vendor Been in Business, and What's the History of Its Business?

The CRM industry celebrated its 28th anniversary in 2007. To the best of our knowledge, no CRM software vendors are older than 23; most are between 10 and 15 years old. This may make the number of years in business less relevant, but we don't think so.

A software vendor such as FirstWave, which began in 1984 as Brock Control Systems, has weathered good and bad times, and through an initial public offering as well as organizational acquisitions and structural reorganizations. Over the years, FirstWave has proven to be a resilient CRM player with products that consistently score high in independent user reviews. While longevity is not necessarily an essential characteristic of a solid CRM vendor, we want to make the point that longevity has a value.

Dozens of outstanding CRM vendors—several of which are today's market leaders—have been in business between 10 and 15 years, have quality CRM software offerings today, and are likely to continue to offer them in the future. For example, McGraw-Hill may have been viewed as a risk-taker when it became the first customer of YOUcentric (now part of Oracle), a vendor that was reasonably new to the CRM industry. McGraw-Hill was willing to take that risk with YOUcentric's Java-based, Web CRM offering and has not looked back since. So, while some vendors are backed by venture capital or others are new to the CRM industry, no hard and fast rules exist about their long-term viability.

In fact, CRM software vendors come and go whether they are established players, such as Sales Technologies (that pulled out of the CRM marketplace in the early 1990s), or new players, such as Corepoint (a CRM vendor that was backed by IBM in the late 1990s but never made it off the ground). So, while the number of years in business is important, that fact alone is not sufficient to determine whether the CRM vendor is appropriate for you.

Question 2: Does the Vendor Have Experience and Customers in Your Industry Sector?

Experience in your particular industry can be quite important. Software vendors who demonstrate their understanding of how your industry works, including your industry's best demonstrated practices within their software offering, may be a real plus. However, you should not be swayed by a vendor's demonstration of industry-specific software, because creating impressive demonstrations using today's software tools are reasonably easy. More importantly, ask questions about the company's active customers in your industry, and whether they are willing to provide you with the names/contacts of these customers. Answers to these questions will let you conduct your own due diligence about how well this particular CRM vendor has met the needs of a live, industry-specific customer.

You may face another dilemma: Suppose a new CRM software vendor does not have specific industry experience yet has software with technology and flexibility that seems ideal based on your specific needs (Pivotal's customer contact center). Increasingly, the industry is seeing a vertical focus from CRM software vendors (Siebel and StayinFront in the pharmaceutical industry), and the need for experience and customers within your specific industry may soon become a moot point.

Question 3: What Is the Vendor's Technological Direction (Web Strategy or CRM Module Expansion Intentions)?

It's important to understand your CRM provider's technological direction and how this direction fits in with your company's technological direction. The best way to determine this is to hold a half-day technology session with the vendor's chief technical officer. The objective of this session is to determine where the vendor is headed (new business modules, new development tools, and the likely time frames for each), to reveal what your specific needs are today and in the future for business functions and technical features, and to understand whether you and the vendor see eye to eye. Don't be surprised if you are asked to sign a nondisclosure agreement, which is standard for these types of meetings.

Question 4: Who Are the Members of the Vendor's Management Team, and What Are Their Backgrounds?

The cumulative background and experience of a vendor's management team can provide insight into its stability and credibility within the CRM market. Ideally, you want to see a mix of business discipline backgrounds (accounting, finance, information systems, and operations) as well as industry background (healthcare, consumer packaged goods, or

CPG) that represents the vendor's product focus and offerings. Also, find out about the companies where the management team members were previously employed. Are those companies thriving and are they still in existence?

Question 5: How Is the Vendor Financed?

Find out about the financial backing of a prospective CRM vendor. Venture capital (VC) groups finance many new companies in the high-tech area, particularly software companies. In many cases, the payback periods for the VC funds are very aggressive, so the venture capitalists want to be paid back in a short period of time. Therefore, the software vendor may feel additional pressure to sell as many seats or licenses as it can as quickly as possible. If the VC organization has dictated an exit strategy by acquisition, there is also increased pressure on the software vendor to do whatever it deems necessary to make the financials look attractive. In other words, go beyond the financial statements when reviewing the financial stability of the vendor.

Question 6: Is Source Code Included with the Product?

More and more vendors are providing tool kits that let the customer make changes to the software without using third-party implementation consultants. Much of the underlying code is programmed into reusable objects. Nevertheless, the lack of a provided source code can limit your ability to customize the CRM system without the help of vendor technicians or third-party consultants. If the vendor does not provide the source code, you need to know why. What happens if the vendor goes out of business? Do you get the source code to ensure your system will continue to function? Read the fine print that explains what is and what is not provided.

Question 7: What Training Is Offered, Including for the End User, Train-the-Trainer, or Systems Administrator?

Remember that over the life of the CRM system, the cost of training can be up to five times the cost of the software. Does the vendor provide any training? Is the training provided in-house, on-site, or online? Does the vendor pass the training responsibility on to the resellers or implementation partners? Regardless of whether the vendor offers some or all of the training programs, ask how the vendor measures the performance of its own trainers, and how it will measure the effectiveness of its own training methods for resellers or users. Does the vendor have structured plans for ongoing training, refresher training, and training for new hires? Is the vendor using the latest technologies to provide training services, such as Web-based training?

Question 8: How Does the Vendor Support Its Software (Does It Have a Guaranteed Response Time)?

Many vendors provide support services as part of their maintenance agreements. Find out what types of support are offered with a maintenance agreement (phone support, Web-based self-service, and/or on-site support). Some vendors offer a la carte support programs such as pay-per-incident or per-support interaction. Are the support services passed on from the vendor to the third-party implementation partner? If the support services are "outsourced" to a third-party company, what certification programs does the vendor have to teach, train, and certify third-party partner personnel?

Question 9: What Is Included in the Maintenance Agreement (What Is the Fixed Number of Upgrades Per Year)?

The maintenance programs provided by CRM vendors can vary in cost and complexity. Get specifics on what exactly is provided by the agreement, its time frame, and who will provide the service and support (the vendor and/or the vendor's implementation/service partner). Ask the vendor how upgrades and updates will be made available, whether via a download from a Web site or via a reseller. Will you have access to a dedicated technician or group of technicians by phone, email, or Web site? Can the vendor guarantee a specific turnaround time for problem resolution? What kind of resources has the vendor devoted to the particular support/service options?

Question 10: What Is the Warranty Period and Bug-Fix Policy During This Period?

Find out what type of warranty policy a CRM vendor has for its products. Many vendors offer a standard 90-day warranty period, but ask the vendor what is included, and if it is exclusive of an annual maintenance agreement. Find out from the vendor how, when, and where any software fixes, updates, and upgrades will be available. Also ask the vendor about the extension of the warranty and any costs associated with the extension.

Question 11: How Does the Vendor Implement the Software (by Itself or via a Third-Party Implementer)?

Most CRM vendors provide comprehensive product suites that employ the services of third-party CRM implementation companies. If the vendor provides the implementation using its own technical staff, how many consultants are dedicated to implementation efforts? Does the vendor provide any type of "rapid implementation" option, and if so, is this appropriate to your own business situation? Ask questions about the qualifications of the vendor's implementation staff; in the case of third-party implementation partners, find out about the type of certification and length of training required to become a vendor implementation partner. If the vendor uses third-party implementation companies, ask how the original vendor ensures quality. Make sure the vendor and/or the implementation partners are using the CRM software for its own front-office operations.

Question 12: How Important Is Your Business to the Vendor?

Will you be an important customer for the vendor? Will the vendor commit necessary resources to ensure the successful implementation of your CRM system? To make sure the software vendor provides appropriate attention, some customers insist that they sign on as members of the software vendor's management board of advisors. Regardless how you do it, secure guarantees from the software vendor showing that it is prepared to commit the necessary resources to make your real-time CRM initiative a success.

Once you have the answers to these 12 questions, apply your business judgment: Find out which of these questions are most applicable to the success of your CRM initiative before deciding which software vendor best meets your needs. When sizing up a CRM software vendor, determine the fit between the direction of your CRM initiative and that of the vendor.

When you have determined this, make the selection and start implementing your CRM system.

Tips for Negotiating with CRM Vendors

The CRM software marketplace growth rate has declined from its peak of about 35 percent annually from 1995 to 2000 primarily because of CRM implementation problems. Many CRM industry analysts consider a growth rate between 10 and 15 percent as a likely rate for 2007 to 2008. This projected growth rate has come about from the emergence of the SaaS CRM model and the increase in CRM demand from the SMB market segment.

And this is good news for CRM software buyers who now have the negotiation advantage. Many CRM software vendors are looking for more business now and are willing to negotiate substantial discounts regardless of what the official company policies suggest.

In fact, I helped one of our clients (a payroll services company) secure a 52 percent discount on the list price from a leading mid-market vendor. In the end, we helped arrange a 500-person license deal for a cost of $682,000 ($1,364 per seat), which was a substantial savings from the initial bid of $1.4 million. In early 2008, I was able to help negotiate a 1,200-person license deal that included all configuration and implementation work for $2 million, ($1,667 per seat) which was again a substantial savings from the initial bid of $3.4 million. Negotiating deals require a good understanding of what can and cannot be negotiated with the vendor.

The following 10 negotiating tips work well in the current buyers' market. You'll need to do some homework to determine the competitive CRM software pricing, or ask a consulting company to help.

1. Be sure you understand the need for each optional software module being recommended by the vendor: "What is the value-added for each of their recommended optional software modules?" Be particularly sensitive to the vendor's desire to scale up its perception of any part of your business (especially if the vendor happens to excel in this area), such as your ebusiness or marketing requirements.

2. Include as many of the vendor's optional modules as you can into the base agreement. This way, you can lock in prices regardless of when the modules will actually be used.

3. Be as definitive as you can in the agreement. Use your company's well-defined business needs and screen designs as exhibits or attachments within the agreement.

4. List and define your deliverables/acceptance criteria within the agreement. Be sure that these deliverables/acceptance criteria have clearly defined metrics, which are important to determine when particular payments should be made within the agreement (see the next point).

5. Spread your payments over the life of the agreement, which should be divided into deliverables/acceptance criteria in phases. Base your payments on the vendor meeting these deliverables/acceptance criteria. While most vendors do not like to link payment to this criteria, more vendors are accepting payments over the project implementation timetable. I remember one vendor president telling me that his software worked well and that all monies had to be paid upfront. Spreading out payments is particularly agreeable when the CRM software vendor also has been contracted to do or assist with implementing any software. Here is one possible payment model: 20 percent of payment upon signing the agreement, 20 percent on the successful accomplishment of an initial set of deliverables/acceptance criteria, 20 percent on the successful accomplishment of the next set of deliverables/acceptance criteria, and the final 40 percent upon the successful accomplishment of a final set of deliverable/acceptance criteria.

6. Consider requesting a site license for your company on a national and/or international basis. When considering site-license pricing, determine the current expected number of CRM users (let's call this variable X) as well as the expected number of CRM users within 12 to 24 months (let's call this variable Y). Negotiate the site license based on a price that is greater than X, which will be list price minus 1 percent (this is the minimum discount amount), and less than Y.

7. Wait between 60 and 90 days before your final acceptance of the system.

8. The maintenance charges certainly can and should be negotiated. Calculate the annual maintenance charge with the percent discount off of the net price (what you actually pay) rather than on list price. While the asking price may be 18 percent, the norm is more likely to be between 12 percent and 15 percent. Start the maintenance charges after the system has received final acceptance; it is not unreasonable to have the maintenance charges begin up to 12 months after final acceptance of the system. Alternatively, negotiate one free year of maintenance either from the date that the agreement is signed or the date the system was accepted.

9. Buy a block of the company's program and project managers' time, or the CRM vendor implementation consultants' time to secure a discount rate.

10. Structure the agreement so your company initially purchases little more than a developer server license and about 15 pilot-user licenses. Then, assuming the CRM vendor is a publicly traded company, time the remaining software purchases around the vendor's quarterly or year-end close.

The current buyer's market will not last forever, but it's quite likely that CRM software vendors will continue to welcome new business. While limits exist to vendor discounts along with a need to ensure a good spirit of partnership when the negotiations have been completed, plenty of negotiation room remains with CRM vendors today.

I often ask, "If one can run a multimillion-dollar equity portfolio on Quicken's 2007 software that costs less than $100 to purchase, why does the per-user cost for CRM software run between $300 and $3,000, with $1,500 being an overall industry average?"

While the CRM software vendors will appropriately suggest the per-user cost of their software needs to be weighed against the value their software delivers, I'm convinced that CRM software prices will continue to come down.

PART 5

Critical
Issues

Chapter 23

Using People, Process, and Technology to Differentiate

Nowadays, most organizations operate in crowded and highly competitive marketplaces. Doing more with less is the norm: Personnel tend to be stretched to the limit; cost-cutting is prevalent. So when new processes and technologies emerge that can help organizations cost-effectively achieve long-term differentiation, they get noticed. Given the need to out-fox the competition and to secure long-term customer loyalty, savvy organizations can apply support capabilities with great success.

Organizations that have successfully developed support capabilities have applied a three-step structured approach—based on people, process, and technology—to achieve long-term product and service differentiation. Here are the highlights of this approach.

People Issues

The people piece of the approach accounts for 50 percent of the overall success. People are naturally resistant to change. Unless properly planned, change can actually be seen as disruptive; people may be hesitant to want to complement products and services with support capabilities to achieve long-term differentiation. To overcome resistance to change, consider the following:

- Be sure that relevant internal and external customers are aware of the pending support changes.

- Take time to help these customers understand what these changes are going to mean for them, such as more efficient and rewarding work.

- Help customers adopt the idea of enhancing support capabilities, and show them the impact that this has had on other companies; take time for training.

- Get customers involved in the change process; invite them to join the discovery team or task force responsible for successfully introducing new support capabilities.

- For those customers who get involved and see the value of enhanced support capabilities, make them your change management agents or ambassadors. Gain their commitment to help others understand the value of enhanced support capabilities.

Simply stated, people make or break a company's ability to develop and successfully implement support capabilities to achieve long-term product and service differentiation. Take time to work with people to drive success.

The Process Element

The process part accounts for 30 percent of the overall success of complementing products and services with support capabilities to achieve long-term differentiation. When implementing the process piece, the organization needs to map out and document key internal and external customer-facing support processes (e.g., processes for customer inquiries, customer requests, problem resolution, customer surveys, etc.).

Look at each identified key process and determine whether it is optimal or could be improved. These are the types of questions you will want to ask to determine the current viability of each identified key support process:

- **Ownership** – Does the process have one or more than one owner? A process may have more than one person or department participating in the process, but successful processes will have only one owner.

- **Metrics** – Does the process have a stated metric (e.g., "We will resolve 90 percent of customer support queries within one hour.")? Remember the words of management guru Peter Drucker, "If you can't measure it, you can't manage it."

- **Interfaces** – What other persons or departments are involved in the process? For example, in a customer support center, sales as well as product development may help to resolve a customer issue. In a successful process, these interfaces are well-greased, and information flows seamlessly across persons or departments.

- **Procedures** – Does the process have clearly stated procedures so that everyone knows how to implement each step of the process, regardless of who is working with the process? The steps of each process should be well-documented and available to all potential users.

- **Integrity** – Is the process practiced the same way for all customers? In successful processes, in addition to documented procedures, all relevant personnel have been trained to apply the process consistently.

- **Vision** – Does the process support the long-term differentiation via support capabilities of the organization? With a successful process, this linkage is obvious.

Organizations often get carried away with process analysis and can get into analysis-paralysis too quickly. Remember to chart out key customer-facing processes initially. This usually consists of between six and 12 processes, but no more. Get these key processes right; where appropriate, subprocesses will follow. If you are stuck determining what constitutes a key process, ask the customers.

Technology Helps

Last of all is the technology piece of the approach. This piece accounts for at most 20 percent of the overall success of expanding your support capabilities. Why? Because there are many fine technologies currently available to help internal and external customers receive increasingly higher levels of support. The issue tends not to be one of actual technology, but rather, it involves the readiness of the company and its customers to absorb and properly use the new technology, such as the process and people side of the equation.

When a company selects its technology partner—specifically, for its software—to enhance support capabilities, the following types of questions are frequently asked:

- Does the software vendor offer both internal support products (IT help desk support software) as well as external support products (customer support center software)?

- Are the vendor's support products integrated seamlessly?

- Does the vendor have a proven track record for implementing these products?

- Does this include experience in the company's specific industry?

- Does the vendor offering include needed implementation and maintenance support for its products (either itself or via partners)?

- How well and easily do the vendor's support products integrate with other CRM software components such as sales, marketing, business analytics, or ecustomer applications? Are the other CRM software components part of the company's or are they third-party applications? How are third-party components maintained?

- Does the vendor work (either through formal or informal alliances) with other relevant vendors that form a part of your enhanced support capability solution, such as with hardware vendors, communications equipment vendors, network vendors, business process consultants, and others?

- Is the vendor's product based on technology that meets current company goals and direction?

A word of caution: It's easy to get overwhelmed or even carried away by the technology piece of this structured approach. Remember, it starts with good internal support processes that are then extended to external customers. Next comes needed change management skills to ensure that people buy into the need for the change with the enhanced support capabilities. Then and only then are we able to turn to technology.

Chapter 24

Ten Steps to Effective CRM Implementation

Recent polls suggest that CRM remains a mystery to many corporate executives despite its many benefits. Why? Because most executives don't understand the processes behind CRM, and they are somewhat intimidated by the technological issues associated with automating CRM tasks.

Given the enormous impact of implementing CRM solutions, it's well worth investing time and resources to ensure that the CRM initiative succeeds. That's why my firm has developed a 10-step approach to help organizations implement CRM systems successfully.

Though we can't guarantee it, our experience over the past two decades suggests that by following the 10 steps listed here, organizations can gain greater confidence that their CRM implementation will succeed. Our experience also indicates that missing any of these steps increases the likelihood that the CRM initiative will be bogged down, fail outright, or become a dinosaur soon after implementation.

Step 1: Organize Your Project Management Team

Initially, you should form a project team consisting of the following members:

- **A project champion**, preferably a senior executive, who will be responsible for ensuring appropriate managerial and financial backing throughout the project. The project champion will be involved about an average of six hours per month during the six- to 12-month project life cycle.

- **A project leader** who has business process and technical skills. This person will be responsible for implementing the project on a day-to-day basis. This will usually be a full-time position during the project's life cycle.

- **A project user group** of CRM end users (staff) who are responsible for providing input to the project leader during the project's conceptualization phase and who test the system during the design and implementation phases. The project user group will be involved about an average of eight hours per month during the six- to 12-month project life cycle.

Step 2: Determine the Functions to Automate

Effective automation at a company starts with a CRM audit, which identifies the business functions that need to be automated and lists the technical features that are required in the CRM system. While several different audit methodologies are available, we recommend one that contains questionnaires, face-to-face interviews with customer-facing personnel (those who have direct contact with customers or serve a support role), face-to-face interviews with customers, if possible, visits with sales representatives in the field as well as sales channel partners, a review of business processes, a technical assessment, and a final report.

You may decide to hire a CRM consultant to conduct the audit, or you may want to conduct the audit yourself. If you choose the latter, start by assigning the task to a project team composed of internal and/or external personnel who are familiar with your sales and marketing operations. You may even wish to send one or more members of your project team to a CRM seminar where audit implementation details are discussed.

Regardless of your approach, the audit step is critical. If the audit is not performed properly, it's likely that you won't be able to implement an effective CRM system. In my experience, companies that took the time to audit properly have more easily and quickly realized the benefits of CRM than those companies that did not. The latter are now paying the price in wasted time, effort, and money.

Automate what needs automating. For example, automating an inefficient business process can be a costly mistake. During my visit with the CRM manager of a leading Italian car manufacturer, it was apparent that he wanted to use the CRM system to "once and for all, control his unstructured Italian sales force." This is not the correct basis for approaching

CRM, and using CRM to try to control a sales force is a grave error. In this case, the company's CRM system never took off.

To ensure that you automate what needs to be automated, your CRM audit should address a "wish list" of how salespeople, marketing personnel, customer support staff, and management would like to improve their work processes. At one company during an audit, the No. 1 salesman expressed a wish: "If only I could get updated information on both my potential client and my competitors prior to the sales call." Remember that the people doing the job know how to do it better. Take time to work with them, and you will learn what needs to be automated.

Step 3: Gain Top Management Support/Commitment

Companies that successfully automate the customer-facing functions view the CRM systems more as a business tool than as a technological tool. Keep this in mind as you approach top management for support.

Top management commitment can be secured by demonstrating that automation can help with the following:

- Support the business strategy since automation delivers the information required to make the key decisions that enable a business strategy to be realized.

- Measure impacts and improves results; this can be gauged according to both tangible and intangible benefits already described in Chapter 1.

- Significantly reduce costs and thereby it pays for itself over a specified time period.

- Document your case for automation based on business impact.

Step 4: Employ Technology Smartly

Select information technology and systems that use open architecture, which makes it easy to enhance and enlarge the system over time. Look for software applications that are modularized and can be easily integrated into or interconnected with your existing information databases. Ensure the technology you select is portable. For example, make sure it uses UNIX, NT, .NET, Java/Active-X, and other such standards. For firms conducting business between the field and headquarters or across regions, select software applications that are network compatible and that permit easy Web connection and/or data synchronization between information on field computers and on regional or headquarter computers. To accommodate future changes, be sure the technology you select can easily be customized as well as modified. In other words, let the technology help you grow.

Although technology is only one step in the overall approach for successfully implementing CRM, it is vital to the functioning of CRM systems. Users should be familiar with the following leading technologies that will continue to drive customer acceptance of CRM in the future.

Object-Oriented Programming (OOP)

Object-Oriented Programming (OOP) is a proven software technique that has simplified software programming for the technical team, and is easier for the CRM end user to use. Recently introduced technology in this category includes the .NET platform that is programmed with development environments such as Java, C++, and Active-X. By using these object-oriented architectures, CRM software vendors provide a framework where new components can plug into. As corporate cultures and business processes change, individual objects (applets and servlets) can be updated, rewritten, deleted, or added, and then quickly distributed and installed throughout the user environment without having to rewrite the entire application, business logic, user interface, or back-office application.

Open Source Technology

Open source code is available free of charge to the general public. The rationale for this is that a large community of developers who are not concerned with proprietary ownership will produce a more useful and bug-free product for everyone's benefit. The open source concept relies on community members to find and eliminate bugs in the program code, a process that commercially developed and packaged programs do not use. The information is shared throughout the open source community and does not originate or channel through a corporation's research and development department. Open architecture in CRM applications is huge in today's marketplace. The ability to integrate with other Web services for mashups (a Web application that combines data from more than one source into a single integrated tool, such as cartographic data from Google Maps merged with real-estate listings on craigslist) is critical. There is a move toward segmentation with application functionality where the specific functionality can be provided as a service. For example, look at companies such as Firepond, which has a software package that can integrate into existing CRM applications and provides extended product catalog capabilities for order entry.

Integrated Development Environment (IDE)

Integrated Development Environment (IDE) provides comprehensive facilities to computer programmers for software development. An IDE normally consists of a source code editor, a compiler and/or interpreter, automation tools, and (usually) a debugger. IDEs are designed to maximize programmer productivity by providing tightly knit components with similar user interfaces, which minimizes the amount of mode switching the programmer must do compared to discrete collections of disparate development programs. IDEs allow the user to simply dive down into the code. But other CRM applications like Siebel have an independent layer that allows the user to extend the application. These IDEs are typically written in a fourth-generation language and should be easy to manipulate and use to extend the application's functionality. These tools depend heavily on a mature object-oriented application that has been abstracted for use by a developer who is not required to understand the code complexities but rather just what he can do with the available objects. Although this feature has been around for a while, IDEs and the user's ability to extend the application are now getting sophisticated.

Software as a Service (SaaS)

One CRM trend is certainly the "No Software" approach taken by companies such as Salesforce.com, NetSuite, and RightNow. Software as a Service (SaaS) is a multitenant application that is redefining an application into an outsourced framework service to build any application. While the concept is not new, it still is not widespread in today's marketplace. In the past, outsourcing your mainframe CICS (Customer Information Control System) environment was possible, but applications still needed to be developed with coding. In today's marketplace, it is technically feasible to build a fairly robust application with little or no coding.

Web and Telephony Integration

Using a single network for both telephone and data communications, integrated business tools simplify customer communications that result in enhanced customer service and improved operating efficiency. Computer Telephony Integration (CTI) is a growing technology in the CRM industry and should be factored into an overall evaluation of CRM solutions in any organization. With the emergence of voice over Internet protocol (VoIP), many integrators are exploring the best way to leverage this broadband capability.

United Messaging (UM)

United Messaging (UM) integrates different streams of communication (email, SMS, fax, voice, and audio) into a single, or unified, message store, accessible from a variety of different devices (common computer application and telephone). Today, UM solutions are increasingly accepted in the corporate environment. The aim of deploying UM solutions is to enhance and improve business processes as well as services. UM solutions that target professional customers integrate communications processes into the existing information technology infrastructure into (CRM) and mail systems (Microsoft Exchange, Lotus Notes, and SAP).

Enterprise Service Buses (ESB)

A new breed of middleware products called Enterprise Service Buses (ESB) offer XML- and SOAP-based integration platforms that can be deployed throughout an enterprise network. By combining messaging, routing, Web services, and message-transformation capabilities into a single technical solution for bidirectional data exchange, ESBs are a strong and growing option in the technical design of a CRM solution.

Profit Optimization Technology

While providing CRM information to other levels of an organization through ESBs and middleware has grown, a new and emerging technology called profit optimization has been shown to be a factor in an overall CRM plan.

CRM applications are a rich resource for data on customer-buying behavior. By applying sophisticated mathematical techniques, these software applications can help companies analyze this data and better understand the segments of customers who buy their goods and services. And, these applications recommend what prices should be charged.

Another way that these applications leverage CRM data is by creating microsegmented models that allow companies to target specific goods and services, promotions, bundles, and, most importantly, prices to specific customer groups. These segmented offers ensure that customers are receiving the products they want and that the price charged realizes the maximum amount of margin available from that segment. Profit optimization is even enabling companies to judge in a split second whether a sales opportunity is good for the company and immediately recommend counteroffers when the deal is unacceptable.

Traditional methods of analyzing these sales opportunities were a rearview-mirror approach to determining which sales were profitable and which were not. Profit optimization allows companies to be preemptory in reacting to changes in their markets.

Profit optimization applications use sales data created in CRM applications (as well as ERP, or Enterprise Resource Planning, and supply-chain manufacturing systems) and push the reach of this knowledge to other parts of the company that may not use CRM directly. For the first time, people in marketing and manufacturing who are responsible for pricing goods and services, and pricing managers who must approve exception-case pricing requests from the field, have all the information they require to do their jobs.

Linux

From a mainstream corporate standpoint, Linux is still in its infancy, and sometimes it's difficult to convince upper management with the confidence to move forward with a technology that is typically viewed as "run by the masses," along with the difficulties of Linux's lack of support of proprietary applications such as Photoshop, PageMaker, and Quicken. However, a number of vendors (SugarCRM, absolutelyBUSY, vtiger CRM) are currently offering CRM solutions based on open source technology.

Acceptance of this new technology has grown over the short term by companies such as IBM, Home Depot, U.S. Postal Service, Dell, Union Bank of California, and others. Linux's growth in the CRM area is beginning to be evident in the marketplace and should present more viable options for corporations over the short- to mid-term timeframe.

Notebook Computers

Sales and marketing personnel who spend much of their time in the field prefer notebook portable computers. Weight restrictions are quickly disappearing as new lightweight batteries are introduced. From our experience, choose equipment of the lighter side; this tends to keep the mobile workers happier. In choosing the hardware, be careful not to compromise on screen size, keyboard feel, and ease of interfacing with options such as networks, CD-ROMs, etc.

Handhelds, Smartphones, and PDAs

Expect to see an increasing number of pen-based portable computers and PDAs being used in niche CRM areas such as inventory management, route accounting, and additional or alternative sales force automation clients. 3Com and Palm One have been supporting the ISV (independent software vendors) community, and this has resulted in several CRM thin-client packages (CRM client software in client-server architecture networks that depend primarily on a central server and focus on conveying input and output between the user and the remote server) running on the Palm platform. Microsoft has been adding to its handheld offerings with new releases of Windows Mobile, previously known as Windows CE and Pocket PC. Many ISVs are developing on the Microsoft platform with seamless integration with Enterprise Applications in addition to Outlook, Word, and Excel. Some vendors have introduced integrated smartphone platforms using Windows Mobile or browser-based applications such as WML, J2ME, and other wireless technology operating on the TDMA, CDMA, and GSM wireless networks.

Another wireless technology that we have seen with ISVs is the BlackBerry platform by Research In Motion (RIM). BlackBerry Enterprise Server (BES) enables secure encrypted data exchanges with a corporate network. With RIM's email and phone devices operating on the Java platform, many ISVs are writing applications for various vertical industries. The company's "push" technology is further enabled with a new BES service called "Mobile Data Server." Currently, no other PDA solutions support corporate security policy as well as the BES.

Voice Recognition

Despite the potential benefits of computers based on voice recognition, we are still several years away from the seamless integration of voice and computer. However, progress has been made in this direction in recent years. This market sector has seen business consolidation activities that have brought more strength to the segment. One key player is Nuance (the dictation pioneer), which offers Dragon RealSpeak and VoCon. Another leader in the market is IBM, which has consistently been maturing its Via Voice product line.

Once inside an application, such as a word processor or email application, the user's continuous speech will be converted to text with about 97 percent accuracy. The difficulty that speech recognition development companies have with voice command and control is that operating systems developed to date have been designed for the keyboard, the integrated pointing device, and the primary interface. In order for voice navigation to be smooth and efficient, a new operating system paradigm will need to be designed. While companies such as Microsoft and Apple are developing these new operating system interfaces, they are still a few years off of delivering a viable product.

Modem Support

Most portable computers have the option of being configured with an internal modem that permits users to communicate to and from the field, including sending and receiving faxes as well as email messages, and to connect to networks such as the Internet or virtual private networks.

Wireless Technologies

The new wave of data communication technologies is already available. Cellular and other mobile communications that permit sales and marketing executives and field service personnel to send and receive data from virtually anywhere will continue to improve their cost performance. They will become the technology of choice for busy, on-the-move sales and marketing executives, without a doubt.

More innovations are expected in the wireless arena. The major problem that we still face is in wireless standards adoptions, especially in the U.S. Currently, ISVs have too many wireless platforms they need to support. The next year or two should help consolidate more wireless technology.

GSM/GPRS is currently the frontrunner in the wireless network arena. Many top wireless carriers are adopting this standard, which has become a proven technology in Europe and Asia. Also, Wi-Fi or 802.11 still has a rapidly growing purpose and user base. Almost all mobile computers now have the 802.11 antenna as a standard feature.

Client/Server Architectures

Client/server architectures permit the two-way transfer of selected new or modified data. This data will be continually updated, with decreased data communications costs since only the changed data is transferred between the clients and the server, and connectivity with existing databases regardless of their location, platform, or data format. This allows a company to maintain its current information technology investments. While several vendors still offer client/server architecture, we are in the middle of major re-architectures. The main problem is that occasionally connected devices such as laptop CRM applications that can operate with connectivity still require client/server architecture. Many vendors are trying to get away from this and go to 100 percent Web-centric. The problem with this approach is that there are still major geographic areas where it is difficult—if not impossible—to achieve network connectivity to the Internet. We are likely to see some form of client/server architecture for several years to come.

"N-tiered" CRM Architecture

"N-tiered" CRM architecture is a growth area. This system architecture accommodates multiple CRM clients—thick (laptops/desktops), thin (browser, WAP, BlackBerry), and bulgy (Palm, MS-Windows CE, Pocket PC). This architecture allows CRM applications and database servers to reside in regional offices with synchronization of information subsets on a regular or real-time basis. Multiple application servers and database servers can be integrated to provide relevant information to the various CRM clients for their particular tasks.

Graphics, Video, and Sound Support

This equipment, which is available today, will continue to improve because of better compression algorithms, larger storage devices in portable computers, and improved multimedia/streaming technology and network bandwidth. Graphics, video, and sound support enhance the sales and marketing personnel's ability to display their goods and services in the field easily, for example, showing color photos of their products and services on the computer rather than carrying around an out-of-date paper catalog. Other areas where graphics, video, and sound are increasingly important are CRM user community training (etraining), product demos, and virtual sales meetings (Informatica, Saba, WebEx, and Microsoft Office Live Meeting).

Step 5: Secure User Ownership

Get users involved early to make sure that the CRM system addresses their needs. One large information technology manufacturer automated its sales force in accordance with the results of the corporate headquarters CRM task force. The staff end-users were not sufficiently represented on this task force and ended up revolting against what they felt was yet another "big brother" system.

Generally, CRM users will respond to a "3X factor" in accessing information from the CRM software package: For every one piece of information that the user requests, the CRM system should provide three pieces of information that the user personally values. The 3X factor will motivate users to use the CRM system.

Remember that satisfied users will want to work with the system, and no one knows better what users need and what they find annoying than the users themselves. Do not be afraid to hand over ownership of the system to the users.

Step 6: Prototype the System

Prototyping your CRM system allows the following to happen: New technology can be phased in, experimentation can be done on a smaller and less costly scale, the system's functionality can be tested, required changes in organizational procedures can be highlighted, and most importantly, CRM objectives can be met. The availability of rapid prototyping software development tools reinforces the importance of testing before you commit.

Step 7: Train Users

Training is a multistep process that should include the following: providing a demonstration to users on how to access and use needed information, ensuring that users are provided with documentation that is understandable and frequently updated, offering online tutorials which can be customized for each user, providing a phone help line to stand by your user, and training the trainers to ensure that new users can be up and running quickly on the system. In many cases, the use of Web-based training will help increase training effectiveness while reducing cost.

At a leading air courier express company, several members of the sales force requested that all electronic information on the CRM system be printed in paper form. This request stemmed from the fact that these users had not been properly trained and did not know how to properly navigate their way around the system to obtain needed information.

Over the life of your CRM system, training will end up costing between one and one-and-a-half times the cost of the CRM system hardware/software. Budget for training accordingly, and remember that the best way to change work habits and to ensure systems success is via effective training.

Step 8: Motivate Personnel

CRM succeeds when users are motivated by the system's ability to help them obtain their objectives. When users understand the strategic importance of CRM, there will be improved user productivity and a positive impact on the company's bottom line.

Trends come and go within an organization, so determine ways to maintain individual motivation and commitment toward the CRM system. Show users their importance and their impact in the CRM system.

Step 9: Administrate the System

One person/department must be held responsible for overseeing the welfare of the CRM system. This person/department must include an information "gatekeeper," who is responsible for ensuring that the information is timely, relevant, easy to access, and positively impacting the users' decision-making needs.

It's one thing to have to be out in the field and using your CRM system with good data; it's another only to find out-of-date or incorrect data. Be disciplined and pay careful attention to information and systems details.

Step 10: Keep Management Committed

Set up a committee that includes senior staff and users from the sales, marketing, and customer service departments as well as from the information systems department. This committee should brief senior management on a quarterly basis concerning the status of the CRM systems project, including successes, failures, future needs, growth, and other metrics. Measure the system's results and relay the impact of the system to management. Secure your system champion.

Ultimately, the benefits of CRM can be substantial, including improved productivity, enhanced customer service, and a strengthened ability to make sound business decisions. To realize these benefits, however, it's necessary to audit properly, to successfully accomplish the 10 steps previously outlined, and to address both technical as well as nontechnical issues.

Chapter 25

Creating a CRM Business Case

A successful CRM initiative is based on a solid CRM business case. The business case is a critical document that describes a company's current CRM-related processes, the desired state of CRM in a company, how the company intends to integrate people, process, and technology to get to the desired state, the costs and expected return of the CRM initiative, the risks and mitigating factors associated with the initiative, the organizational/operational impact of the initiative, and CRM program metrics against which success/failure can be measured. The CRM business case is as relevant to smaller CRM projects as it is to multiple CRM projects within a larger enterprise-wide CRM program.

An organization that embarks upon a CRM initiative but that fails to create a comprehensive CRM business case risks the success of the CRM project from the start. The CRM business case should not be an option. Not only should it be done, but it also should include precise metrics to measure throughout the life of the CRM initiative. Despite early claims of high failure rates in CRM initiatives, companies today that take the time to create a comprehensive CRM business case containing the following metrics greatly improve the likelihood of success. Remember the words of management guru Peter Drucker who reminded everyone, "If you can't measure it, you can't manage it."

The following information will help any business start crafting a comprehensive CRM business case.

Executive Summary

- **CRM program background** – Provides the reasons for launching the initiative, current business issues that CRM is likely to address, and the impact that CRM is likely to have both internally as well as for customers.

- **CRM value proposition** – Describes which CRM value proposition components are applicable for the CRM program and offers measurable program impact. The CRM value proposition is based largely on metrics identified in the appendices that follow.

Each CRM initiative will have its own value proposition. Here is one example of a company's value proposition for a 150-person, multifunctional CRM effort:

At a high level, the CRM initiative for this company promised to:

- Deliver more productive reps (freeing up 18.5 hours per week currently spent on unnecessary administrative work) leading to higher close ratios (from 22 percent to 28 percent over an 18-month period)

- Reach new customers with more customer seminars (increase the number of annual seminars from eight to 12)

- Improve lead efficiency and speed (baseline of three days to get the lead out to the sales rep, decreasing to one day over a 12-month period)

- Lower mailing costs (annual promotional mailing costs to decrease from $340,000 to $180,000)

In a more detailed view, the same CRM initiative promised to deliver the following:

- **Productivity impact each week** (a result of on-the-job efficiency because staff didn't need to chase information):

Each sales rep	18.5 hours (2+ day per week)
Each sales manager	5.8 hours
Tech services department	20.2 hours (2+ days per week)
Marketing department	36.8 hours (4+ days per week)
Each product manager	6.0 hours
Total (for the entire CRM user base)	**1,182 hours (148 days per week)**

- **Revenue impact per annum** (higher close ratios as a result of jobs being done more effectively):

Territory sales reps (total)	$ 3.55 million
Sales managers (total)	$ 1.47 million
Tech services department	$ 0.30 million
Total	**$ 5.32 million**

- **Cost savings per annum** (as a result of no longer sending annual product catalogs to all customers, but rather specific catalogs and targeted mailings to customers based on known areas of interest):

  Marketing department savings, $234,950

- **Financial breakeven at 16 months** (sufficient contribution has been generated from the CRM system through month 16 to pay back all CRM-related costs through month 16)

CRM Value Proposition Guidelines

For the past decade, my firm and others have conducted research into the CRM value proposition. While each CRM value proposition is unique, here are some generic guidelines for creating a CRM value proposition. Companies that successfully implement a CRM initiative benefit from one or more of the following six CRM value proposition components:

- **Enhanced productivity** – Expect a 10 to 20 percent annual increase in the productivity for customer-facing personnel, resulting from having needed customer information readily available. With proper discipline and incentives, this productivity improvement leads to a 5 to 10 percent increase in annual sales.

- **Lower costs** – A 5 to 10 percent decrease in costs for sales, marketing, and customer service general and administration. This benefit results from the company knowing its customers and servicing them better and more efficiently.

- **Superior employee morale** – A 10 percent decrease in turnover rate, resulting from more satisfied customer-facing employees, along with a better pool of candidates applying for customer-facing job openings.

- **Better customer knowledge** – A complete, comprehensive customer profile as defined by customer-facing personnel and customers within 18 months of launching the CRM initiative.

- **Higher customer satisfaction** – A 10 percent increase per annum between 100 percent customer satisfaction and current satisfaction ratings. This results from customers who receive desired information promptly and completely.

- **Improved customer loyalty/retention** – A 10 percent annual increase in customer "wallet share" (the percentage of the customer's overall revenue and profit potential realized through individual and company's efforts), and a 10 percent annual improvement in customer retention rates. These gains are made because customers like to do business with a company that cares about their relationship.

In addition to CRM program background and a CRM value proposition, the Executive Summary section of any CRM business case should include the following:

- **Initial project scope and timetable** – Provides high-level goals, milestones, and dates associated with the successful implementation of the CRM initiative.

- **Business sponsorship** – Describes the role of top management in approving the CRM business case and in actively participating in driving the success of resulting CRM projects (participation in the CRM oversight board that reviews the accomplishment of metrics every six months).

Financials

- **Detailed financial information** – Includes estimated costs for hardware, software, communication, consulting, training, internal costs, and other total-cost-of-ownership components needed to realize a successful CRM program. This also provides estimated revenues resulting from the CRM program, including identification of the breakeven point and the resulting ROI.

Recommended Technical Solution

- **Insight into key technical issues** – CRM technical alternatives are considered, along with the description of the proposed CRM technical solution, interfaces with existing company systems (ERP systems), disaster recovery policy, hot spare policy (from the company on the failover mechanism to provide reliable system configurations), and support/help desk policies. This section tends to have heavy input from by internal IT personnel.

Key Risks and Mitigating Factors

- **Key technology risks and mitigation** – This includes lack of scalability, inappropriate security procedures, difficult data synchronization, and lack of data quality strategy.

- **Key user risks and mitigation** – Bad or inappropriate training can lead to an inability to use the system properly, or users don't perceive the value of CRM.

- **Key management risks and mitigation** – This includes a lack of management commitment to CRM, lack of management support for CRM, or management attention shifted from CRM to a more attractive initiative.

Operational/Organizational Impact

- **Key processes affected** – Describes the processes that have an impact or will be impacted by the CRM program, including how processes will be enhanced.

- **Organizational issues** – Provides the number of personnel affected by the CRM program; also identifies how the CRM program may impact job descriptions, individual performance requirements, and compensation.

- **Organizational buy-in** – Details a CRM program communications plan along with appropriate change management issues that need to be addressed to ensure the success of the CRM initiative.

Appendices

For each CRM business functional area (time management, sales, sales management, telemarketing/telesales, customer contact center, marketing, business intelligence, ebusiness, and other), there is a high-level description of potential areas of improvement. For example, this may include key activities, the current state of these activities including the time spent per activity, and the likely benefits and results of the CRM system quantified in time saved, monetary gain, and/or cost savings achieved.

The appendices highlight common CRM business functionality such as a common customer profile or a limited number of common management reports needed across all customer-facing functional areas. Identifying common CRM functions is important for the overall success of a CRM program since common business functionality allows multiple business functions/departments to share common information on an as-needed basis. The appendices may also include unique CRM system customer-facing functionality needs. Unique needs may be important because of circumstances such as cultural differences within a global company. However, unique needs should be kept to a minimum, if possible, since significant costs are associated with fulfilling unique needs. These unique needs often lead to incompatibility of business processes and, ultimately, to an inability to share or report against common customer information.

In the end, each CRM business case is unique, and that is why it's difficult to provide a sample or generic CRM business case. The CRM business case is not optional; it must be measured quarterly to ensure that the CRM initiative stays on track. By using the CRM business case effectively, a company can proactively achieve CRM initiative success.

Chapter 26

Getting Your CRM Business Prioritization Right

When choosing a CRM solution, organizations should refer closely to their list of requirements, which typically includes business, functional, technical, and user-friendliness/support items. These items are derived from the organization's early CRM brainstorming sessions, field/corporate visits, questionnaires, and business matrices employed, including the technical infrastructure review.

That requirements list can be quite extensive. Nevertheless, in our experience, it is not always feasible or wise to try to deliver on all defined business functions during the first CRM system release. Here are a few reasons why:

- While all business functions may seem important, experience suggests that once a CRM system is implemented, users employ considerably less than 100 percent of its available functionality.

- Too many business functions tend to overwhelm the capabilities of even the best technical staff, and this may lead to confusion between the functions needed and those that would be nice to have, which can delay the delivery of high-priority functions.

- The CRM initiative changes the way customer-facing personnel work, and this can be a shock to the user. Overwhelming users with too many changes too quickly can actually produce lower productivity and a longer technological assimilation period.

For these reasons, we suggest starting small and building CRM system functionality in phases. To ensure that there is a clear understanding of which business functions will be implemented first, second, and so on, the business functionality list should be prioritized.

Prioritizing those business functional requirements can be difficult. If you are implementing a multifunctional, integrated system, it is likely that the business functional requirements list will contain requirements from job functions, including sales, sales management, marketing, customer service, and top management. It's also likely that each of these job functions will view its own requirements as the most important ones for the system. Clear rules for prioritizing business functional requirements can eliminate internal politics that can lead to inappropriate prioritization, which may have long-term and unfavorable results.

Here are our suggestions to avoid potential problems and to prioritize a business functional list to help ensure maximum results:

- Coordinate a prioritization meeting. Invite senior managers who are responsible for sales, marketing, and customer service to a session (which should last no longer than three hours). In addition to this group of senior managers, invite potential system users (a representative or two from sales, one from marketing, and another from customer service), preferably individuals who have participated in the brainstorming session, field/corporate visits, and questionnaire exercises.

- During the prioritization meeting, potential system users should brief senior management on how the business functional requirements list was created and what each desired function means. The senior managers should also brief the potential systems users about the company's key priorities, based on business strategy and direction.

- Next, participants in the prioritization meeting should discuss how each proposed business function supports both the company's key priorities as well as the needs of potential systems users. Compromises will need to be made during this part of the meeting.

- Participants of the prioritization meeting should then prioritize the business functional requirements list (No. 1 being the most important function to automate, No. 2 the second most important function, and so on). Responses to this prioritization exercise should then be tabulated.

- Finally, participants should review the prioritization exercise results, discuss the remaining disagreements, and agree to a final prioritization list, which will be used for the internal system specification or for a Request for Information/Proposal to external vendors. In the end, disagreements or difficulties should be worked out by referring to the company's business strategy and direction. The value of a prioritization meeting includes: 1) a final list of prioritized business functions; and 2) buy-in from senior management and users regarding the direction for the CRM system.

My firm once coordinated a prioritization meeting for a large consumer goods company. Within 30 minutes after the user and senior management briefings started, it was apparent that the marketing director felt he owned the system, and the sales manager really wasn't interested in it. Acknowledging the long-term dangers of this situation, we asked a few pertinent business questions, including how sharing marketing and sales information could benefit each party; this line of questioning forced these two directors to address the need for an integrated CRM system. This type of situation is not uncommon. In fact, it serves as a reminder that while the prioritization meeting should be structured, some flexibility must be built into the timetable for issues that may arise.

Support Requirements

A second element in your CRM software selection process will be an initial list of user-friendliness/support requirements. These requirements come directly from early brainstorming sessions, your field/corporate visits, questionnaires, and any business matrices that are employed.

User-support requirements are essential since many potential users of your CRM system may not be familiar with the CRM software you select, with using CRM software in general, or even with using other computer systems. To complicate the process of determining user-support requirements, CRM software is being developed for hardware platforms other than desktop or laptop computers, including handheld devices and wireless devices. Pay attention to these requirements; too many good CRM systems have failed because user-support requirements were overlooked.

Who decides on the user-support criteria? It's actually a collaborative process, but the users should have a major voice. This decision must not be left up to technical or managerial personnel. Only by trial and error will your company learn the correct level of user support, since this level differs from company to company and from system to system.

Here are some of the key user support requirements that you should take into consideration when specifying and designing your CRM system:

- **Graphical User Interface (GUI)** – For thick and thin client CRM interfaces, Microsoft (MS) Windows GUIs and browser GUIs predominate. Some vendors have developed GUIs that mimic those of MS Outlook. Vendors have been recently taking cues from the Web and designing interfaces that mimic the interface of a Web browser. This makes sense, because most new CRM software being developed is based on Internet/Web platforms and technologies. Handheld devices such as PDAs use a different GUI due to its smaller screen size. Regardless of the interface, consider these key questions: Does the screen layout appear to be cluttered, or does the screen layout appear to be well-designed in terms of ergonomics and flow? Have the screen fields been laid out in a logical manner? Is it easy to get to a secondary or a support screen from the main screen?

- **System navigation** – This is the ease that users have moving from field to field within a screen, from screen to screen, as well as from function to function within the system. Several studies confirm that system navigation is a key success factor for user acceptance of the system. While system navigation may be a subjective issue, let the users inform you whether the system navigation is easy to implement. Navigation schemes for CRM software primarily use MS Windows or Web browser metaphors, which should be familiar to most computer users. Different functions of the software are now often being ported down to handheld and wireless devices, which have their own navigation schemes.

- **Intuitiveness of the system** – This is a tough requirement to define since each user will have a perspective on the definition of intuitiveness. Screen design, graphical user interface, and system navigation all have an impact on the intuitiveness of the system. Based on my firm's findings, users feel that an intuitive system reflects the developer's knowledge of the customer-facing processes behind the interface. In a nonintuitive system, users may instead feel that technical personnel who are out of touch with critical customer-facing functions, such as sales, marketing, and customer service, designed the system.

- **System effectiveness** – Increased competition between software vendors has led to divergent philosophies within the industry about what constitutes effective functionality. The business principle driving this split is defined on how a company can best take advantage of its information resources to increase sales. Some software vendors have answered this question by incorporating a sales methodology, which requires the user to input a substantial amount of data to provide a more extensive profile of the contact, account, or opportunity. Other vendors have chosen to simplify the user's responsibilities; they require less data input and offer a more appealing screen design, with colors, shading, and easy-to-read text to increase user support and program use. This is where the software buyer must decide what is more effective: acquiring more information or offering a simpler data entry environment.

- **Customer self-service via the Web** – The influence of the Internet and the Web is affecting CRM initiative efforts in many ways. The vendors involved in more advanced Web interaction technology are offering online Web pages that provide customers with a "window" into some customer service portions of the corporate knowledgebase (subject to security restrictions). Using the customer service Web pages, a user can perform operations without the assistance of a customer service representative. Users might input service request information, check on the status of a problem resolution, request technical documentation, and search FAQs, or request a follow-up from a customer service representative. What Web self-service support capabilities are provided by your short list of vendors?

- **Help functionality** – Most users prefer a field-sensitive help function rather than a screen-sensitive help function, since less work is required by the user to find specific answers to users' questions. Another important help function requirement is the ability for the systems administrator (internal or external to your company) to modify (add, enhance, or delete) or to customize the wording within the help function. The ability to customize the help function is particularly important if the system contains specific business processes that are unique to the company and which users may need to refer to regularly. Lastly, does the help function contain the user documentation online so users can leave their often heavy user documentation books at home?

- **Online chat** – What interaction channels are available to customers as an alternative to making a phone call, sending an email, or searching a knowledgebase to get answers to support questions? Increasingly, vendors are offering an online chat feature that lets customers interact with customer service representatives via a company Web page. Typically, this interaction entails typing in questions and receiving feedback via a dialog box, which displays the questions and answers. This capability augments the other customer self-service features that a vendor may provide.

- **Online training** – Does the vendor offer modes of training in addition to the standard training options for classroom training provided on-site or at a company location? With the increase in Web-based CRM applications, more Web-based online training is now available. So, users can participate in training exercises via the Internet without the limitation of geographic location (travel). Trainees can log into a scheduled session, which is held using Web-based collaboration services such as Saba or WebEx. Some CRM vendors offer Web-based CRM applications training via OEM agreements with companies such as KnowledgePlanet. Online training is particularly suited to periodic training, because there is typically less material to present. This online training capability lets users increase their skills without spending additional time away from work; the vendor can provide the same quality of learning as the on-site training at a lower cost of delivery.

- **User documentation** – Is the documentation comprehensive and up-to-date? Are there practical examples in the documentation, including screenshots of software functionality? How do system users receive documentation updates? Can updates be delivered electronically? Can the user documentation be accessed online while the user is on the system?

- **Internationalization** – Does the vendor offer multilanguage and multicurrency versions of the software? What types of translation capabilities are provided for local versions of the CRM solution?

What international support office locations are available to customers who have global CRM system implementations?

- **Data synchronization** – Is the process of sending and receiving data to/from the field with headquarters a "one-button" operation, or do you need extensive training? And how simple is it for the user to determine what went wrong and what to do to correct the problem if the phone line or wireless modem disconnects in the middle of data synchronization?

- **System support** – Given the importance of this topic (training, help desk, and systems administration) and the impact that system support can have not only on users but also on the overall success of the system, there is a separate chapter on this topic (see Chapter 11, The Necessity of Training).

Here is an example of how one company addressed the user-support issue. A few years ago, a large international pharmaceutical company implemented a comprehensive CRM system for its sales and marketing personnel. To ensure the system was user-friendly, the company invited sales and marketing personnel to participate in the project from the inception. Specifically, as the in-company system was built module by module, the sales and marketing personnel were given the right to veto any screen as well as to reject the navigation, the help function, or any feature, as unfriendly.

While this approach led to a longer than expected development period as well as a few battles between users and developers, the users ultimately owned the system they created based on their own needs and their own user support criteria. Today, sales and marketing personnel at this company still connect to the CRM system daily. This shows that by letting the users define and approve user support, you greatly enhance the likelihood of the overall system's success.

The requirements analysis portion of the CRM software selection process is important to the success of the CRM initiative. Take the time upfront during the implementation process to carefully consider and prioritize the business functional and user-friendliness/support requirements for any CRM system investment.

Chapter 27

Outsourcing CRM

Until recently, implementing a CRM software solution meant one of two options: engaging an external implementation company that has received implementation training/certification by the software vendor, or using your internal IT resources to implement a software solution.

Neither of these options is optimal. By using an external implementer, you are theoretically buying expertise and experience. But be prepared to pay an "implementation multiplier" of between .5 and 1.5 times the price of your software. And make sure those assigned to your CRM implementation project are skilled and available during the entire process. Imagine if an implementer said that your assigned project manager would remain on the job only until they receive a higher bid from another customer. This actually happened to one of our clients. The replacement project manager was inefficient, and the implementation came in nine months late and 100 percent over budget.

Using the company's internal IT resources also has its own list of pros and cons. Once the CRM software vendor has properly trained your IT personnel—do not cut corners here—you can look forward to substantial cost savings in the long run. You also gain internal expertise. But remember that your internal resources will be on a learning curve initially.

The deficiencies that exist by using external implementers and internal IT resources will also help drive other viable implementation options that warrant your careful attention.

Option 1: Implement Using a Combination of Internal/External Skills

A leading payroll services vendor was scheduled to implement a 2,000-person CRM system. External implementation quotes hovered at about $6 million. In today's economy where "more for less" has become a realistic request, the customer turned down the external implementer option and decided to make arrangements to have six internal IT professionals receive implementation training from the CRM vendor. Three external CRM software implementation experts (one project manager, one software customizer, and one software integrator) also joined these six individuals. They also engaged a leading CRM authority to join their project implementation team and provide overall implementation guidance. The cost for this combined internal/external skill set was less than 20 percent of the $6 million alternative.

This option is driven by the availability of well-qualified CRM software vendors and implementer personnel who are looking for work.

Option 2: The Vendor Owns the Implementation

A leading oil and lubricants manufacturer had a 400-person CRM system to implement and asked the CRM software vendor to implement the system. Until recently, CRM software vendors only developed software, leaving the implementation to selected partners. But as vendors need successful implementation reference sites, this trend slowed. In this case, the CRM software vendor accepted the challenge and placed a total of four internal project managers and developers on the implementation. This project was finished on time and below budget, with an implementation multiplier of .9 (a figure within the recommended implementation multiplier range).

The willingness of vendors to take on their own implementations appears to be a growing trend. Pivotal's purchase of Software Spectrum is an example that has increasingly allowed Pivotal to take on more of its own implementations using internal Pivotal resources.

Option 3: Application Service Providers (ASP)

A number of companies do not want the hassle of owning their CRM implementation. They may lack sufficient internal implementation resources or the budget to hire external resources. In these cases, an ASP (application service provider) or SaaS (software as a service) is a viable option, particularly for those companies that leverage this as a stepping-stone to their own CRM system. (The term ASP is a new name for the old practice called "outsourcing.") The driver behind this option is lower start-up costs; you can also write off all ASP fees as an expense item. Be prepared to give your company's critical data to the ASP, and understand it may not be cost-efficient for the ASP to tailor the CRM software to every company need. Among the CRM software vendors who offer ASP services are Onyx, FirstWave, Salesforce.com, RightNow, Siebel, NetSuite, CrystalWare, and others; specialized ASPs offer CRM services, such as USi and NaviSite.

Implementation costs typically take the largest bite out of a CRM budget. The CRM industry, which has now passed the ERP industry in revenue per annum as the largest software application area, depends heavily on successful implementations to propel its future growth.

In addition to external implementers and internal IT resources, there are other attractive implementation alternatives that you can investigate. You may find a better alternative.

Understanding the ASP Model

What is an ASP and why is it a relevant acronym in CRM? It's important to understand the history and growth of ASPs, the applicability of the ASP to your organization's CRM efforts, and which companies are among the leading ASP vendors.

Today's chief information officers (CIOs) are being asked to roll out electronic commerce initiatives including CRM and eprocurement in weeks, not months; they are also being asked to adapt or draw up entirely new strategies at a moment's notice. In addition to these dynamic business pressures, CIOs are wrestling with labor issues, speed of technological change, and the emergence of broadband networks. All these forces support the ASP value proposition.

Although analysts' predictions for the growth of the ASP market have been slow to materialize, researchers such as IDC are predicting sales of $24 billion for ASPs by the end of 2007, meaning that the funding should continue for existing and new ASP players. The message is clear that while the ASP model may be ideal for your organization's CRM needs, it is prudent to research the financial stability and long-term viability of the ASP you are considering.

ASPs had their start between the 1960s and the 1980s when businesses sold time shares on mainframe computers and hosted subscribers' applications. Model 3270 terminals functioned as thin clients. Mainframe tools and networking protocols provided control over and insight into usage, reliability, availability, performance, and service levels.

These time-shares or outsourcing companies even owned or leased the communications network. Mutual trust between provider and customer was possible because the provider controlled the quality of deliverables, and the customer could validate that quality.

With the advent of client-server computing, the technical industry's progress toward distributed and open technology caused an unintended side effect. Somewhere in the evolution from old to new, precise control and measurement of service levels were lost. Not surprisingly, fewer providers of application services remained.

Within the CRM industry today, we are seeing it come full circle. ASPs are now integrating new technology with meaningful, measurable service-level agreements and can deliver efficiently. ASPs are also winning corporate customers back with messages of security, reliability, and cost containment.

Many examples of best-in-class companies have moved their data and applications onto an ASP site. This has been complemented by communications infrastructures that have moved from private networks to frame relay connections (an efficient data transmission technique used to send digital information quickly and cheaply in a relay of frames to destinations from one or many end points), the Internet, or private VPNs (virtual private networks).

In the simplest terms, an ASP uses the Internet or private extranet to host, manage, and support software applications for companies. ASPs make it possible for enterprises to access enterprise-class software solutions without deep investments in the software, hardware, and personnel to support those solutions. The basis of the relationship between the customer and an ASP is a contractual service level agreement (SLA); ASPs provide software, infrastructure, and operations support as well as application services for a predictable monthly subscription fee.

Why are so many companies suddenly feeling comfortable with something that was treated as questionable-at-best only a few years ago? One of the primary points is the scarcity of raw intellectual talent, forced by the World Wide Web itself. The demand for information technology specialists is so high that companies are often unable to find or to afford the talent they need to run their critical applications. Even when they do find the talent, they are under constant threat of losing those specialists to headhunters. Information technology employees are now holding jobs for months, not years or decades. Intellectual capital is going out the door just as fast as it is coming in.

According to an old proverb, "There is nothing new under the sun." For those of you who have been around the SFA (sales force automation) market long enough to have gray hair, you will remember a company in Atlanta called Sales Technologies. In the 1980s, Sales Technologies had large mainframe-based SFA systems; remote sales personnel synchronized to these mainframes. When the company was still in business, Sales Technologies primarily served the pharmaceutical and petroleum industries as a true pioneer in an SFA ASP.

Several pessimists suggested that ASPs might only be able to thrive in small- to mid-sized businesses. Sales Technologies proved this theory to be wrong; its well-designed business model attracted larger corporations that were willing to sign up for these types of service offerings. Some CRM vendors (Neteos) that had originally offered its solution only via an ASP offering found that following the ASP route exclusively can be dangerous since some companies do not want to place all their eggs in one ASP basket (Neteos eventually went out of business). Increasingly, CRM software vendors are offering ASP services and providing software on a licensed basis as well.

Application developers and independent software vendors view the ASP arena as a new channel to deliver their applications. Of course, some big questions remain about how the application developers will react since this movement represents a major shift in the revenue model. The shift is from higher upfront revenue for each customer to longer ongoing revenue in much smaller increments from potentially many more customers. The pay-as-you-go model of renting applications makes the revenue a three- or four-year equivalent to traditional license fees. But not all application developers are buying into this model.

Despite the promise of a growing ASP market, several CRM vendors have been forced to make significant changes to their ASP model or to their ASP teaming partnerships, or to stop offering an ASP option altogether. For example, Siebel closed its sales.com offering in 2001, although Siebel re-entered the ASP market with its Siebel CRM OnDemand product in 2003. Many ASP vendors also have gone out of business, including AristaSoft, marchFIRST, FutureLink, and Agillon.

Judging from this mixed track record, it's best to look carefully at a vendor's long-term commitment to the ASP model. In fact, if you opt for the ASP model, I recommend that your ASP contact provide mitigation for these types of risks.

In researching ASPs, I identified several vendors that can address CRM needs. Some of the following ASPs listed are sales focused, whereas others have greater enterprise capabilities. This list is representative not comprehensive. For more details about each company, check out Appendix D.

Broad-Based ASPs

EDS, www.eds.com

IBM, www.ibm.com

Jamcracker, www.jamcracker.com

Oracle On Demand, www.oracle.com/ondemand

Concur Technologies, www.concur.com

USi, www.usi.net

Small- and Mid-Size Business ASPs

NaviSite, www.navisite.com

TeleComputing, www.telecomputing.com

NetSuite, www.netsuite.com

CrystalWare, www.crystal-ware.com

Onyx, www.onyx.com

Pivotal, www.pivotal.com

Salesforce.com, www.salesforce.com

RightNow, www.rightnow.com

Vendors are approaching the emerging ASP market segment from all angles. Some ASPs are providing only point solutions, such as SFA. Other vendors are providing an integrated suite of CRM, ERP (Enterprise Resource Planning), employee portals, and data warehousing. Several vendors have formed new corporations or business units to address specific market segments, such as SFA. Much of the new ASP funding is directed at ASPs that specialize in specific vertical industries.

As outlined previously, ASPs have several different pricing models. Application vendors such as Oracle have a business model where you buy the software license, pay the maintenance fee, and then pay them to host your application.

USi and others let users rent the application and hosting services for a monthly fee. In almost all cases, users pay for set-up and implementation costs. With certain ASP providers, these costs can be almost as expensive as hiring a systems integrator. Be careful to evaluate the details carefully before signing any ASP contracts.

The next-generation Web services vendors such as Salesforce.com, NetSuite, and RightNow provide subscription-based pricing that is typically much less costly than ASPs that host traditional CRM packages.

Key challenges to the success of ASPs revolve around the network bandwidth to let the applications perform at a necessary level for consistent, acceptable service level agreements (SLAs) and 24/7 availability. While most companies are still undecided on the future, the companies providing robust integrated application suites seem to be gaining momentum.

Will ASPs become the way of the future? This is still the subject of many debates. Voice mail supplied by the phone company is the equivalent of outsourcing your answering machine service for a monthly fee. Many consumers feel comfortable with an outside organization managing this mission critical service. But questions still remain about the control and security of CRM data. Many businesses do not feel comfortable housing mission critical data at some ASP site, and prefer instead to have that data located at the company site.

Overall, the ASP market is still developing. Vendors are still working on service definitions and priorities, network availability, and bandwidth issues as well as partnership strategies. According to a recent ASP Industry Consortium survey, 56 percent of companies currently renting business applications from an ASP have less than 500 employees. The survey indicates that small- to mid-sized companies are still the largest market for the ASP model.

Renting applications seems as if it would be a logical solution for many businesses. However, time will tell. Companies have been touting the promise of computing as a utility for several years.

Companies deploying CRM might consider ASP as a potential software delivery method. But, be forward-thinking in your business model. To date, ASPs have not really addressed requirements including call centers or customer interaction centers. Does this mean that your organization should outsource only half of your CRM application, if you need call center functionality as part of the CRM system?

There are also varying levels of willingness among ASPs to integrate their applications with your existing legacy applications, ranging from import/export integration only to more complex integration capabilities. Don't be surprised if an ASP company lets you know that you have to manage your own legacy systems. Again, does this provide a good business case if you still have to have an IT department just to manage your legacy? If you interface your legacy applications to the ASP, the third-party ASP company's mixed-bag approach to application hosting makes it unclear where accountability lies. So, pay attention to which integration services the ASP will provide.

Adopting Service Level Agreements (SLAs)

While some ASPs use co-location facilities and buy bandwidth from network carriers, other ASPs try to control every aspect of their service. This impacts the important issue of the ability and willingness of ASPs to offer varying levels of SLAs. The SLAs offered by an ASP generally covers only the services that the ASP controls directly, including availability, functionality, and performance, from the applications to the network. The SLA should include, but not be limited to, the following:

- Purpose of the SLA

- Description of service

- General payment terms

- Duration of service

- Termination conditions

- Legal issues such as warranties, software ownership, etc.

- Start date of service indemnities, limitation of liability, etc.

- Installation timetable

ASPs also are struggling with the customization issue, and this does not appear to be going away anytime soon. Shared services always means more generic offerings. However, many companies customize applications unnecessarily. To help with customization, ASPs also are turning to more configurable solutions that customers can tailor to their needs without expensive source code customizations.

In the final analysis, there are benefits to the ASP model. For example, one benefit is enabling specific CRM software to be deployed quickly and requiring little IT infrastructure. But be careful in your due diligence, be realistic with your expectations, and make sure the ASP can meet the prioritized business requirements already predetermined for your CRM system.

Chapter 28

Addressing CRM Security Risks

Nothing in this world is gained without risk. When you are about to launch a new application that has taken months in the making, or are about to sell your wares over the Web, or are letting your field service reps get to their data over the Net, you realize there will be risks involved. The growth of CRM and ebusiness is exposing organizations to more access than ever before. Too many variables exist in hardware, firmware, operating systems, middleware, applications, and networking for anyone to account adequately for all the possibilities. In fact, the only truly secure system is one that is switched off and good to no one.

According to Robert Richardson, director of the Computer Security Institute, "Information security is a complex undertaking, but it is also an essential one in the current, highly networked world. Organizations that hope to thrive have to create a culture that willingly funds, trains, and empowers an enterprise information security function, because attacks happen with regularity and their impact can be significant." In the Computer Security Institute's 2007 Computer Crime and Security Survey, the following range of attacks and abuses were noted:

- 59 percent detected employee abuse of Internet access privileges (for example, downloading pornography or pirated software, or inappropriate use of email systems)

- 52 percent detected computer viruses

- 50 percent reported losses from the theft of laptops or mobile devices

- 26 percent detected phishing where their organizations were fraudulently represented as sender

- 25 percent detected denial of service attacks

By addressing the security of company infrastructures, we can address the threats that put our CRM and ebusiness networks at risk. Information systems security policies primarily address threats. Without any threats, policies would be unnecessary, and users could do whatever they wanted with information. Unfortunately, threats exist and information systems security policies are necessary to provide a framework for selecting and implementing countermeasures against them. A well-designed information security policy defines an organization's objectives of the information system and outlines a strategy to achieve these objectives. An enforceable written policy helps ensure that everyone within the organization behaves in an acceptable manner with information security.

A security policy establishes what must be done to protect information stored on computers. A well-written policy contains a sufficient definition of "what" to do so that the "how" can be identified and measured or evaluated.

A company must have concise and easy-to-understand policies that can be implemented and enforced, while balancing protection with productivity. But, more importantly, they must define responsibilities and how violations will be effectively handled. No matter how diligently a company maintains a security policy, it is impossible to remove all the security risks. One reason is that there are so many areas for security breaches to occur in the enterprise CRM and ebusiness environments. These include the following areas.

Remote Access:
- Laptops (e.g., viruses, password protection, applications and operating systems, encryption, personal firewalls, encryption devices, token management, enterprise firewalls, and data back-up)

- PDAs/Web phones (e.g., password protection, virus protection, enterprise firewalls, encryption, and potentially wireless encryption)

- Virtual Private Networks, or VPNs (e.g., enterprise firewalls and network-provider password management)

- Remote Access Service, or RAS (e.g., RAS server passwords and enterprise firewalls)

- CRM application-level security (e.g., workgroup, user, and field level)

Partner Relationship Management (PRM):

- PRM/CRM application security (workgroup, user, and field level)

- Demilitarized Zones, or DMZ (extranet passwords and log-on passwords)

- Partner versus competitor data and information security issues

- Public Key Infrastructure, or PKI (an arrangement that binds public keys with respective user identities by means of a certificate authority)

ebusiness/ecommerce:

- CRM, portal, Web self-service, and ebusiness application security (user and field level)

- PKI

- VPNs and Web services

Call Center Email:

- Virus protection

- Help desk access

Enterprise Email:

- User list management

- Lightweight Directory Access Protocol or LDAP (used for email user management)

- Password management

- Server email attachment virus protection

- Web access management

Enterprise Security:

- Intrusion detection

- LDAP (used in firewalls, segmentation, authentication, and email user-management authorization)

- Password management

- Network-operating system password management

- Virus protection

- DMZ

- Firewalls (external and office-to-office) network, proxy, and packet filter gateways

- Internet access (surf control)

While not all security holes can be plugged, companies should strive to define an acceptable level of risk at a reasonable cost. Identifying the threats or risks that your enterprise may face will help identify any vulnerabilities and will assist in selecting the appropriate security protection measures. Management today must learn the new industry terminology and be proactive and aware of security issues. Prior to setting security policy, the following are critical trends and areas where more education is needed.

The Human Factor

The people in your organization are the weakest link. Everyone in your organization, from the customer service representative at the call center to the sales executives equipped with wireless enabled laptops, can inadvertently—or intentionally—create a security breach. One aspect of human behavior is a given: If you try hard enough, you can find someone who will believe nearly anything. Hackers know this and often create plausible stories to entice information from your employees. Unwittingly, your employees open the door to these attacks often innocently, such as passing an email along to someone else. The malicious employee is the individual who intentionally inflicts damage to the network. This type of damage can consist of anything from releasing a virus, stealing information, and poisoning data, to bypassing security controls to play games on company time. All statistics show that millions of dollars are lost each year as a result of employee security breaches.

Of course, people outside your organization who inflict chaos are commonly known as hackers. The Internet provides them with potential access from anywhere in the world. Some of these people are looking for some sort of intellectual high, while others are fueled by more treacherous motives, such as revenge or stealing for profit. In any event, no intrusion is innocent, and no intrusion is benign.

The other people issue involves the difficulty in attracting and keeping skilled staff. Lack of skilled staff leads to another common threat to an organization's network from the inside, which can be as simple as mis-configuration of servers and firewalls from the manufacturer or from the system administrators themselves. From this, a common theme is emerging: education. The people involved with setting the policy and making the system secure need to make intelligent decisions. The threats to your CRM network can come in many forms, from disgruntled employees and corporate espionage to lax system administrators, faulty products, and poorly educated users.

Systems and Software

Other risks to the CRM enterprise reside on our own PCs. Malicious code (sometimes called malware) can take different forms: a computer virus, a Trojan horse (a program that purports to do one thing but creates a security vulnerability), or active content such as Java and ActiveX programs. Other harmful agents are the worms, such as Nimda and Code Red, that can distribute themselves without people actively distributing them. Ebusiness is especially vulnerable because the Internet is the lifeline of these viruses. The good news is that some good virus protection tools exist, but they must be coupled with prudent user behavior to be effective. Antivirus software has also been developed for PDAs, but there are also threats because of access to networks by Web cell phones (WAP and WML). The immediate need is to secure the network where these devices communicate. Companies must look at company firewalls and even personal firewalls for employees with home-based PCs who connect via a cable modem and DSL.

Software vendors make installing software easy. Even if you know nothing about software, you can use the system defaults. From a security standpoint, you only open a potential security door by allowing all options. Any capabilities and services that you don't plan to use should be turned off until they are needed to reduce the number of attack points. Firewalls are only as good as their configuration. Eliminating risk through this method is known as hardening and offers fewer entry points into your network. Because networks are in a constant state of change due to upgrades and add-ons, constant adjustments are being made to the software settings. This only adds to the frustration of assuming that the settings for a particular software installation are secure. It is almost impossible to prevent new security holes from appearing as software is changed.

Complex software combinations among the various ebusiness systems, CRM suites, and other ERP components makes it practically impossible to evaluate the overall systems software in sufficient detail to discover and resolve all potential security exposures. In some cases, users count on each software component being well-designed from a security standpoint and strive to minimize exposures resulting from combining and integrating the software. Many times, system administrators must take it on faith that the components will enforce acceptable security.

To set up a system to successfully manage security risks, a set of management requirements must be established. These imperatives may require management adjustment, but these imperatives are in lieu of an accepted industry-wide measurement system. How do companies judge the risks embedded in their current ebusiness systems? How do they determine if the investments related to reducing risks are warranted? The essential elements of risk and cost involve the following:

- What resources need to be protected?

- What is the cost of loss or compromise?

- What is the cost of protection?

- What is the likelihood of loss or compromise?

- What is the cost to an organization?

The 2007 Computer Crime and Security Survey reported that 46 percent of respondents experienced a security incident within their organizations in the past 12 months. There were 46 percent who reported an average loss of $345,005, up from $167,713 in 2006. The average annual loss was $239,000 per respondent for the past three years.

The IT manager has no proven mechanisms to compute the company's vulnerability, because the effectiveness of security countermeasures defies quantification. Unfortunately, in the real world, we deal with budgetary constraints, so choices have to be made. You need to consider the probability of a security breach versus the expense. IT managers can develop metrics that may not be foolproof but still allow for guidelines as the cost of security measures are evaluated. The following list is fictitious, but it could be a guideline for developing a way to answer the previous questions:

- The cost of installing a firewall is $25,000 ($1,000,000 worth of protection); the risk of compromise is 50 percent.

- The cost of adding audit analog lines is $2,000 ($50,000 worth of protection); the risk of compromise is 5 percent.

- The cost of developing a security policy is $40,000 ($1,000,000 worth of protection); the risk of compromise is 75 percent.

A company's senior management should—with the approval of the board of directors—decide which risks should receive what level of attention and investment. The decisions must be documented and must guide all implementation plans for ebusiness. Sometimes problems arise and are handled by whichever manager is involved at the time. The decisions that these managers make must be aligned with the set security policy.

According to industry estimates, budget allocations for security policies should be set to about 5 percent of the company's IT budget. Instead, security budgets are usually embedded in individual projects such as the ebusiness or CRM project, which effectively raises the cost of the ebusiness or CRM project. A dedicated budget based on the risk assessment should be allocated and reconciled with individual business unit budgets.

Developing the Security Policy

First, securing a network can ensure the following goals:

- Confidentiality

- Integrity

- Availability

Since no single technology or process can be implemented in the name of total security, the aim is to develop a defense through an in-depth strategy.

Start with important security principles and corporate security standards. Use the following guidelines in this development:

1. Appoint a high-level executive with company-wide responsibilities to enforce and develop security policies consistently across an organization.

2. Ensure that security policies are holistically defined and enforced across the ebusiness and CRM environment, from applications to networks to security for physical servers, laptops, and hand-held devices. Since the IT systems belong to the company, they are designed to further the interests of the organization. Enforcing the policy is essential. Organizations must hold specific individuals accountable for incidents as well as holding managers accountable for risk and budget decisions.

3. Make sure the lines of business are actively involved and support the CRM security strategy, ebusiness, and investments. Since line-of-business executives make the majority of the ebusiness and CRM funding decisions in many organizations, not having their buy-in can lead to productivity losses from corporate security investments as the business units continue to be inconsistent and unpredictable as they "reinvent" security within their applications. The key to success is not only the do's and don'ts but also providing a sense of why.

4. Think and plan ahead. Think at least six to 12 months ahead while giving the lines of business the tools needed to build a secure ebusiness environment without creating a security infrastructure that will become yet another legacy infrastructure within a few months. This includes deploying Web-only security solutions that will not be able to integrate with existing applications as real-time customer access demands naturally grow with Web site usage.

5. Understand the links among ebusiness, CRM security, and customer satisfaction. In our real-time business, customer intimacy, loyalty, and satisfaction are imperative. A complex security infrastructure, despite its security-oriented benefits, may impede customer satisfaction. Enforcing policies such as password guidelines that ensure single sign-on can tighten security and

increase customer satisfaction. We have found organizations can require partners and employees to use up to seven different passwords. This becomes a burden, and your user community will become lax when this much effort is required.

6. Create a single, well-known focal point for security incident reporting. Even with intrusion detection in place, break-ins will occur, but any hope of containment needs to be dealt with quickly. All users can assist with this effort, but a well-designed system will facilitate containment.

7. Enforce good administration practices. Control the administration consistently from a central policy but allow flexibility to delegate certain administrative security tasks to business units, partners, or others based upon the needs of the growing business.

8. Develop authentication rules. The most common method is using passwords for access, but you should look at others, such as smart cards, security tokens, and encryption. Make sure that the password rules are spelled out and enforced.

9. Implement active content screening tools (virus protection) and establish rules for downloading from Internet sites and email attachments. This could possibly be an education issue; you may also want to include what types of network traffic should and should not be allowed.

10. Use open standards. Using multivendor, open standards in vendor selection and product choice is a key requirement to current and future flexibility and interoperability.

11. Beware of any vendor who promises a complete security solution with only its product portfolio. Strong business partnerships are critical in end-to-end security control and management.

12. Implement an ebusiness privacy policy. Protecting personally identifiable data is important to maintaining brand equity as well as to conforming to existing and developing privacy legislation.

13. Don't stop updating policies and checking security. Review your organization's information protection or information security programs. Get assistance, call on experts, and use available tools.

For example, Microsoft offers its free Microsoft Security Assessment Tool that is designed to help organizations assess security weaknesses in the current IT security environment and provide specific guidance to minimize these weaknesses.

14. Ensure that data is backed up frequently. A good policy might include details about which systems need to be backed up, how often, who will perform the back-up, etc. This can also be incorporated into a disaster recovery policy. You want to make sure you can recover quickly from any loss. Create a contingency plan that covers all possible scenarios that could result in a loss of data and property.

15. And finally, educate, educate, educate. Annual or semiannual security training for end users and administrators is a must. To maintain a strong security posture, members of an organization should know what to look for concerning security risks. Knowing how to report problems or incidents is also essential in maintaining that posture. Make sure administrators are educated on current technology and can adequately secure your CRM network.

Dealing with computer security and information privacy assurance is critical to the future of ebusiness. While the technology community is offering new solutions to security problems, IT managers must put this technology through a systematic risk-management process. While most companies do not handle security management efficiently yet, a focused effort can lead to notable improvements within a year. This focus includes analyzing risks, setting a specific security budget, and creating a security policy. Remember that CRM and ebusiness security is vital for the success of the real-time CRM system.

Chapter 29

Eight Key Implementation Issues

The CRM industry needs to improve the level of implementation professionalism. In my opinion, few, if any, implementation shortcuts are available.

With this in mind, let's look at the eight key CRM system implementation issues. The following eight issues refer to post-CRM software selection implementation, which assumes a company has specified a software vendor of choice or agreed on internal specifications for the CRM system.

1. Prepare for Your CRM Implementation

Preparation means that you and/or your systems implementers need to create the following:

- A financial plan that demonstrates a commitment to the required financial resources for personnel, equipment, and integration activities.

- A clear project methodology to ensure that the project stays on track and within budget. There is no one best project methodology, but use of one is non-negotiable.

- An implementation plan for your project that lays out each to-do step, assigns responsibility as well as a date for each item, and provides milestone checks for those items.

- A communications plan that describes the types of internal marketing communications that you intend to produce during the implementation of the CRM project. For example, this includes weekly communications via emails to all potential users, a CRM notice board on your intranet, printed material from your executive sponsor, and discussions at quarterly sales meetings; while the exact content of the communications differs for every project, typical communications include weekly project implementation accomplishments, training/support schedules, user issues, and success stories, pilot outcomes, and the like.

- A training plan that describes in detail who will be trained, when the training will occur, where the training will be held, how many participants will be in each training session, number of trainers, and the training materials to be used.

- A support plan that describes first-, second-, and third-tier support, and that outlines help desk/support intentions (support hours).

2. Set Up an Effective CRM Project Management Team

Successful CRM implementation requires an effective project management team that consists of the following personnel: the CRM project leader, the executive sponsor, one or more representatives from sales, a representative from marketing, a representative from customer service, the CRM software vendor, a representative from the system implementer, and an external CRM advisor.

Typically, the project management team meets once a week for about four hours to review the project implementation plan. The previous week's implementation deliverables need to be reviewed and categorized into the following color-coded achievements: green (fully accomplished), yellow (minor action items that remain on the to-do list), and red (not accomplished). In addition to reviewing the previous week's to-do items, the project management team also needs to discuss the coming week's to-do items and identify any issues that are likely to impact the full accomplishment of each item.

The project management team may occasionally also want to call upon heads of the subproject management teams to provide the project management team with a status report on the subproject team's deliverables.

Subproject management teams often include the following entities: a business process sub-project management team (responsible for modifying and/or creating new business processes that will be supported by the

CRM system); a help desk subproject management team (responsible for creating the help desk/support plan, which includes help desk scripts, help desk hours of operation, etc.); a training subproject management team (responsible for creating the pilot training plan, the roll-out training plan, and post-roll-out training); and a quality control subproject management team (responsible for ensuring that project implementation is realized at the highest standards of quality standards).

3. Integrate Legacy and Third-Party Information Systems

If not carefully planned, integration is an issue that can delay the on-time implementation of a CRM system. Integration deals with which type and what quantity of data your company intends to bring into your CRM system; this may include information from legacy systems as well as from third-party sources. You will need to determine what data conversions need to be performed to get the data into your CRM system in a usable format and what data needs to be populated into your CRM system. Since not all data formats are compatible, integration can be a tricky issue. All too often, companies try to integrate too much information from too many systems into the CRM system. My integration advice is simple: Don't bite off more than you can chew. It is better to integrate less and complete your CRM project on time than to integrate more and have the project delayed.

4. Customize Your CRM System

Customization is a necessary part of all CRM systems. For example, the graphical user interfaces (GUIs) can be customized to reflect the specific needs of each user or each user group. For example, while the sales reps want the opening screen to show all opportunities, the customer service rep may want the opening screen to show all outstanding customer service incidents. In addition to user GUIs, business functionality within the system can be customized. For example, if your company publishes textbooks for university students, you will likely need to customize your CRM system to accommodate the need to send review copies or "comps" to professors, since a comp function is not standard in most off-the-shelf CRM systems.

If not carefully monitored, customization can become another activity that delays CRM implementation. All too often, users want to customize too much too quickly. To prevent this from happening, have a customization plan that clearly describes the phases in your customization efforts before you start your customization. And remember the 80/20 rule: If you can get 80 percent of your customizations completed on time and within budget, forget about the remaining 20 percent.

5. Pilot Your CRM System

The objective of piloting your CRM system is to test the system before you start. A good CRM implementation should include one or more pilots when important feedback is gathered from system users about the likes/dislikes of the emerging system. To prepare for the pilot(s), you should develop a plan that describes what the pilot is trying to accomplish (proof of concept and increased productivity) and describes the metrics that the pilot will be measured against. One or two pilots should be run simultaneously because one pilot may not include a mix of users that represent the larger group that will be using your CRM system. Each pilot should consist of 10 to 12 users (e.g., eight sales reps or eight customer service reps and two to four managers). The pilot should last between three to six weeks. You should have a clear understanding of what constitutes a successful pilot; you may need to pause your CRM roll out if the pilot falters.

Training the pilot users properly is critical. Remember that pilot users are your live systems testers. They will know little, if anything, about the system, and it is unlikely that you will have well thought-out user training materials or documentation for pilot users. As a result, it becomes your responsibility to ensure that pilot users have been properly trained. Poor training may lead to poor pilot results; if training is managed properly, this can easily be prevented.

Pilot measurements also are important. How will you judge the success or failure of a pilot? For the IT division, success may simply mean getting the new CRM system to exchange data with existing legacy systems. Yet for the sales division, success may mean proving that it takes less time to create and send a customer proposal, and so, productivity has increased.

Unless all parties agree on metrics prior to the pilot, the pilot's success or failure becomes a subjective measurement, which can be dangerous. My firm recommends three measurements for a pilot: ease-of-use of the system as measured by the users, proof-of-concept as measured by the IT department, and business impact as measured by business management. Establish a baseline for each of these three measurements prior to the pilot as well as a measurement scale, and then measure results during and directly after completion of the pilot.

6. Roll Out Your CRM System

The roll out of your CRM system will mean collecting many small, yet significant pieces that the subproject management teams have been working on through completion of the pilot. So, there should be a roll-out plan that describes each of the pieces associated with the roll out in great detail, including who will be trained, where the training will occur, and for how long. Training is not restricted to roll-out training, and it should include pre-rollout training, such as for computer literacy. (You do not want non-computer literate users to participate in your CRM roll-out training classes.) Your roll-out plan will also describe the exact content and timetable for each roll-out training session, as well as the test that all users must pass prior to graduating from roll-out training class.

When planning a roll out, you should employ pragmatic timing: People take vacations, children get sick, emergencies occur, etc. So, your roll-out plan needs to have contingency options in case there are glitches (and there always are). Your roll-out plan should also describe how you intend to update the system for field or remote users and demonstrate exactly how system updates will work once users return to their respective day-to-day jobs. Do not underestimate the complexity of a CRM system roll out, especially if the implementation is global, which can be considerably more complex.

7. Support Your CRM System

Supporting your CRM system is the next area of concern. Do not underestimate the impact of excellent support; this can greatly impact the success of your CRM system. You should have a support plan that describes the levels of support your company offers to system users, the hours of operations of the support function, and the procedures to escalate a support issue that may not be easily resolved. For example, your support plan needs to define who is your company's first-tier support (an internal help desk, an 800 number, or your boss), who is your company's second-tier support (your systems administrator or IT department), and who is your company's third-tier support (the CRM software vendor). Your support plan needs to clearly describe the international hours of operation for your support or help desk. Is it 24/7, or is only from 8 A.M. to 5 P.M. weekdays? Your plan also needs to describe the role of your systems administrator.

More often, companies that are implementing CRM are turning to third-party CRM support companies to provide support for the system. Companies such as C3i in New Jersey specialize in this area and offer a full line of training and support services, including a "hot spare" (a failover mechanism to provide reliability in system configurations) program that guarantees delivery of a ready-to-use replacement PC in the event that your PC crashes or is stolen. Whether you create your own support function, default to support by your CRM software vendor, or use a third-party support company, take the time to create a clear, comprehensive support plan. There is nothing worse than being in the field, logging onto the CRM application, and not getting information because of a support issue.

8. Grow Your CRM System

One of the most important CRM implementation issues is the ability to grow your system. This means growing system functionality beyond the initial roll out and the initial business functionality. A key factor will be your ability to maintain enthusiasm for the system among its users and to help users manage the changes that inevitably take place when applying technology to day-to-day business circumstances. From a management perspective, you will need to measure and demonstrate the system ROI and business impact if you are to receive continued system funding. Our experience with several hundred CRM-related system implementations worldwide over the past two decades suggests that successful companies grow their CRM system using a phased, pragmatic approach.

Remember that there are eight key implementation issues associated with the successful implementation of your CRM system:

1. Prepare for your CRM implementation.

2. Set up an effective CRM project management team.

3. Integrate legacy and third-party information systems.

4. Customize your CRM system.

5. Pilot your CRM system.

6. Roll out your CRM system.

7. Support your CRM system.

8. Grow your CRM system.

It's important to pay careful attention to each of these key implementation issues, getting each issue right. In the past, systems implementation was considered a weak link in the CRM industry, which needs to be strengthened considerably for continued strong growth. Needless to say, this presents an excellent opportunity for CRM systems implementation service providers. The complexity and weaknesses in implementation also explains why many CRM software vendors have now decided to implement CRM systems themselves.

Chapter 30

CRM on a Global Basis

Are there substantial differences when a CRM system is implemented internationally versus in the U.S.? What are the differences, and do they need to be taken into account before implementation, or can they be addressed after?

In this chapter, we respond to these and other important questions/issues associated with implementing CRM on a global basis. We will look at key similarities between an international versus a U.S.-only implementation, key differences, and lessons that should be explored when implementing an international CRM project.

CRM is now a global business. While the CRM industry started in North America (particularly in the U.S.), the European and the Asian CRM marketplaces now are in growth mode. The Gartner Group predicted that worldwide CRM software revenue will exceed $7.4 billion in 2007, an increase of 14 percent from $6.5 billion in 2006. The worldwide CRM software market is expected to grow an average 12 percent per year to a figure of $11.4 billion by 2011. This growth stems in part from North American companies opening offices overseas, as well as from emerging European and Asian CRM software vendors and third-party players that specialize in CRM consulting, integration, and training/support. Several leading non-U.S. providers of CRM software have also customized their software for the North American market with some success.

In today's increasingly global marketplace, more companies are specifying an international CRM system from the outset. While the international implementation of CRM was usually launched after the U.S. system was up and running, both versions of the system now often get specified, customized, and implemented simultaneously.

With these two observations in mind, let's turn our attention to key similarities and differences between an international and a U.S. implementation.

Key Similarities

1. Use of a Structured Methodology to Prioritize Business Needs

My firm has worked with several international CRM projects in the past. This experience has taught us that whether the CRM project is in North America, Latin America, Europe, Asia, or elsewhere, the company that uses a structured methodology ensures that global business needs rise to the top of the business prioritization list, where appropriate.

For example, one European company sold mining and construction equipment to North and South America (about 50 percent of its global sales), Europe (about 30 percent), and Asia (the remaining 20 percent). The initiative to implement a CRM system, which came from the top executive of North and South American sales, began with a brainstorming session and field visits with top U.S. and Canadian managers.

The initiative quickly met resistance from European managers who had been planning to implement their own CRM initiative but with a different methodology. After extensive transatlantic discussions, the board decided to make the CRM initiative a global project. Shortly after, my firm met with company managers in Asia, Europe, and South America, and we applied the same methodology to all parts of the company. This was important since the company had recently launched a global account management project, and the proposed CRM initiative played a critical role in ensuring that the global account management project was implemented in a similar manner in all parts of the world.

2. Effective Data Synchronization

Whether the CRM project is U.S. or global, the data synchronization portion of the initiative needs to work effectively. Data synchronization is the exchange of customer files and other information from field personnel with headquarters personnel or systems, and vice versa. The importance of data synchronization cannot be underestimated, particularly if the CRM system is designed to support file-sharing across borders for a global account management system. Remember that all countries do not have similar technical capabilities (data communications), which may be required to ensure that proper data synchronization occurs in more than one country. Plan this aspect of any global CRM system carefully. Web-based CRM systems can usually eliminate this need for synchronization because the CRM data is centralized and available only when a user is connected to the CRM system via the Web. For a more in-depth look at data synchronization issues, refer to Chapter 16, The Importance of Data Integrity.

3. Proper Training and Support

Regardless of the scope of the CRM initiative, the training and support processes remain an essential ingredient in U.S. as well as international projects. For example, a U.S. food manufacturer, which then did about 30 percent of its global sales within Europe, launched its global CRM initiative. The company immediately created a training and support plan for users in the U.S. and in Europe.

During the initial training sessions, it was clear that although the company sold the same products on both sides of the Atlantic and that the American and European personnel had similar training and support needs for the new CRM system, substantial differences existed in computer literacy levels within the company. As a result, two needs were established: first, the need for a consistent global training program for the new CRM system; and second, sufficient customization within the training program to support the different levels of computer literacy. Of course, adequate CRM application and hardware support is also essential. So, it is important to check the support options in the country where the CRM systems will be implemented; vendors may offer different levels of support and options depending upon geographic region. For a more in-depth look at CRM training issues, check out Chapter 11, The Necessity of Training.

Key Differences

1. Differing Business Needs

Not all companies, particularly those with global operations, can implement a similar business strategy. This implies that divisions or regions of the same company may have different business needs for CRM support. For example, a U.S. high-tech manufacturing company had a distribution channel strategy in Europe that differed considerably from the one in the U.S. While the business strategy in the U.S. is based on the growing independent reseller distribution channel, the one in Europe is based more on the Value Added Reseller (VAR) distribution channel. (The Asian business strategy is generally based on joint ventures with companies in the host country.)

This difference in distribution channel strategies has a considerable impact on what information needs to be gathered and distributed within this company's proposed CRM system. For example, needed sales and marketing information can be gathered from VARs since they purchase directly from the European office. But it is more difficult to obtain sales and marketing information from independent resellers who often buy from VARs or from large original equipment manufacturers (OEMs), many of which really don't want you to know too much about what they are doing.

These business issues should be discussed before you launch an international CRM system, and the differing needs should be identified at the start. Although a common business strategy or a common set of business needs may not be possible or even desired, these differences still need to be understood and taken into account when designing and implementing your CRM system.

2. Differing Technical Infrastructures

Another area that often appears in a global CRM system concerns differing technical infrastructures. For example, my firm assisted one of the world's leading global oil companies in its efforts to install its second generation of CRM software. While the company's U.S. technical infrastructure had been based primarily on a distributed client-server basis supported by an emerging data warehouse, the European technical infrastructure had been based on a mainframe computer in one European country and connected to 16 other European countries via data communications leased lines.

The hardware in place for this company's field personnel also varied considerably depending on the location. Given that data synchronization across borders in Europe can often be difficult, the company decided to try a solution using Lotus Notes servers in each European country. This strategy differed considerably from the approach that was suggested for the U.S., which had little difficulty with data communications or data synchronization. For mobile CRM (mCRM), U.S. wireless standards differ from other parts of the world, and the infrastructure and usage of mobile technologies in Europe is more advanced in some ways than in the U.S. The message is clear: Assess the technical infrastructure carefully in regions where you may roll out a CRM system.

Given that differing technical infrastructures can be costly in the long term to maintain and support, one of our clients formed a global technical infrastructure team that was asked to develop a global technical infrastructure recommendation based on common ground: database standards, middleware tool sets, software applications, programming languages, common hardware, and communication standards.

3. Issues of Internationalization/Localization

Since countries use different languages, have different currencies, work with different financial statements, and have different laws about gathering information on customers and individuals, international CRM systems need to take these differences into account. The need for customized offerings has become more critical with the emergence of the Euro, triangulation, the growth of wireless communications, and other internationalization/localization realities. For example, my firm worked with a leading air courier express company that had offices in more than 100 countries around the world and many internationalization/localization issues.

Although the manager of its international CRM system would like to have a common core module in all offices around the world (facilitating global account management or financial reporting), this manager also recognized that different countries require program customization recognizing each unique environment without harming the common core module. Customization often poses a challenge to an international CRM system, and while it may seem outdated or unreal, many of today's CRM software packages won't do an adequate job handling multiple languages, currencies, or date formats.

Recommendations

What should be kept in mind when implementing an international CRM project? Three specific recommendations follow:

- **Recommendation 1** – If possible, international implementation issues should be considered before the initial implementation of your CRM system. If this means delaying the project by a few weeks or months, this time will be well spent. Planning upfront will save considerable time later.

- **Recommendation 2** – While similarities exist, so do substantial differences between the implementation of an international and a U.S. CRM system. Although striving for as much similarity as possible is a priority, differences do and will exist; some sort of vehicle must be used to address and ideally resolve these differences early in the project.

- **Recommendation 3** – Plan your international CRM efforts carefully, and be sure to create and work with one or more international superuser groups throughout the life of the project. In addition to providing input for addressing and ideally resolving differences early, the superuser group plays a critical role in coordinating the involvement of different players in an international CRM system. In particular, these include top management (the funders), the information technology team (the builders or technical supporters), and field/headquarters personnel (the users).

Most of those companies that have taken time to acknowledge and incorporate these three recommendations into their international CRM system have done well. As is always the case, doing your homework first increases the likelihood of success.

Chapter 31

CRM in Government

After years of dismissing CRM for the public sector, government organizations are now often finding that aligning business processes more closely to their technology investments can lead to increased productivity and customer satisfaction.

In fact, analysts report that the government sector is one of the hottest growth markets for CRM. Government spending on CRM software is expected to grow 30 percent in 2007, reaching $2 billion in sales.

Of course, while the government doesn't sell many products or services, and most agencies aren't using CRM to increase revenue, there are several reasons why CRM can be applied effectively in the public sector: cost reduction, product and service improvement, better customer knowledge, and higher employee morale. To achieve these benefits, agencies often use conventional software, call centers, and online services offered by retailers. Even though government agencies aren't driven by profit, they do want to do a better job serving the public and becoming more efficient. So, CRM is closely related to "egovernment," using technology such as online services to make it easier to pay taxes, for example.

Meanwhile, with the advent of government-wide initiatives such as the President's Management Agenda (PMA) mandates on egovernment and the Federal Enterprise Architecture (FEA), federal IT managers have been challenged to re-architect IT infrastructures within their agencies.

To increase efficiency, reduce complexity, and cut the cost of designing, implementing, and managing information technology (IT), Congress and the White House initiated a reform movement in 2001 now recognized as the FEA, which is largely derived from the enterprise architecture methodology developed by John Zachman and other well-known theorists. The goal was to create an IT architecture that would help map an organization's business processes with its IT systems, enabling private and public sector institutions to free up funds for more value-added, mission-critical activities. The FEA initiative has grown into a fully sanctioned federal regulation. Even with budget-withholding "sticks" (measures to withhold money unless FEA regulations are met in government agencies) to enforce compliance, the process of adjusting agency missions to match changing goals takes time.

Gone are the days when agencies invested in custom IT initiatives are championed by department heads or individual project leaders. Instead, government oversight organizations such as the Office of Management and Budget (OMB) and the Government Accounting Office (GAO) are driving compliance, withholding key budget dollars for agencies that haven't moved quickly enough to align agency IT investments with transformational mandates.

While the actual results of this transformation are just starting to trickle in, the federal government is now working to successfully re-engineer its processes. Via the PMA on egovernment and the FEA, the message is clear: Federal IT managers must modernize and transform their operations to be more effective, efficient, and responsive to citizens (G2C), government suppliers (G2B), and other government agencies (G2G).

In most cases, the goal of federal mandates involves consolidating information systems, especially those that support common operations across agencies. This way, federal agencies can better pool resources and save money, while improving the quality of those services.

The current federal mandates address critical frustrations in which current processes, legacy systems, and stovepipe IT systems (a legacy system that is an assemblage of inter-related elements so tightly bound together that the individual elements cannot be differentiated, upgraded, or refactored) will need to be replaced by performance-based business models and modernized IT solutions that can help accelerate the pace of the government's migration to real-time operations.

While the OMB, GAO, and other agencies may have set the standard for transformation and modernization, the process of motivating federal agencies to enforce compliance is a separate, more challenging undertaking.

Today's agency IT leaders face tremendous pressures driven by the need to do more with less and to meet federal mandates or risk losing funding for critical IT investments. Worldwide government agencies are challenged with the multiple concerns of efficiency, cost effectiveness, and providing quality service. Recently, budgets have been affected by requirements for security and other areas that were not originally foreseen when the mandates for CRM automation began. As public sector officials look across their increasing domain of responsibility, the entire organization can be viewed as an opportunity to achieve real improvements in efficiency and economy, enabling savings to be redirected to the improvement of service delivery to constituents.

Collectively, the federal government transformation mandates are forcing agency IT managers to inventory IT assets currently in use and create enterprise architecture plans that will help them simplify, unify, and secure IT infrastructures. According to various 2005 reports in *Federal Computer Week*, the OMB estimated that the government could save $3 billion in the next few years by consolidating common applications and technologies. This estimate may be conservative.

Now, with the reality of FEA regulatory requirements, the PMA and egovernment initiatives (all designed to promote the use of Web technology to transform operations, to cut costs, and to improve both efficiency and service), the government's goal is to gain clarity and transparency into IT operations.

Providing business case evidence to justify each IT investment is considered a first step toward unifying government operations and improving services for constituents. And that's where government CRM initiatives can make a difference.

Key Government CRM Drivers

The forces driving agencies to use CRM include the desire to provide better constituent services, more closely align business and technology goals, avoid fraud, and meet growing demand for better (Web-based) self-services.

Unlike for-profit organizations where timely and efficient customer service translates to bottom-line results, government agencies—sometimes unfairly—are considered slow to respond to the needs of their constituents. While many government organizations strive to provide high-quality services, many are hampered by budget constraints, outdated or unwieldy processes and IT systems, and the sheer volume of constituents they must support.

Perhaps the biggest growth area in CRM over the next three years will be in the public sector, especially within state and local governments. In fact, my firm expects the government sector to spend at least $2 billion on

CRM software over the next three years and at least $3 billion on CRM services over the same period.

Government is the No. 1 growth sector in the CRM industry today. Currently, the three most common areas for governments' CRM investments are 311 initiatives (phone calls for non-emergency issues), case management, and billing capabilities. Whatever the investment, one thing is certain: The results are promising for government agencies that embrace CRM.

Industry Input

According to Input Inc., a global database and analytical research provider specializing on the government market, the U.S. federal government will spend about $79 billion on IT-related contracts in fiscal year 2007. A five-year forecast on federal government IT spending conducted by Input Inc. in 2007 projects that spending will grow from $79 billion in fiscal year 2007 to $102 billion in fiscal year 2012 to produce an average annual growth rate of 5 percent each year. Concerning the federal IT spending in 2007, nearly half of the government's IT budget will be spent on homeland security-related matters. Overall, 21 out of 27 civilian agencies received an IT budget increase, with the Department of Housing and Urban Development, the Labor Department, and the Interior Department receiving the largest wedge of the IT budget. Another report released by Input Inc. in 2007 indicates that state and local governments are next in line to see a boost in IT spending. U.S. state and local government spending on IT products and services will grow at a compound annual rate of 6.6 percent, from $55 billion in 2007 to $77 billion in 2012.

This same Input Inc. report also finds that economic growth at the state level has been widespread; a majority of city and county officials are optimistic about their jurisdictions' financial and economic situations. This economic environment combined with population growth and a trend toward states and localities setting their own economic, environmental, and social goals, makes the state and local market an increasingly attractive market for IT vendors.

One industry trend is expected to drive significant growth during this period: the national effort to transform healthcare through the implementation of health IT. Interoperable communications, intelligence fusion, and information sharing will be the focus of ongoing homeland security and justice and public safety spending. Consolidation of data centers and outsourcing of IT infrastructure will be common as federal government agencies, states, and localities modernize the core technologies behind general government services.

The Government Value Proposition

Federal agencies need to understand CRM's value proposition, including the following aspects:

- **Enhance customer-facing processes** – CRM enables agencies to create "clean" processes—replacing old, outdated functions—with new optimized systems to improve service delivery (streamlining delivery of passports, for example) to constituents. These preselected optimized business functions also provide the ability to measure and further refine each step to fine-tune key services, as needed.

- **Improve productivity/reinvest savings** – With the right information coordinated in a single database instead of spread among 20 different applications, government workers can spend less time searching for things, which, in turn, creates more time for relevant work. Easier access to key information can create a time savings of 10 to 20 percent in each work day, which could be applied to providing better services or speeding responses.

- **Facilitate results-based management** – The ability to justify IT investments and measure return on investment (ROI) is critical for government audiences today. A CRM initiative forces agencies to think of creating efficiencies and speeding ROI.

- **Provide better comprehensive customer knowledge** – Constituents of all kinds can be better served by government agencies when they set up initiatives to gain a 360-degree view of each constituent type. When more pertinent information is collected, it's easier to speak in the same voice to each constituent, whether inside another agency or outside the beltway. Extensive constituent profiling also enables agencies to create the kind of self-service applications that can dramatically reduce costs and speed services delivery.

- **Enhance relevancy by tailoring information** – If you can successfully profile each constituent audience, you can more easily tailor messages to better serve their needs. The goal is to provide more—and better—services in a more timely fashion.

- **Better serve customers and partners** – Raising the customer support bar, whether via self-service initiatives, such as the IRS has created for tax preparers, or 311 initiatives for state and local government audiences, helps deliver more—and better—services for those key audiences.

- **Increase satisfaction and loyalty** – Better services, created by tailoring processes to specific target audiences, will delight those constituents, build loyalty, and ease the ability to gain funding for more similar projects in the future. The upside—and downside—is that satisfied customers will demand more.

- **Achieve superior employee morale** – The average government employee does work that involves many mundane, remedial tasks each day; when an agency tailors its services to proactively serve customers, employees tend to be much happier at their jobs.

The bottom line: CRM brings value by helping agencies provide more relevant products/services, enabling higher customer satisfaction, and easing the ability to fund new agency initiatives.

The primary benefits that government agencies can expect to derive from the successful implementation of CRM include the following:

- Better processes that support specific constituent audiences

- Higher work force productivity

- Happier constituents

- Enhanced government decision making

- Promotion of service-centric push

- An eased ability to secure funding

For example, several intelligence community (IC) agencies have found the CRM initiatives in place so far have provided a way to create comprehensive customer profiles that can be shared within the agency and across IC agencies, as well as to enhance intra-agency customer-centric business processes. Initiating better processes have led to higher productivity and better morale among employees. In addition, IC customers (e.g., the White House, State Department, Justice Department, U.S. Military, other domestic and international IC agencies, etc.) report being happier. CRM has also helped IC agencies make better decisions and provide input into national intelligence community decisions; more information is available in the NSA case study presented later in this chapter.

Challenges to Government CRM

Although the benefits of implementing CRM may outweigh the risks, federal agencies still face a serious set of challenges to rival the success of any CRM initiative.

First—and perhaps foremost—is the problem that arises from "the full-plate syndrome." As most federal workers can attest, doing more with less is the norm in most every government organization. Because their days are filled with so many activities, the ability to accept change or do things differently can be a truly daunting challenge. The old mantra of "If it ain't broke, don't fix it" is a well-understood concept: Why stop and learn a new way of doing things when the old way did indeed get the job done? The only way to help ease the government's painful full-plate syndrome is to take something off that plate, or at least, reprioritize what's on it. Intensifying an agency's focus on better serving constituent needs may help alleviate the pain of changing processes a bit.

Another key challenge relating to people is gaining top management support. This can best be achieved by closely tying mission goals to proposed CRM enhancements. Internal culture issues may negatively impact the adoption of a customer-centered CRM initiative. That is why it's important to find and deal with those managers who currently rule or desire to protect specific "fiefdoms."

Another potential challenge comes as constituents get a taste for improved services. Most constituents expect better service now. It's a product of the Web culture, and an increasing inability to tolerate slow, unhelpful, and overly bureaucratic processes.

Another well-documented challenge for most federal agencies is the existence of roadblocks to sharing information and knowledge. There is still a great need for federal initiatives to "fix" this problem, which remains a widespread challenge to the success of an agency's CRM initiative.

On the process front, the single biggest challenge facing federal audiences today is the need to create constituent-centered processes (both internal and external). By definition, this means building interdependent and aligned activities and processes that directly interface with the customer during request, fulfillment, delivery, and use of an agency's products and services.

And finally, don't underestimate the need to find the best, most secure technological solutions that still remain accessible and acceptable to users.

At most government agencies, customers demand better and more information. Meanwhile, tight budgets and closely watched CRM business cases are the norm. Many government agencies also struggle with an internal culture, and the need to be open to change. For example, while information sharing remains important within the intelligence community, sometimes the sensitivity of information leads to less than optimal information sharing.

Increasingly, government agencies are challenged to provide quality service that's efficient and cost-effective. Recently, budgets have been affected by requirements for security and other areas not foreseen when federal mandates for CRM initiatives began. As public sector officials scan their increasing domain of responsibility, it's important to consider the entire organization as an opportunity to achieve real improvements in efficiency and economy, enabling those savings to be re-invested to improve service delivery for all constituents.

Government Case Studies

National Security Agency (NSA)

The NSA, a division of the Department of Defense, is serious about emerging from isolation and adapting best business practices to continuously improve its ability to protect and defend the U.S. 24/7/365.

Without a bottom line that reflects profit margins, the NSA still understands that its mission includes a key CRM objective, providing the best possible service to the nation, measured in the timeliness with which it delivers the right information to the right person at the right time.

In a nutshell, the NSA coordinates, directs, and performs highly specialized activities to protect U.S. information and produces foreign intelligence information. The NSA's mission is to understand the secret communications of foreign adversaries and protect the U.S.'s own communications. While the NSA sits on the frontier of communications and data processing, it is also an important center of foreign language analysis and research within the government.

The NSA also employs the country's premier code makers and code breakers. Considered the largest employer of mathematicians in the U.S. (and perhaps the world), the NSA performs two key tasks: Signal Intelligence Directorate (SID), which searches for weaknesses in adversarial codes and systems, and Information Assurance Directorate (IAD), which designs cipher systems that will protect the integrity of U.S. information systems.

For this example, the NSA focused on the SID, which groups its customers by need, including the following:

- National policymakers

- Law enforcement

- Intelligence community partners

- Military commands

Customer requests are received through formal processes, based on intelligence community-approved priorities, ad hoc requirements, and the National SIGINT Operations Center, which receives crisis requests 24/7.

Since September 11, 2001, ad hoc requests have poured into SID through multiple channels, overshadowing all others and making it difficult to track and fulfill customer requests in real time. Meanwhile, the NSA's customers expect timely responses with intelligence that can be ordered and fulfilled at the click of a mouse.

To improve the NSA's responsiveness, the organization implemented the following three programs to improve customer relations:

- **Account management** – This program focuses on customer needs and how to channel customer input into SID decision making, using a team of account managers and senior executive account managers who work with each set of customers to understand how they work and find better ways to support their intelligence needs. SID is working on improving ways to integrate feedback gathered from all channels, and then, mining that data for insight into how NSA can enhance customer relations.

- **Customer support plans** – Completed annually, these plans create a service-level agreement for national customers to provide a snapshot of current products and services as well as the goals each customer has for the services needed. These plans are monitored quarterly, and they are currently being expanded across the entire SID to enable the directorate to have a common view of the customer and speak to the customer in a consistent manner.

- **Customer contact center** – These centers are being created to relieve account managers from handling tactical problems that contact center personnel can solve, leaving account managers to concentrate on more strategic relationship goals. The vision is to enable a contact center to serve as the front door to SID, enabling customers to have all questions answered, and shop the variety of services SID offers. So far, it's been difficult to automate workflows involved in submitting and fulfilling customer requests in real time. Instilling a "customer service culture" in the NSA is another big challenge, as well as training personnel in contact management, CRM, and marketing/communications. Technologically, out-of-the-box contact center solutions tend to fall short in providing the tools that connect numerous and complex information sources.

In a public forum, the NSA's deputy chief of customer gateway at SID likened the challenges, "to retooling a fighter jet, while in flight. And not only are we in flight, but we are also in the midst of a dogfight."

Yet the deputy chief maintained that CRM is a catalyst for government transformation. To properly represent NSA to customers, the deputy chief believes every person's skills must include customer service. Creating that culture of customer service is a key goal for the NSA. The agency is also working to improve marketing, communications, and the education of the work force, customers, and partners to better ensure the success of its customer service focus.

IRS Offers Eservices Online

The IRS continues to roll out a series of online eservices, primarily aimed at authorized tax practitioners and financial institutions, to stimulate electronic filing, speed tax problem resolution, provide better constituent services, increase online self-services, and help lower costs.

Since August 2003, many taxpayers have registered to use the new online eservices, created using a CRM application suite, such as the efiling system for tax return. Of 136 million individual income tax returns filed in 2007, more than half were completed electronically. The new online eservices have been more successful than anticipated as stated in an October 10, 2005 *Government Computer News* article written by Jason Miller, which reports that the IRS efile system has lowered the cost of processing corporate tax returns by 79 percent, from $2.45 per tax return to 52 cents each. It has also lowered the processing tax return error rate to 1 percent from a previous figure as high as 36 percent. Overall, the new eservice offerings have saved the IRS more that $7.9 million by reducing the cost of paper processing and decreasing the time it takes to process requests and provide responses to inquiries from taxpayers.

One of the new IRS eservices is an online tax ID-matching capability offered to financial institutions that has already matched more than 11 million tax IDs with the IRS files to verify amounts recorded on 1099 forms. Richard Skorny, deputy associate chief information officer for program management at the IRS, maintained that the IRS simply couldn't offer this type of service to financial institutions previously, because the matching process was too cumbersome and time consuming. "Now, we can match individual requests, or up to 100,000 files at once," he said.

Another eservice is a transcript delivery system that enables authorized tax practitioners to access the prior year IRS transcripts of taxpayer returns. Instead of calling or requesting transcripts in writing, which took days to months for a response, tax return transcripts are now accessible online in minutes.

To use this service, tax practitioners must first provide power of attorney authorization, which is also part of the online eservices. Once he or she is authorized, a tax practitioner can also gain access to 1099 and W-2 forms filed with the IRS and help clients resolve IRS tax problems usually within three business days. "We believe these online services will change the way tax practitioners do business with the IRS," said Skorny.

The new suite of eservices allowing tax practitioners to represent their clients electronically is called the IRS Electronic Account Resolution (EAR) service, which lets tax practitioners resolve client IRS account problems securely via the Internet. The IRS's goal is to provide a response to tax practitioners within days instead of weeks.

In 1999, the IRS started looking for a solution to help improve the agency's ability to respond to about 88 million taxpayers who call for assistance annually. The Web-based services have supplemented a traditional call center that lets the IRS handle more critical calls.

The IRS' eservices CRM initiative took five years to roll out because it involved re-engineering numerous processes inside the IRS. For example, because signatures are so important to the IRS, "[W]e had to put extra effort into validating electronic signatures when moving tax services to the Web," said Skorny.

Testing the new processes involved customers, the practitioners, the IRS staff, and financial institutions. The entire initiative was also complicated by the need to adhere to emerging FEA mandates. Security and responsiveness were also key issues.

With its Web-based self-services and automated transactions, the IRS hopes to better focus its resources in frontline tax administration. "The overall goal is to provide better services, at a more reasonable price," said Skorny.

City of Des Moines

The City of Des Moines, Iowa, successfully built a Citizen Response System (CRS) to manage and automate inquiries from 200,000 city residents. As many as 9,000 incoming calls are handled each month by the CRS, and then they are quickly and efficiently dispatched to 20 different city departments for action.

In an effort to become one of the best-run cities in the U.S., administrators for the City of Des Moines wanted to automate the way it received, managed, responded to, and ultimately resolved requests from its 200,000 residents. The variety of requests from residents represented a fairly broad range of issues, incorporating trash pickup, potholes, fallen branches, snow removal, and animal issues such as barking dogs and cats stuck in trees. The city had previously implemented Front Range Solution's HEAT Service and Support software to assist its internal IT help desk in managing calls and providing problem resolution for users of its computer and network systems.

After examining a range of possible software solutions, the city process improvement team decided to leverage its internal support experience and decided to implement HEAT as the logical extension of its current program, now aimed at external customers (residents of Des Moines).

According to reports on this CRM example, one of the major challenges was the complexity of dealing with multiple city departments, most of which had never documented their processes or procedures. More often, knowledge of how a particular issue was managed was handed down between employees, and a major part of the implementation process was understanding, documenting, and then codifying the city departments' processes into the HEAT application software. As an example, the CRS application had to integrate with the city's pavement and sewer management software and with a geographic information system (GIS) used to map the location of the civil infrastructure within the city. An SQL server database was used as the repository of information for the CRS application, which enabled the access and sharing of data by other departments and applications.

Perhaps most importantly, the city is providing better levels of service for its residents and is enhancing the quality of life and the level of comfort and safety of its residents while reducing the costs associated with managing these issues.

The city also benefited from the business process review that was used to identify and document internal procedures; more than 1,250 different types of calls, inquiries, and service requests were identified. The city was also able to pinpoint areas where the departments could improve performance. Ultimately, the CRS/HEAT system gives the city staff not only the ability to see where they need to make improvements but also the ability to see where they shine.

PART 6

The
Future

Chapter 32

The Evolving Real-Time Enterprise

The CRM industry has come a long way during the past 20 years. What started as a sales force automation (SFA) opportunity in the early 1980s, soon emerged into an SFA, customer service, and support industry in the late 1980s. Marketing was added to the equation in the early 1990s. Later in that decade, business analytics and ecustomer applications were added to the mix of CRM applications. CRM application suites emerged with the entry of enterprise resource planning (ERP) players. The late 1990s was a "golden age" for CRM, with 30 to 50 percent annual growth that helped propel CRM to the No. 1 position in software application license revenues worldwide. By the way, CRM still retains the No. 1 position among software application license revenues and will continue to do so for years to come.

The turbulent dot-com crash in 2001 meant a considerable decrease in CRM growth rates and a closer look at the CRM value proposition. The CRM failure rates were bantered around as much as its benefits, and the entire software industry was under attack for not meeting customer expectations. Stock prices of CRM public companies crashed, resulting in a real wakeup call.

Today, CRM software vendors that once relied on third-party integrators to install their software now install more of those in-house. The vendors that also once simply sold CRM software are now increasingly offering complementary business-process and change-management services. CRM software vendors commanded high prices for their wares, and by using systems integrators, those inflated prices increased higher still. Following the dot-com crash, a new alternative was born in the form of application service provider (ASP) hosted solutions. The result? Software and implementation prices have dropped dramatically in recent years. And with the entrance of Microsoft in the CRM space and Oracle's purchase of PeopleSoft and Siebel, the industry received another stamp of approval. Today, CRM has achieved best-practice status within most industries.

In 2003, most industry watchers looked for a year of renewed growth in the CRM industry. CRM software vendor revenues, as well as CRM implementation service revenues, started to rebound. Customers, vendors, and implementation firms finally understood that CRM is not solely a plug-and-play technology solution. They started to grasp the significance of getting the right mix of people, processes, and technology to drive CRM success. Back-office/front-office integration is on the rise. Consolidation among the software vendors is also increasing within the industry. CRM software vendors started creating vertical market software solutions to differentiate themselves. Self-service applications and other customer support applications have also become more popular. Wireless has become the norm; industry forecasts indicate that 80 percent of all CRM applications will be wireless ready by the end of 2008. Meanwhile, the ASP (application service provider) or SaaS (software as a service) model continues to grow.

Government CRM—The Next Big Boom?

While chairing a recent CRM conference, an FBI agent came up to me and held out his badge. "Oh dear," I muttered, "what could I have done?"

It turned out that this fellow was simply seeking advice about the Bureau's CRM initiative. A few hours later, a woman from the Defense Logistics Agency (DLA) came over asking about the DLA's ambitious CRM initiative.

In fact, there are a growing number of short-term CRM initiatives at civilian federal agencies, organizations including the Bureau for Public Debt and the U.S. Postal Service, military offices such as the DLA, and intelligence agencies including the National Security Agency and the National Reconnaissance Office.

Today, government agencies are under increasing pressure to control costs, improve productivity, and deliver better products and services much like their private sector counterparts. But separately, these government agencies face their own set of CRM challenges.

For example, suppose Agency X is a global postal service. Faced with increased pressure from private sector competitors, Agency X decides to compete by creating and offering a better service than the competition. The agency takes time to learn more about customer needs, segments the customer base, and puts together a unique offering per identified segment. Agency X then decided to implement a CRM initiative to realize its service-driven initiative.

Initially, the troops seemed fired up. Then, Agency X noticed some resistance from personnel who were required to make needed process changes. As one Agency X employee asked, "Why do we have to change processes that have served this agency and its customers well for more than 50 years?"

Although it's not atypical to see this sort of reaction to any CRM initiative, it presents a particular challenge in the government sector. Unlike in the private sector, managers may not be able to provide enough incentives to help motivate change. Also, buy-in tends to be made on a horizontal level (the agency head, Congressional Oversight Committees, labor unions), which can lead to drawn-out negotiations, major delays, and even the demise of meaningful CRM initiatives.

Suppose Agency Y is a member of the intelligence community. This particular agency gathers intelligence, and interprets and provides it to a number of customers including the president, his cabinet members, the military, law enforcement officials, and other members of the intelligence community. Agency Y turned to a CRM initiative as a way to better serve its customer base, which seemed to make sense until the head of Agency Y asked the CRM leader to present a business case justifying the expense.

Unlike the private sector, Agency Y could not argue about revenue enhancements, and it couldn't justify the initiative on cost savings, which might translate into a budget reduction. This meant that Agency Y had to justify the CRM initiative based largely on improved customer service and satisfaction, which are not easy metrics to obtain in the intelligence community.

With continued belt-tightening and the help of federal mandates such as the Federal Enterprise Architecture (FEA) and the President's Management Agenda (PMA), justification efforts for new technologies such as CRM can include "cost avoidance," which is agency-speak for anything that reduces costs.

Despite the challenges, the CRM opportunity in government remains strong. There isn't a single federal, state, or local agency that isn't under increased pressure to control costs, improve productivity, or deliver better products/services to internal users or external constituents. And there isn't a single government customer who wouldn't appreciate lower costs or better products/services. CRM has a long and impressive track record of delivering these benefits and more, when properly implemented. For a more in-depth look at this topic, turn to Chapter 31, CRM in Government.

The Future = RTE

So where is the industry headed over the next few years? CRM increasingly integrates front-office applications (sales, marketing, customer service) with back-office applications (ERP applications for finance, human resources, manufacturing, and inventory control), with ecustomer applications (Web shopping, Web self-service, and permission-based marketing), and with supply-chain applications (B2B exchanges). With all of those bases covered, what could a person consider as the inherent weakness in the current CRM scenario? Right now, the weakness is obvious. These many differing software applications are being stuck together using proprietary pipes that are expensive to implement and often require high-maintenance middleware solutions to run effectively.

And this is where the evolutionary start of the Real-Time Enterprise (RTE) begins. RTE technology seamlessly links different applications with a common, standards-based open architecture "pipe" based on .NET and J2EE technical architectures. The RTE pipe offers easy and open integration links based on XML, a business workflow or business process engine, and real-time analytics capabilities. Now disparate applications can be put together in a cost-effective way. CRM software suites are no longer required. Best-in-class software "point" solutions will grow and be used more often.

While the technology advances of .NET, J2EE, and XML help propel the growth of the new emerging RTE industry, another significant issue will also factor into the equation: the entrance of the federal government. Given the need to drive down costs and to better manage customer/constituent relationships (both internal and external), government agencies are significantly stepping up their acquisition and use of CRM software. And this will likely drive CRM and RTE revenues much higher in the future.

RTE Defined

RTE is the process of interconnecting a company's entire operations via internal and Internet applications to enable all information to be shared in real time. This allows the company to function like a 24-hour nerve center, instantly alerting individuals to changes in customer demand, competitive situations, inventory, availability of supplies, and profitability.

But the concept behind RTE is not new. Air-traffic controllers, big city police forces, and energy/utility/stock traders all function in real time. Inevitably, nearly every company operates at least partly in real time. But the idea of large businesses operating in real time—all the time—is relatively new.

Take a look at the following companies: Amazon, Best Buy, Cisco Systems Inc., DaimlerChrysler, Dell, Department of Defense, eBay, Federal Express, GE, Google, Hewlett-Packard, KeyCorp, Morgan Stanley, Motorola, PJM Interconnection, The Limited, Tyco, United Parcel Service Inc, U.S. Steel, and Wal-Mart.

These companies have become RTEs by spending enormous amounts of time, money, and resources over a number of years. Look at their names carefully. Notice anything about them? You should. Each of them is a leader, most often the No. 1 company in its respective industry. They have all been able to successfully achieve sustainable, competitive advantage.

The good news is that any company (even yours) can now leverage the lessons these companies learned that helped them accomplish full-time RTE status.

A Natural Progression

The migration toward RTE status seems to evolve in a natural progression, supported by RTE process and technology enhancements. On the process side, many enterprises today are truly global companies with global processes that work around the clock. With the steady lengthening of regular business hours, the Internet provides customers with the ability to be inside your company at all hours. On the technology side, the market has progressed from batch processing to online processing to client/server processing to Internet processing. Increasing computer capabilities and speed have driven entirely new business processes such as real-time decision making or email. Greatly reduced technical infrastructure costs including those for hardware, storage, and bandwidth are clearly a reality today.

RTE Vision

In an RTE, the majority of software applications move to the Internet. Advancements in Internet technology mean that regardless of the computer device (PC, handheld PDA, notebook computer, iPhone, television, or any other device), comprehensive, complete, and personalized software applications are accessible from anywhere at any time. The old "software application clients" are reserved for a dwindling number of remote users who conduct a large portion of their business off-line.

Internet software applications contain browsers that offer individual users personalized processes that are backed up by applications to these processes. In other words, each Internet application knows who you are, when you log on, what your preferences are, and which business processes and information needs to address, and optimizes your Internet experience each time.

Real-time processing architectures are already available, based on lessons learned by the early adopters. These architectures contain new software components including entitlement, personalization, change notification, multitier supply-chain integration, performance management, multilevel partner relationship applications, global synchronization/integration, and wireless communications.

In an RTE, every piece of information is current. Whether you are the customer, the distributor, the internal order taker, a member of your finance department, or a tier-one, -two, or -three supplier, you will immediately know about shifts in demand because new opportunities or competitive situations will automatically trigger new supplies, billing requirements, and more.

The Value Proposition

The value proposition for RTEs is so strong that more and more companies have proactively opted to become RTEs. Execution efficiency and structural efficiency comprise the RTE value proposition. On the execution efficiency side, RTEs can expect the following:

- **Reduced costs** – This includes significantly reduced IT infrastructure/integration costs (which accounts for an average 30 percent of an IT department's budget), an average 20 percent reduction in the cost-per transaction, and an average 15 percent reduction in inventory costs. For example, one customer of U.S. Steel's Straightline Source subsidiary, which provides real-time, online information visibility to manage supply and to reduce inventory management costs aimed at optimizing steel procurement, realized a 15 percent decrease in inventory levels, a 10 percent reduction in procurement costs, and a 90 percent cut in communications time in 2005.

- **Operational excellence** – This includes accepting orders in real time and ensuring product availability, optimizing order management and fulfillment, and linking real-time activities with demand planning. For example, DaimlerChrysler's Mopar Parts Group, during the first year of its RTE system, was able to increase its average four-day fill rate from 96.5 percent to 98.5 percent, which resulted in $20 million savings in reduced safety stock and $10 million savings in excess transport charges.

- **Enhanced productivity** – An increase of 10 to 20 percent per employee per annum (four to eight hours per week for an average 40-hour workweek) is the norm, since personnel no longer have to waste time tracking needed information. With discipline and incentive, increased productivity leads to increased revenues. For example, the Tyco Adhesives' warehouse/distribution center in Franklin, Kentucky, within the first month of implementing its RTE system in 2005, realized greater than 100 percent productivity increase, from 2,350 line items picked and shipped on a good day to today's average of 5,800 line items. Inventory accuracy also increased from 98 percent to more than 99 percent.

- **Better decision making** – This results from having more timely information and being able to act on it to enhance decision making. The better decision making at PJM Interconnection, which manages the electric grid for the mid-Atlantic states in real time while coordinating supply from greater than 650 power generation companies, provides electricity for Pennsylvania customers at prices that are on average 4.5 percent below the national average.

- **Customer delight/loyalty** – Customers appreciate responsiveness with order information, financial information, support issues, etc. For many years, Dell's real-time order and fulfillment system resulted in more than 97 percent customer satisfaction and helped propel Dell to the No. 1 slot in the computer industry. Some of Dell's more recent problems can be attributed to the company taking its eyes off the customer delight/loyalty ball. While these problems are being corrected now, the impact has been significant and Dell has dropped to the No. 2 slot in the computer industry in terms of sales.

On the structural efficiency side, RTEs can expect to produce sustainable, competitive leadership. In fact, when properly implemented, RTEs can achieve oligopoly or even monopoly positioning within their industry. For example, Cleveland-based KeyCorp is one of the nation's largest bank-based financial services companies with assets of about $92 billion. Its RTE has helped the bank achieve its strategic direction of offering integrated financial services nationwide and enabling customers to have all their financial service needs fulfilled in real time. In fact, its RTE has enabled KeyCorp to provide new bank products/functionality 12 to 18 months sooner than most of its peers and to achieve higher Internet banking penetration into retail banking clients than its peers, all of which support its sustainable, competitive leadership position.

By opting to become an RTE, companies of all sizes and industries are realizing value propositions based on powerful execution and structural efficiencies. These companies are creating and sustaining leadership positions within their respective industries, leaving their competition wondering how to catch up.

RTE-Enabling Technologies

Today, wireless technologies open an array of new opportunities to collect, distribute, and analyze information that enables better, faster customer responsiveness, and real-time operations for many organizations. The impending wireless Internet promises to spur productivity by collecting data that could never be tracked before and by making information available exactly when it's needed. This will speed automation, allowing people behind a cash register to do more productive work. According to Tim Bajarin, president of Creative Strategies Inc. (introduced in Chapter

21, A Wireless World), wireless technologies (Wi-Fi, WiMAX, and RFID) can help companies achieve RTE status with a high-level productivity boost and allow users to access and execute information quickly.

He cites Lockheed Martin, which currently builds fighter jets (primarily F16s) in a manufacturing hangar about 1-mile long and ¼-mile wide. The company found it could reduce the time it takes to build each plane—from six to four months—by providing mechanics and engineers with Wi-Fi connections and tablet or notebook PCs. Usually, the professionals building fighter jets spend the majority of each day on top of, or inside, each jet. Every time a question or a problem cropped up with a particular step in the assembly process, the engineer would climb down from the plane and walk through the enormous hangar to a computer station to refer to the manufacturing plans and call for technical support. When 500 "super-secure" Wi-Fi nodes were added, these workers could stay on the aircraft and still get the answers they needed to complete each jet's assembly. This use of wireless technology has dramatically increased productivity and enabled a swift and significant ROI, according to Bajarin.

While Wi-Fi, or 802.11, is designed for wireless access to information within a 200-foot radius, WiMAX is a large area networking architecture that expands the limits of wireless access from 200 feet up to 50 miles; WiMAX can deliver up to 70 Mbps of throughput at its highest rates. Wi-Fi, WiMAX, Bluetooth, ZigBee, and Ultra-Wideband are types of wireless networking technologies that push wireless networking into every facet of life, from cars and homes to office buildings and factories. These technologies will usher in a new era for the wireless Web. They will work with each other and with traditional phone networks so people and machines can communicate like never before. People in formerly isolated towns will find themselves with fast Internet connections if they have access to WiMAX. On the highway, drivers will be able to use a laptop or PDA to check the weather or the traffic a few miles ahead, thanks to 3G cellular networks and eventually WiMAX.

Since 2005, these technologies have attracted an estimated $4.5 billion in venture capital (VC) investments. WiMAX and other wireless network technology could compete with other wired and wireless architectures, such as hard-wired cable, DSL, and cellular-based wireless services, for an array of real-time applications, including voice over Internet protocol (VoIP) and real-time, location-based services. Because of the ease of implementation, compared to the effort involved in wired broadband cable connections, Bajarin envisioned cable- and telcom-based companies delivering wireless broadband high-speed Internet and VoIP alternatives to home audiences in broader numbers and going mainstream by 2009 as WiMAX wireless networks are built. Sprint and Clearwire, the leading network providers of WiMAX services, expect to have at least 90 percent of the major metropolitan areas in the U.S. covered by their WiMAX networks by this date.

On the current wide-area networking front, the next generation of high-speed 3G wireless cellular radio services are already poised to enhance the use of VoIP for call centers and other low-cost calling operations. According to Bajarin, Verizon, Sprint, AT&T, and all the major carriers are driving these 3G broadband wireless wide-area services, which feature data speeds of up to 5 megabits, and are already providing advanced wireless capabilities in most major metropolitan areas of the U.S. With prices for wireless connectivity and access to Wi-Fi hotspots starting to drop and the addition of next-generation 3G wireless cellular services, the ability to send and receive information in real time will drive the acceleration to RTE, according to Bajarin. These wireless technologies are well-designed to help sales, marketing, and field service products move from overnight batch processes to real-time operations.

For example, VoIP is also likely to grow more popular in call centers and other environments because these wireless high-speed broadband links won't require national or international toll charges, according to Bajarin. And the new wireless broadband network technologies will allow easier real-time collaboration, integrating layers of currently more complex services offered by cellular suppliers. The simpler, easier technological solutions will deliver a low-cost alternative to traditional wired line architectures, said Bajarin.

Organizations should match their primary business needs to the wireless devices available to keep costs under control. If leads and pipeline updates are needed in the field, go with a handset solution. These devices support two-way text messaging as long as the information being sent is concise, such as prospect names and phone numbers. You may also want to consider upgrading to a Java-enabled handset for off-line memory and the ability to use the CRM application when outside the wireless coverage area. If the sales force needs to create and edit information in the field, via email or with a CRM application, invest in a more text-friendly device such as the BlackBerry. Again, upgrading to a Java client provides local processing power and data storage for important customer information. However, if heavy data entry, extensive computing power, and large data storage are required in the field (as with Lockheed Martin) and the cost of equipping the sales force with separate cellular voice service isn't a deterrent, laptops with wireless modem cards fit the bill. BlackBerry devices may also handle form and quote generation if the engines that drive these services are available in the office, or via a hosted CRM service.

Another important technological innovation is radio frequency identification (RFID), which primarily focuses on replacing bar codes on boxes or pallets of products to better manage delivery and distribution of products as part of financial and product tracking services. This technology is quickly picking up in supply-chain management applications today. Wal-Mart and the Department of Defense, among others, mandated that all suppliers place RFID tags on boxes in 2006. That's because RFID tags provide more information than traditional bar codes, identifying the contents of a box or pallet by colors, sizes, styles, etc. The key benefits of RFID include improved information on inventory status, better tracking and management of assets, and enhanced customer service and responsiveness.

Another key technological ingredient is the Universal Application Network (UAN). Led by Microsoft and Siebel and backed by 50 hardware and software suppliers so far, this XML-based Web services architecture is designed to enable software developers to write code in such a way that if one element changes in inventory, that element is changed across the enterprise's financial, inventory, distribution, manufacturing, and sales systems. UAN architectures are expected to make it easier to link wireless technologies into corporate applications such as Oracle databases or PeopleSoft human resources or financial applications. Sales, support, and marketing personnel need access to customer information from anywhere at any time. UAN will let users use multiple products in the enterprise so that changes made in a PeopleSoft application are reflected in the Oracle database and other financial systems. While the boost in Lockheed Martin's productivity shows promise for revolutionizing manufacturing processes, Pepsico, Wal-Mart, and other large corporations are starting to incorporate wireless technologies and next-generation UAN architectures to enhance the real-time delivery of information.

Lastly, there are emerging camps in the RTE technology marketplace. One is commonly referred to as the open proprietary vendor solution

(Salesforce.com with its new AppExchange, SAP with its NetWeaver environment, Siebel with its UAN environment, Microsoft with its .NET). All these claim to be open architectures, but they are actually open within their proprietary systems. The vendors think that they can offer real-time functionality by having applications added onto their open proprietary environment.

The other is commonly referred to as the middleware camp, consisting of an emerging group of vendors such as Tibco, BEA, or IBM Websphere. This camp is more open and less proprietary, but it has fewer real time and CRM modules that are currently written for its environment, so more are middleware technical infrastructure companies than real time or CRM modularized companies. It is not clear which of these camps will emerge as the long-term RTE winner, but what is important is that both camps are capable of allowing for RTE functionality to take place. It's a matter of time to see which camp will emerge as the winner or the best alternative within a specific identifiable market segment.

An RTE Timetable

The leading technology/business publishers are likely to refer to RTE as the "greatest business accomplishment of the decade." The evolution of the RTE decade will fall into the following three distinct periods:

- **2002–05: Incubation** – During this period, you read and heard a great deal about RTE. Companies moved toward real-time status, along with more RTE vendors, more RTE case studies, etc. Many RTE conferences took place, and many RTE white papers were written.

- **2006–09: Hot new market** – There were many RTEs in 2006 and 2007, which will translate to many more viable RTE examples to follow. Many case studies that are published will document the RTE value proposition. Venture capitalists begin to fund real-time enterprise technology vendors, and you can also expect to see early real-time technology vendors go public. Those companies that proactively become RTEs will begin to pull away from the pack. Their market leadership accomplishments will become regular, recurring stories in the leading business press. Competitors will begin to wonder what happened.

- **2010: RTE moving full blast** – Just like in the early days of CRM, there will be an increasing number of new real-time technology vendors, consultants, and analysts in the industry. RTE companies will be profiled in case studies that appear in multiple industries and in various media and publications. More companies will budget appropriate funds to become RTEs. Leading RTEs will sustain and enhance their leadership positions. Their reach will cut across entire demand-and-supply chains. Mobile communications and browsers will become the norm for those who use RTE systems. Customers will enjoy working with RTEs. Venture capitalists will invest heavily, and the market capitalization of RTE vendors will soar.

RTE Vendors

The following three sets of vendors will play a prominent role in the rise of the RTE industry:

1. **The existing players** – eGain, HP, Infor CRM, NetSuite, Oracle, RightNow, Salesforce.com, SAP, Teradata, TIBCO, and others have identified RTE as a part of their future direction.

2. **Web-services players** – BEA, IBM, and Microsoft .NET can be found in this group. Microsoft has made a significant commitment with .NET, the software giant's platform for XML Web services. In recent discussions with senior Microsoft executives, I learned that Microsoft is looking for .NET to become the programming model for RTE, and Microsoft would rather encourage third parties to build these applications on top of the .NET platform than to build its own RTE applications.

3. **The new guard** – While Aleri, Antenna, Nokia, and others are taking the lead here, it's too early to tell which of these RTE vendors may become a future RTE industry leader.

Early RTE Adopters

Microsoft has spent millions establishing its RTE initiative called Agile Business; Siebel is pushing forward with its RTE offering called Universal Application Network. Recent advances in real-time analytics from companies such as Teradata are adding fuel to the RTE fire. Leading IT consultancies such as the Gartner Group now track the RTE industry. In January, a Gartner survey found that more than 20 percent of CIOs at Global 2000 enterprises cited RTE as one of their top-five investment areas.

Why have global leaders such as Amazon, Cisco, Dell, eBay, Federal Express, General Electric, U.S. Steel, and Wal-Mart committed millions of dollars to build RTE capabilities? The RTE value proposition rests on reduced costs, operational excellence, enhanced productivity, better decision making, customer delight and loyalty, and sustainable competitive leadership.

As an example of the RTE value proposition in action, PJM Interconnection is a regional transmission organization that plays a vital role in the U.S. electric system. PJM ensures the reliability of the largest centrally dispatched control area in North America by coordinating the movement of electricity in all or parts of Delaware, Maryland, New Jersey, Ohio, Pennsylvania, Virginia, West Virginia, and the District of Columbia. PJM's members transact much of their business on PJM's Web site. Using online tools that provide real-time data about the electric system, PJM triggers the buying and selling of power among its members, arranges transmission service, schedules contract purchases, carries out business strategies, and makes critical business decisions. The RTE business model lets PJM rapidly add new members and provide lower prices to customers.

Improved business process tools have helped companies easily link supply-and-demand RTE processes. New integration tools have also helped.

Finally, one more RTE driver is the wireless revolution. With the wireless industry growing at an annual rate of more than 30 percent, it is only a matter of time before companies work in real time over wireless networks.

CRM Drivers

CRM plays a driver role in creating the RTE, primarily because CRM already has many of the RTE building blocks in place. Many companies have already implemented CRM systems that connect suppliers, internal customers, distribution channel partners, and end users. Sales, marketing, and customer service CRM applications interconnect. Data gets shared across company personnel who touch the customer.

The CRM industry also has considerable integration experience. While not always completed with excellence, the industry has successfully integrated dispersed data sources and has learned many lessons along the way. In addition, many CRM initiatives and supporting systems, if not most, include the implementation of customer touch programs. These customer touch programs cut across demand and supply chains, which is a critical success factor for realizing RTE status. And perhaps most importantly, there is the emerging Net generation. These future leaders tend to be active ecustomers and users of today's CRM systems. They do not question the value of the RTE. Instead, they question why it's taking so long to get there.

Today, it is no longer an option to optimize your customer relationships. Given the more knowledgeable and less loyal customer base today, particularly the Net generation, no organization can risk securing anything less than outstanding customer relationships. That means having up-to-the-minute customer knowledge and providing support from anywhere, anytime; this defines CRM's future with real-time CRM solutions.

Real-time CRM solutions result from the explosion in Web services and hosted applications, wireless expansion, and businesses accepting the Web as their primary platform for engaging customers. As the CRM industry continues to develop more sophisticated real-time CRM solutions, organizations will have the opportunity to revolutionize their customer relationships using valuable real-time CRM tools and techniques.

You'll need to stay informed about key developments in the people, process, and technology related to real-time CRM solutions. Top management teams of best-in-class companies have already reached this conclusion, including several from our own customer base.

At AAA Mid-Atlantic, for example, where we have worked closely with its top management team for years to help deliver a world-class CRM initiative, real-time CRM solutions have meant putting new business processes into place to create and use real-time customer profiles to perform real-time customer service, and to perform real-time cross-selling and up-selling.

At a global financial services company, we helped its sales and marketing management team develop a technical infrastructure and execute business functionality that supports working in real time at all times. At the core of these improvements is a real-time, Web-based, world-class customer-self service capability.

Real-time CRM solutions are being propelled by the following key business drivers that will expand in importance over the next decade:

- The need to be increasingly customer-focused, especially the ability to understand the strong demands of the Net generation

- Increased competition and the need to maintain long-term differentiation through real-time customer service excellence

- An increased emphasis on better market segmentation and on understanding the growing real-time expectations from leading, attitudinal-based market segments

- The need for tighter linkages between front-office and back-office processes and technology systems to ensure a real-time understanding of your customers

- The need for improved business analytics and metrics (customer-balanced scorecards) so decision makers can be quickly alerted to key marketplace and buyer developments

Several years ago, Bill Gates spoke about "information at your fingertips anytime and anywhere." The future of CRM, especially real-time CRM solutions, has already begun to deliver on this vision.

RTE Critical Issues

Becoming an RTE is now within the reach of almost every company, provided RTE vendors, analysts, the media, and users can work together to address the following critical issues:

- **Effective integration of people, process, and technology** – While the RTE proposition includes significant infrastructure enhancements for most companies, RTE is considerably more involved than a pure technology play.

- **Success by example** – The RTE value proposition will catch on more via successful case studies than by marketing promises or media hype.

- **Helping potential RTEs to understand how emerging RTE components fit together** – For example, the key is knowing how technology, end-to-end business processes, and required areas of change management complement each other.

- **Laying out clear, pragmatic road maps** – This process will help companies become RTEs.

RTEs of all sizes and industries already realize the value propositions of powerful execution and structural efficiencies. These companies are creating and sustaining leadership positions within their respective arenas. The competition is wondering how they will catch up, if ever. With this in mind, the time is right for executives worldwide to enhance their knowledge of RTEs and become drivers of what will become the "greatest business accomplishment of the decade."

Chapter 33

Ten Steps for Creating a Real-Time Enterprise

The real-time enterprise (RTE) concept requires interconnecting a company's entire operations via internal and Internet applications, and enabling all information to be shared in real time. As we noted before, this allows the company to function like a 24-hour nerve center, instantly alerting individuals to changes in customer demand, inventory, availability of supply, competitive analysis, and profitability.

Many companies today are already reaping the execution and efficiency benefits that result from becoming an RTE, including Cisco, Dell, and Wal-Mart. What can we learn from these and other RTE companies? Each will confirm the importance of using a structured approach for creating the RTE.

My firm has formulated the following 10 steps for creating the RTE, along with overall timeframes involved in the process of moving toward RTE status.

Step 1: Analyze Your Current Building Blocks

Successful RTEs build on current investments in the area of CRM, SCM (supply-chain management), and ERP (enterprise resource planning). I believe CRM is the driver behind the RTE. Why? Because CRM systems already connect suppliers, internal customers, distribution channel partners, and end users; CRM already shares processes and data across sales, marketing, customer service, and executive functions; and CRM already moves data in CRM, SCM, and ERP applications.

So start by analyzing what CRM systems and initiatives you now have in place. Look for an understanding of how best to exploit these efforts to become an RTE. For example, how can you leverage or expand your current CRM processes? How can you leverage or expand on the people changes that you already have in place? How can you leverage and expand your current technology? Run similar analyses for your SCM and ERP building blocks.

Step 2: Create an RTE Road Map

Creating an RTE road map includes creating a clear vision of how your company will function as an RTE, along with people, process, and technology components. Your road map will lay out which RTE processes need to be in place and how to accomplish them, what your RTE people issues are and how to overcome them, and which RTE technologies are needed and how to implement these technologies over time. Your road map also will describe how you intend to reach out to your suppliers and customers, usually through focus groups, to validate your emerging RTE vision.

Step 3: Prioritize Processes and Functions to Automate

Next, you want to prioritize the RTE processes and which RTE business functions to automate. For example, assume your RTE vision suggests you have three major business processes that require enhancements to become an RTE. You'll need to agree on which of these three business processes you will implement first, second, and third. In other words, the RTE road map (Step 2) leaves you with the total picture of the RTE "puzzle," and in this step you are deciding which pieces you should be adding and in which order.

Step 4: Secure Supplier, Partner, and Customer Buy-In

To secure buy-in on the supplier, partner, and customer side, determine and communicate what's in it for each of them. In other words, why should they be interested in participating in your RTE? You will want to meet with them to allay their fears, to talk through their value proposition, and to discuss key benefits to participating in your RTE. One of the most effective tools in this step will be your RTE communications plan.

Step 5: Demonstrate RTE Value, Gain Top Management Support

To accomplish this step, you will need to build a value proposition based upon both execution (lower costs per transaction, higher revenues per employee) and structural efficiencies (securing sustainable, competitive advantage). You can also include soft efficiencies (higher customer delight and intimacy), but the RTE value proposition has to have enough substance so top management overwhelmingly concludes that the value far outweighs the cost. Here's a hint: Wrap your RTE value proposition within your RTE business case. This is a critical step in that it is a potential stop point, a point where management can say, "I'm just not convinced, and either drop it, postpone it, or send your RTE efforts back to the drawing board."

Step 6: Launch Change, Training, and Communications Programs Early

In an RTE, people work differently; they are very visible. They can't dust things under the rug, there are no private C drives. So you have to talk to people about how this will affect their day-to-day jobs, and describe what a day in the life of the RTE will be like. You will need to determine whether they need to be retrained on emerging RTE processes and on the use of RTE technologies to support these processes. You will also want to launch your RTE communication program intensively at that point.

Step 7: Use Real-Time Technical Architectures and Applications

With the explosion in new real-time technical architectures and applications, you'll need to begin to understand them. They include impressive advancements in integration and messaging environments, new network capabilities, new supply-chain applications, entitlement capabilities, and more. There are new, efficient ways to trigger RTE processes and workflow that allow one RTE software application to impact multiple other RTE software applications, all in real time. Smart browsers know who you are when you come in; they know what processes to evoke and how to optimize your customer experience each time you access the RTE. And they are attractively priced.

Step 8: Execute Your RTE Road Map in Small, Executable Steps

We have all learned from our CRM, SCM, and ERP experiences that tackling too large a technology project can spell doom from the start. If you are going to implement a winning RTE, remember to tackle the job in small bites and lots of successful quick wins. In today's economic climate where questions immediately get raised regardless of the investment type (let alone a large investment and commitment like creating an RTE), what executives are looking for is measurable quick wins; the one thing that will kill your RTE is doing too much too quickly and not being able to show the value of what you have done. Small, accomplishable steps will also help you to secure continued buy-in from top management.

Step 9: Deliver Strong RTE Analytics and Operational Excellence

Make sure that at each step of your RTE road map implementation, you provide analytical feedback that reinforces the business value of your RTE to your top management team. At each stage of implementing your road map, deliver the comprehensive analytics and document your quick wins. On the operations side, document operational excellence, which means writing down RTE procedures, policies, and job description changes so that they can be repeated throughout your RTE implementation. Be sure to drive operational excellence throughout the implementation of your RTE road map; the importance of this cannot be underestimated.

Step 10: Measure, Record, and Communicate RTE Success

This closes the loop with Step 5, where you have demonstrated RTE value and gained top management support. The way to sustain continued support is by measuring your quick wins throughout the implementation of your RTE road map, and then recording and communicating these wins on a monthly or quarterly basis to your top management team, your internal RTE users, and your suppliers, partners, and customers on the outside. Ongoing measurements, recordings, and communication need to happen throughout the lifetime of your RTE.

As you move through the various steps in this process, plan on accomplishing Steps 1 to 5 in about two to four months (three to six months for a more bureaucratic company), and plan an additional six to 12 months to accomplish Steps 6 to 10 with the understanding that these steps will be done in two-month deliverables. Putting it all together, plan on eight to 16 months to create your RTE (nine to 18 months for a more bureaucratic company). Speaking pragmatically, a quick win is possible within four or five months, but if you want to achieve sustainable, competitive leadership (as Cisco, Dell, Wal-Mart, and other RTEs have done), think eight to 16 months ahead.

Whatever overall timeframe you end up with for delivering RTE excellence, keep this advice in mind: Don't expect or promise too much too quickly; you want to ensure your real-time success.

Chapter 34

The Future of CRM: Real Time

Let's venture forward five or 10 years and explore what working in real-time CRM is like, where "always-on, always connected" becomes the prevalent way to conduct business.

The Net generation, also known as the Millennials, are between ages 12 and 32. This PlayStation generation is the first age group to be born into digital technology exclusively, and they are accustomed to 3D images and the World Wide Web; email to them is old-fashioned, and they don't even know what a typewriter is. Most importantly, your Net Generation customers and employees will expect you to conduct business with them and through them in an always-on, always-connected real-time way. As this generation enters the work force and becomes your customers, access to information any time and any way they want it will be normal business procedure for them, and they will expect the companies they deal with and work for to provide this level of real-time connectivity at all times.

This always-on, always-connected concept is a result of the move from an analog to a digital world, which my firm forecasts as being completed by the year 2030. In the digital world, broadband rules, every mobile device has a wireless connection to the Internet, and all computing devices are connected to each other, synchronized, and always up to date. In other words, working in real time becomes the norm for conducting business.

From the hardware perspective, computing devices that rival earlier PCs are already small enough to fit into your pocket. Just look at Apple's iPhone and other smartphones that are already on the market. A decade ago, cell phones were mainly a luxury item used by doctors, lawyers, and real-estate agents. These phones basically did one thing: made mobile phone calls. Today's cell phones are already multifunctional; they house applications such as GPS devices, video phone services, cameras, email, real-time news updates, and Internet browsing. They are getting lighter, smaller, and more powerful and will always connect to your office, your customers, or your family from anywhere in the world. These small, portable devices become the lifeblood for businesspeople who live in the always-on, always-connected real-time world. And as the Web becomes a key way to deliver applications, smartphones with full Web browsers will make them even more powerful.

On the software side, the idea of an all-in-one CRM application by 2012 will be replaced by plug-and-play, best-in-class business functional modules that build in best-in-class business processes. All remaining horizontal CRM applications will be replaced by vertical solutions that optimally fit industry-specific business models.

These hardware and software technology advancements have already had a significant impact on CRM and will continue to do so as they finally allow companies and customers to easily work in real time, all the time. In sales, this means real-time inventories and collaborative selling where the buyer plays an active role in the sales process. In service, this means the pervasive use of self-service that builds on extensive real-time knowledgebases as well as vendors who instantly alert customers to anything important (RFID tags attached to products as well as navigation systems that alert companies and customers to product movements in real time).

In marketing, this means automatic re-segmentation of markets based on real-time information, auction-based pricing, and collaborative customers who actively participate in real-time product testing and feedback. In business analytics, this means real-time reporting with actual intelligence-based recommendations coming directly from your applications. Remember: This always-on, always-connected concept will come with every piece of digital information and will be capable of being shared instantly.

For many years, I have suggested that CRM is a business approach that integrates best-in-class business processes that internal and external customers buy into and that real-time technology also supports. Finding the right formula for the new people, process, and technology integration mix in an always-on, always-connected real-time world will not be easy. And here comes the twist: While technological advances will inevitably occur, working in real time still requires that you establish those necessary processes that optimize the customer experience each time they visit you online. Because at the end of the day, we're all people who make our buying decisions based on a good customer experience.

Chapter 35

Web 2.0 and the Digital Client

At a recent CRM conference, industry pundits gathered to discuss what the future holds for CRM: Author Malcolm Gladwell (*Tipping Point*) suggested that the CRM industry needed to reframe its value proposition; in my chairman's address, I spoke about the state of our industry in its healthy transition and continued growth, the application of wisdom, and the emergence of the digital client; author Stan Davis (*Blur*) challenged the audience by suggesting that to secure continued growth and innovation, the CRM industry must adopt a new life cycle that embraces Web 2.0 developments and accepts the digital client as a key source in this transition. These keynotes were followed by a session with Tim Bajarin, Patrick Bultema, and myself called the "Future of CRM: The Digital Client," part of which I would like to share with you.

After we discussed the characteristics of Web sites that form the current core of Web 2.0 (Wikipedia, craigslist, Google, Facebook, MySpace.com, YouTube, and LinkedIn), we asked the audience some provoking questions: How much does it cost to secure products and services on Web 2.0 sites? (Answer: Nothing; they are all free.) Who is the customer in these Web 2.0 sites? (Answer: Any and everyone.) How do you define a Web 2.0 customer? (Answer: Any individual who invests personal resources with an organization in exchange for value.) What's the value proposition for Web 2.0 sites? (Answer: The exchange of user-generated content and social networking.) Are there really significant numbers of Web 2.0 site visitors? (Answer: Yes, including 56 million who have viewed the Evolution of Dance video on YouTube.) What's the value of these Web 2.0 sites? (Answer: How about more than $160 billion in market capitalization for Google, which equals about five times the market cap of General Motors and Ford combined.)

After we reviewed why John Chamber, Cisco Systems, Inc.'s CEO, recently concluded that "This collaboration that kids [discovered] through social networking is the future of business," we tackled three tough questions. Here are some of the highlights:

Why will the digital client drive the future of business?

In the U.S., there are currently 75 million Generation Y (less than 23 years old) digital clients and 750 million worldwide; by the year 2015, Gen Y will account for 45 percent of the world's population. The members of Gen Y have known only digital technology their entire lives. At a recent focus group of youths (13 years and younger), only one person knew what a typewriter was, and this person had seen one in the Smithsonian Institute.

When members of Gen Y grow to more than 3 billion digital clients worldwide in 2015, there will be 3 billion people using digital devices and will expect an always-on, always-connected access to the Internet in their digital devices. Consequently, the explosion in demand will be from Gen Yers who will be digital clients.

Gen Yers are the key drivers behind Web 2.0; according to a 2006 study from the Kaiser Family Foundation, Gen Yers spend an average of 8.5 hours per day digitally connected. The Gen Y population is spending 90 percent of its time on average researching products and services on the Internet before making a major purchase, and 50 percent are also purchasing products on the Internet. This demand for digitally connected products is evident as members of Gen Y are responsible for purchasing 270,000 iPhones during the first three days that iPhones went on sale in the U.S. in June 2007 and were on track to purchase 3 million iPhones by December 2007. Gen Yers are providing much of the free user-generated content for Web 2.0 sites and are commercializing social networking. They feel that always-on, always-connected to each other and to the Web is an inalienable right. But most importantly, digital clients are now increasingly the buyers/influencers of your products and services. Simply said, digital clients represent the future of your business; they are not going away, and you cannot avoid them.

The impact of Gen Y is prevalent as two major companies, Apple and eBay, continuously reinvent themselves to target the digital demands of Gen Yers. Apple previously was known for its personal computers, Apple and Macintosh. When the profit margins from personal computers began to decline, Apple began reinventing itself for the changing marketplace. Much success in recent years stemmed from the realization that the digitally connected generation will buy digitally connected products for their personal use, including iPods and iPhones. With Apple's recent successes in the marketplace, it's evident that Gen Yers, or digital clients, will drive the company's future.

eBay is another organization that continuously reinvents itself to meet the demands of the digital client generation. eBay originally started out as an Internet auction business, then it moved into the digital payments industry when it purchased PayPal. In recent years, it has moved into ticket sales with the acquisition of StubHub, then into long-distance phone calls with the acquisition of Skype, and into classified ads with the purchase of Kijiji. It has also moved into social networking with the acquisition of StumbleUpon. While some may argue that eBay is moving too quickly (witness the significant write-off that eBay incurred with its Skype write-down [recording a loss on the purchase of Skype]), few are able to mimic the "digital client DNA" that seems to be a permanent part of eBay's business approach.

For the digital client generation, using multichannels is the norm. In fact, many consider it an expectation. For example, a AAA member who begins a transaction (e.g., an emergency road service call, a travel inquiry, or an insurance claim) will usually start in one channel (e.g., visit an AAA branch or direct mail) and go through several additional channels (e.g., phone or online) before the transaction is complete.

Yet, the need for multichannel options is one of the most misunderstood norms of the digital client generation. Most businesses are still thinking that multichannel means offering and resolving a transaction through one unique channel, regardless of the channel (e.g., phone, in-person visit, email, etc.). It is actually more correct to call this approach "multiple-channel," since the digital client uses one or more channels to resolve an issue, but each time the digital client stays in the channel of choice. In other words, no flow or exchange of information happens between channels.

The digital client views this multiple channel as an old-fashioned, inappropriate approach to conduct business. Rather, the digital client expects organizations to offer a multichannel approach where the resolution process for a transition can be seamlessly transferred from one channel to a second, third, or fourth channel without interruption until the transaction is finally complete. As previously stated, the concept of being always-on, always-connected in relation to completing transactions is seen as an inalienable right by the digital client, and businesses must adapt to this expectation if they intend to survive over the long term.

In addition to multichannel, the always-on, always-connected digital client has another expectation that I call "business in an instant," which is depicted in Figure 35.1.

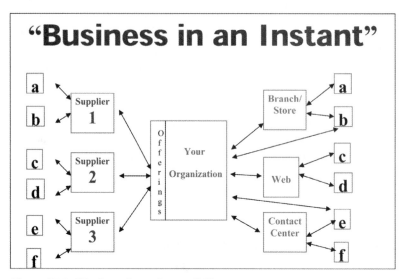

Figure 35.1   "Business in an Instant" diagram

Business in an instant is a natural outcome of achieving CRM in real time. This diagram shows how digital clients (denoted as the a through f boxes on the far right of the diagram) expect to be able to connect to your organization in real time via the distribution channel of their choice (e.g., branch/store, Web, contact center, or directly to your organization) to determine your offerings/inventory and their availability. Digital clients furthermore expect that you have established links in real time with your Tier 1 suppliers (suppliers 1 to 3 in the diagram) and that they in turn have established links to Tier 2 suppliers (shown as a through f on the far left of this diagram). With these real-time links in place, digital clients can easily query about the availability of your products or services. If your product or service is not available, your organization will automatically trigger a request to your Tier 1 (or even Tier 2) suppliers to determine when the product or service can be made available. In other words, by linking together all players involved in the supply/demand chain, and utilizing CRM applications that help manage the relationships between these players, information flows in real-time across the supply/demand chain and the digital client successfully realizes "business in an instant."

My friend Tim Bajarin reminded us that the always-on, always-connected digital client lives within a digital ecosystem that extends beyond technology, drawing on normal human impulses (i.e., the need to communicate) and absorbing only those technologies that meet its goals. Which technologies? These are the Web 2.0 technologies including blogs, wikis, videos, RSS feeds, widgets, and podcasts, each of which supports the social movement for humans to communicate with one another. For long-term survival, organizations need to master these new technologies and apply them in ways that attract and keep their digital clients. This means moving CRM beyond real time, leveraging Web 2.0 technologies, and successfully driving the next generation of CRM 2.0 applications.

Three basic tenets of Web 2.0 will impact the future of CRM: user-generated content, social networking, and disintermediation. These three tenets come together in a type of perfect storm for Web 2.0 company leaders such as MySpace.com, Facebook, Wikipedia, and YouTube. The content of these Web sites is completely user-generated. More importantly, the success of these Web sites has set the expectations of digital clients in mind for the way they will conduct business in the future with an organization; simply said, they will not be forced to use outdated business models that too many organizations still insist on using. Each of these sites has a tremendous impact on the future of the Internet marketplace, yet each site has few employees (MySpace has only 300 employees for its 80-plus million user base, while Wikipedia and YouTube have only 25 employees each).

But take what John Chamber said about the impact of social networking a step further: Social networking (a $2.5 billion market today) with user-generated content is a preview of tomorrow's business models and the recipe for an organization's long-term survival.

What does this mean for organizations that want to leverage the latest advancements, but at the same time, do not want to simply chase the "Next Big Thing"?

The following two examples showcase companies that have adopted social networking to drive their future.

Example 1: Pfizer, the pharmaceuticals company, announced in September 2007 that it had entered into a collaborative agreement with

Sermo.com, the fastest-growing social networking site for doctors, which has been endorsed by the American Medical Association. At the time of the announcement, 30,000 doctors frequented Sermo.com and an additional 2,000 doctors were joining it each week. Sermo.com offers doctors a way to network with their colleagues to discuss their medical cases and/or problems as well as post their own personal information and medical questions for other doctors to answer. Sermo.com expects to open its fast-growing, social networking site to doctors outside the U.S. in 2008. The Pfizer management sees this collaboration with Sermo.com as an appropriate method of changing its current situation of high costs and tremendous inefficiencies in its relationships with doctors.

The challenge for Pfizer was to convince doctors to sign up with Sermo.com while simultaneously respecting their desire for privacy. As an inducement, Sermo.com prohibited any advertisements on its Web site. Pfizer and Sermo.com worked out a deal that established the ways drug-makers can best communicate with physicians online, including the provision of clinical trial feedback as well as on-demand drug and disease information to physicians. The Sermo.com site gives its members a sense of belonging to an interactive online social community where they can publish and receive feedback on numerous medical issues. For Pfizer, the Sermo.com site serves as an efficient way of letting doctors obtain information on its drugs, improving relations with the medical community, and getting assessments from physicians on its clinical trials. Pfizer also sees Sermo.com as a stimulus to reignite growth within the company and prepare itself for the changing drug market. Other major pharmaceutical companies have noted Sermo.com's success and are also expected to create their own physician social networking sites. It is likely that Sermo.com will provide a model for organizations to deal successfully with critical distribution channels (i.e., doctors in this case), while working within this distribution channel's social networking environment.

Example 2: The American Automobile Association (AAA) celebrates its 105th anniversary in 2008. While most of us know AAA as the "towing" company, which is still the principle reason why members join AAA, times have changed. AAA has acknowledged the need to move away from traditional marketing techniques and begin experimenting with new, innovative marketing techniques including social networking and user-driven content (known as "member communities" in AAA parlance). But there is one problem: The average age of a AAA member is 53, and unless AAA intends to go into the retirement home business, which isn't likely, now is the time to reach out to a younger generation and sustain AAA's relevance to its future member base.

In 2005, AAA Southern New England, based in Rhode Island, stepped up to the plate and launched its INsider program, targeted at the teen population (ages 13–16). The program is a membership marketing promotion for teens designed to increase their awareness of AAA membership benefits. It is marketed through various methods including online, AAA branches, AAA Horizons publication, high school sports publications, and AAA trip sweepstakes. The program shares AAA information and its benefits on a regular basis through direct mail, Web pages, email messages, a quarterly newsletter, and a soon-to-be-announced AAA member community where members can share their user-driven content with other members and nonmembers. Program participants receive a membership card, which provides them with benefits including discounted admission to amusement parks, movies, and sporting events. Additional benefits include automatic entry for sweepstakes and raffle prizes, along with free driver education information.

To secure Gen Y members above the current membership number of 25,000, AAA Southern New England has agreed to spend five times more within its marketing budget on teens than 20 years ago. The AAA Southern New England executive team felt confident that the five-fold increase in the teen marketing budget would be more than offset by additional AAA memberships and long-term revenues. And so far, the results look bright: INsider spending in the AAA Southern New England branches are up 10-fold over the past two years, and annual INsider parent spending is up more than 15 percent each of the past two years from 2005 to 2007.

While AAA Southern New England is the only AAA club currently offering an INsider program aimed at the digital client, the remaining 61 AAA clubs in North America are watching this effort. My prediction, based on the need for AAA to penetrate the digital client segment, is that other AAA clubs will follow with their own version of an INsider offering.

I predict that the impact of social networking on marketing will be tremendous. During the next eight years, as the always-on, always-connected generation joins the workforce, individual interconnectivity will continue to blossom and self-publishing will explode within and outside the workplace. As a result of social networking, the information playing field will be leveled as all organizations have the same access to social network-ing sites and the opportunity to collect and analyze the similar information to support their marketing efforts. The main marketing impact will be an increase in niche aggregation, which is the sophisticated filtering of social networking sites to separate relevant and irrelevant buyers on these sites. Organizations will also be forced to move from producer-driven to con-sumer-driven thinking to penetrate identified market segments with increasingly relevant products and services. Perhaps of greatest impor-tance is that social networking will offer entirely new branding opportuni-ties for organizations including Pfizer, AAA, and even yours.

From our discussion, we can conclude that there is a strong need to embrace Web 2.0 technologies such as social networking and to extend brand awareness to digital clients. All this must be done carefully, which implies that we need to do the following:

1. **Know your customer base** – You must know your customer base well. Are they digital clients? What are they interested in? What are their profiles? What do you need to do to keep them as customers?

2. **Understand executive tolerance** – Each company's executive tol-erance for Web 2.0 technologies, such as social networking, will differ. For example, my firm works with a large financial asset management company in Baltimore, Maryland. One executive at this management firm said that while social networking probably had a place in the consumer-to-consumer (C2C) world, the exec-utive management team was not convinced that the social net-working marketing approach was appropriate for its business-to-business (B2B) model. The team contended that customers (financial asset managers) rarely chatted with one another on the Internet. But in fact, doctors also used to say the same thing before Sermo.com was created.

3. **Carefully protect the brand** – Experimenting with Web 2.0 tools such as social networking implies considerable risk. Good infor-mation travels fast on the Internet; bad information travels even faster. So you have to be careful and protect the brand as you expand your Web 2.0 efforts. For example, if a social networking experiment does not work out for your organization, you must

know when and how best to pull the plug to minimize any damage to the long-term value of your brand.

How can your organization begin to create its digital client road map?

Mastering the digital client roadmap, which is likely to be based on Web 2.0 tools and techniques, is no easy task. Here are your first 10 starting points:

1. Immerse yourself in the Web 2.0 culture to understand it. This means learning about search engine marketing tools, search engine optimization, blogging, and other social networking techniques, or hiring a professional to ensure that your blog/social network site is compliant, catchy, and fun.

2. Ramp up your knowledge of social networking through participation. Join a few social networks, create a blog, start downloading podcasts, or have fun producing your own online videos.

3. Keep your eyes open to Web 2.0 and digital client developments outside of your industry. Study new Web 2.0 companies like Yellowikis, a Wikipedia-like site for open business listings. This new site has the potential to shake up the $22 billion Yellow Pages industry.

4. Conduct research among your client base regarding their Web 2.0 desires. Are they digital clients? What Web 2.0 applications are they interested in? What is their profile? What do you need to do to keep them as customers?

5. Understand executive tolerance. Each company's executive tolerance for Web 2.0 technologies' will differ. Figure out the best way to secure approval for potentially disruptive behavior brought on by Web 2.0 technologies.

6. Consider purchasing a Web 2.0 company in your industry. This may make better sense to jumpstart your efforts and secure executive approval.

7. Ensure that all information that you offer your clients is accessible via mobile devices. Mobile devices are at the cornerstone of the digital client's Digital Ecosystem.

8. Hire Generation Y employees (and put at least one on your Board of Directors). This will help propel digital client business in an instant thinking.

9. Don't neglect security when utilizing Web 2.0 capabilities. Many of the technologies are new and not necessarily proven. Be sure to have a well thought-out Web 2.0 security plan.

10. Carefully protect the brand. Good information travels fast on the Internet; bad information travels faster. So you've got to be careful and protect the brand as you expand your Web 2.0 efforts. If, for example, a social networking experiment does not work out for your organization, you must know when and how best to pull the plug so as to minimize any damage to the long-term value of your brand.

In this book, I have tried to show why CRM in real time is the key to the future of all organizations. The always-on, always-connected digital client demands CRM in real time, plus a lot more. Winning organizations have understood the significance of CRM in real time and have already begun to use Web 2.0 tools and techniques, often in the form of new CRM 2.0 applications. My prediction is that any organization not actively participating during the next 12 months in at least two experiments involving Web 2.0 tools and techniques aimed at the digital client is destined to follow the almighty typewriter into the Smithsonian Institute.

In fact, finding the best way to work with the digital client will be the topic of my next book.

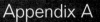
CRM Sales Process Example

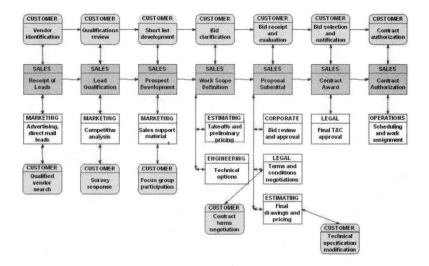

This figure illustrates the mapping of a global manufacturing company's existing sales process. Mapping a company's existing sales processes is one of the essential steps for successful CRM implementation.

Level 1 Process Flow Example

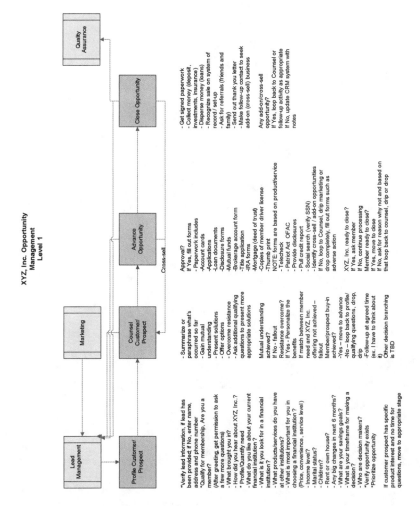

This figure shows the Level 1 process flow example (hypothetical company, XYZ, Inc.). Level 1 is the highest level of the process steps for a CRM implementation.

CRM System RFP Example

BUSINESS FUNCTIONS	DESCRIPTIONS
Contact Management	
Contact profile	
Organization chart	
Contact history	
Account Management	
Account information	
Business relationships	
Activity management	
Order entry	
Order history	
Sarbanes-Oxley compliance features	
Sales contract generation	
Quote/proposal generation	
Sales Management	
Opportunity management	
Sales cycle analysis/sales metrics	
Territory alignment/assignment	
Activity reporting	
Mapping tools	
Expense reporting	
Lease management	
Time Management Tools	
Calendar	
Task lists	
Email	
Fax	
Transaction log/audit trail	
Customer Contact Center	
Customer self-service	
Automated Email response	
Interactive calendar/workforce management	
Interactive support/multimedia portal management	
Customer Service	
Incident assignment	
Incident escalation	
Incident lifecycle management	
Problem resolution database/search	
Incident reporting	
Order management	
Return authorization management and analysis	
Service level agreement/warranty management	
Field Service	
Call handling/dispatching/scheduling/workforce management	
Inventory management	

Problem resolution management	
Time and expense reporting	
Remote knowledge management tools	
Wireless application ability	
Wireless application ability mode	
Telemarketing/Telesales	
Call management	
Scripting	
Call recording	
Call statistics/reporting	
Auto-dialing	
Marketing	
Campaign management	
Marketing (media) encyclopedia	
Predictive modeling tools	
Product/price configurator	
Search engine marketing	
Customer lifetime value	
Customer survey management	
Literature fulfillment	
Letter writing/mail merge capabilities	
Lead Management	
Optimization	
Incubation	
Qualification/prioritization	
Routing	
Tracking	
Partner Relationship Management (PRM)	
Channel program management	
Opportunity management	
Reporting capabilities	
Sales management	
Marketing	
Lead management	
Eservice	
Knowledge Management	
Information feeds	
Search engines	
Inference engines	
Document management	
Business Analytics	
Pre-defined reports	
User-defined reporting	
Pre-defined queries	
Ad hoc query generator	

Automatic roll-up/drill down capabilities	
Forecasting/planning tools	
Graphical or statistical modeling tools	
Dashboard/portal interface for key indicators	
Notification of Web site updates/changes	
Alert/alarm capabilities	
Ebusiness	
Personalization	
Portal capabilities	
Content management	
Storefront	
Order/transaction processing	
Cross-selling	
Online customer behavior analysis and reporting	
Supply Chain Management	
Eprocurement	
Interfaces to B2B exchanges/software packages	
Logistics management	
Product lifecycle management	
Project Management	
Project tasks/deliverables	
Contractor/subcontract relationships	
Project resource allocation	
Time/expense management	
Six Sigma workflow methodology module	
Employee Relationship Management	
Job postings/application qualifications	
Employee performance	
Employee training, skills	
Compensation management	
Equipment management	

TECHNICAL FEATURES	DESCRIPTION
Workflow	
Process configurability	
Alerts/notifications	
Task reassignment	
Workflow personalization	
Architectural Consistency	
Are all your software modules on the same architecture?	
Are all your software modules seamlessly integrated together?	
Technical Specifications	
Desktop/laptop operating systems supported	
Handheld operating systems supported	
Application server operating systems supported	
Wireless technologies supported	
Scalability	
Users per application server	
Web services capability	
XML integration	
SOAP integration points	
XSLT & CSS support	
ERP integration	
Interactive voice response integration	
Point solution integration	
Specific links/hook into third party business intelligence software	
Bulk email distribution	
Email brought into CRM system without integration with local resources	
Telephony switch and/or PBX integration	
Software programming language(s) used for development	
Software architecture(s)	
Current architecture release date	
First software release date and platform(s)	
Last software release date and platform(s)	
Security architecture	
Network single sign-on compliant	
Directory support	
Minimum hardware requirements for desktop/laptop client	
Minimum hardware requirements for application server	
Minimum hardware requirements for handhelds	
Toolkits used in software development and customization	
Database servers natively supported	
Application server software	
COM and/or CORBA compliant	
Laptop databases supplied with package	
Handheld databases supplied with package	
Database protocols	
Connection mode	
Client-to-server synchronization	
Server-to-server database synchronization supported	
Portal technology tools supported	
Speech recognition supported	
Thin-client supported	
Source code available/included	
Office productivity package integration	
Bi-directional integration with groupware platforms	

IMPLEMENTATION	DESCRIPTION
Integration	
EAI tool	
EAI vendor partnerships	
OTLP integration capabilities	
Batch integration capabilities	
Integration templates, examples	
Pre-defined integration points	
Implementation Team	
Internal consulting services for implementation	
Size of internal consulting services	
Partner network for implementation	
Size of partner network	
Partner certification process	
Certification classes/average class duration	
Certification exams	
Administering certification exams	
Re-training/re-certification process	
Time and Cost	
Typical implementation duration for 50 users with minimum customization	
Typical implementation cost expressed as a ratio to software license cost	
Configuration	
Add business specific fields-types	
Modify list contents	
Restrict data entry to predefined pick lists	
Identify required and non-required fields	
Modify forms	
Set permissions for different user groups at the form level	
Set permissions for different user groups at the record level	
Set up workflow processes	
Customization	
Creation of calls to external business application	
Dependent lists	
Creation of application behavior based on values entered into particular fields	
Creation of business specific forms and tables that integrate with the customer's application and database	
Data Conversion	
Import of records from multiple sources via data import tool	
Available data import formats	
Dynamic field mapping capability through the user interface	
Creation of relationships between records via the import tool	

REAL-TIME FEATURES	DESCRIPTION
Real-time dashboard	
Real-time analytics	
Real-time currency conversion	
Real-time accounting integration	
Service-oriented architectures functionality	
Rapid application development tools	
Workflow building tools	
Business object configuration	
Mobile-device implementation	

USER FRIENDLINESS/SUPPORT	DESCRIPTION
Help function	
Help menu	
Context-sensitive help	
Detailed error messages	
Internationalization	
Multi-currency	
Multi-lingual module support	
Translation capabilities/integration	
Foreign office locations	
International support	
Training	
Range of available options	
Training charges	
Support	
On-site support	
Phone support	
Toll-free number	
Technical and user documentation	
Web, bulletin board, online forums	
Maintenance/support charges	
Software warrantee period	

Top CRM Software Solutions

Enterprise Solutions

1. Amdocs CRM v. 6 from Amdocs Limited (www.amdocs.com)

2. C2 CRM v. 8.0 from Clear Technologies, Inc. (www.clear technologies.com)

3. CMS 9.0/Oncontact V v. 5.2 from Oncontact Software Corp. (www.oncontact.com)

4. ExSellence 5.0 from Optima Technologies, Inc. (www.optima-tech.com)

5. FirstWave CRM v. 3.1 from FirstWave Technologies, Inc. (www.firstwave.com)

6. growBusiness Solutions v. 3.1 from Software Innovation ASA (www.software-innovation.com)

7. Infor CRM from Infor (www.infor.com)

8. mySAP CRM from SAP AG (www.sap.com)

9. Onyx 6.0 from Onyx Software (www.onyx.com)

10. PeopleSoft CRM from Oracle's PeopleSoft (www.oracle.com/peoplesoft)

11. Pivotal v. 9.0 from Pivotal Corp. (www.pivotal.com)

12. Salesforce.com from Salesforce.com (www.salesforce.com)

13. Saratoga CRM 6.5.3 from Saratoga Systems, Inc. (www.saratoga systems.com)

14. Siebel 8.0 from Oracle's Siebel (www.oracle.com/siebel)

15. Tibco Process RM v. 9.0 from TIBCO (www.tibco.com); update 7.0 from update software AG (www.update.com)*

*There was a tie for the 15th position

(Source: ISM's Top 15 CRM Software Selections for 2007, ISM, Inc., Bethesda, Maryland)

Small Business Solutions

1. Ardexus MODE v. 5.5 from Ardexus, Inc. (www.ardexus.com)

2. C2 CRM v. 8.0 from Clear Technologies, Inc. (www.clear technologies.com)

3. CMS v. 9.0/Oncontact V v. 5.2 from Oncontact Software Corp. (www.oncontact.com)

4. Goldmine v. 7.0.3 & HEAT from FrontRange Solutions, Inc. (www.frontrange.com)

5. Maximizer Enterprise 9.5 from Maximizer Software, Inc. (www.maximizer.com)

6. Microsoft CRM 3.0 from Microsoft Corp. (www.microsoft.com)

7. NetSuite CRM v. 11.0 & NetSuite v. 11.0 from NetSuite, Inc. (www.netsuite.com)

8. Powertrak v. 8.02 from Axonom, Inc. (www.axonom.com)

9. Relavis CRM 7.0 from Relavis Corp. (www.relavis.com)

10. RightNow CRM v. 8.0 from RightNow Technologies, Inc. (www.rightnow.com)

11. Sage CRM 100/200 v. 6.0 from Sage Software (www.sage software. com)

12. Sage SalesLogix v. 7.0 from Sage Software (www.sage software.com)

13. Salesforce.com from Salesforce.com (www.salesforce.com)

14. SalesPage CRM from SalesPage Technologies, LLC (www.sales page.com)

15. Salesplace 2006.3.2 from Interchange Solutions (www.sales place.com); Siebel CRM OnDemand from Siebel Systems, Inc. (www.siebel.com); StayinFront CRM v. 9.3 from StayinFront, Inc. (www.stayinfront.com)*

*There was a three-way tie for the 15th position

(Source: ISM's Top 15 CRM Software Selections for 2007, ISM, Inc., Bethesda, Maryland)

Sources to Assist in CRM
Software Selection

Publications

Many magazines that feature CRM-related information provide articles about CRM software and issues that are specific to areas such as ebusiness, lead tracking, sales force automation, and more. Magazines that have regular coverage of CRM issues include:

- *CRM*

- *CIO*

- *Computerworld*

- *InfoWorld*

Other publications feature material about CRM, computer and software issues, and sometimes software reviews and analysis. These publications include:

- *EWeek*

- *Information Week*

- *Mobile Enterprise*

- *Selling Power*

- *Sales & Marketing Management*

- *Wireless Review*

- *PC Magazine*

A word of caution: Articles found in some of these publications may be based solely on vendor input, whereby vendors fill out and return the magazine's standard form along with promotional literature and brochures. Take note if the magazine has actually tested and analyzed the software in question.

Trade Shows/Conferences

Trade shows and conferences can be an excellent way to find out more about CRM automation (e.g., destinationCRM's annual conference exhibition). Speakers with expertise in this field can provide useful information. Trade shows and conferences also often have a vendor exhibition attached to the show or conference, where you can view CRM software.

To decide which trade show or conference you should attend, we recommend asking the vendors, who will provide trade show or conference brochures along with free passes to the exhibition. There are several regional events coordinated by chapters of Sales and Marketing Executives International (SMEI) and the CRM Association. The American Marketing Association also has conferences where sales and marketing automation is a regular topic. More information on dates and locations of the trade shows can be obtained by searching the Web.

Attending a CRM conference can provide a wealth of knowledge about industry trends, vendors, and products. In addition, these shows typically offer excellent seminars conducted by leading experts. But because there's much information available and you have only a few days to take it all in, you need to prepare a game plan. Here are a few guidelines:

- **Assess the show** – Start by learning what the show has to offer. Ask the conference promoter to send a show guide with information on the technical seminars and special presentations, as well as an exhibitor listing and exhibition hall floor plan. Study the brochure and use it to schedule your activities. To avoid any scheduling conflicts, be sure to list the seminars you want to attend, including date, time, and room number. Once you get to the show, prepare a list of potential vendors to visit.

- **Determine your goals** – To ensure that all of your company's CRM issues are addressed, make a list of goals you want to accomplish at the conference. If you're the only person from your company attending the show, ask colleagues for their input.

- **Develop a specific plan for seeking expert advice** – Plan to meet with seminar speakers. Be prepared with a list of questions about your project and issues that you want addressed. Set up a time to meet with experts when they have more time to discuss your project. If that isn't an option, keep a list in hand and talk to important speakers immediately after the seminar. Speakers are interested in furthering the industry and helping CRM projects succeed, so don't be shy.

- **Research show exhibitors** – Use the Web to gain preliminary information about a company's niche, products, and customers. If you need more in-depth information, talk to a representative. You'll save valuable time at the show by focusing only on those companies capable of matching your project's technical and business requirements. Be sure to take advantage of all these vendors being located in the same place by arranging a demon-stration of each promising CRM software package.

- **Talk to the show promoter** – Conference promoters can usually provide additional tips and information to help take the stress out of attending an out-of-town conference. For instance, many provide shuttle bus service to and from the conference center through selected hotels. Also, ask about hotel and airfare dis-counts that might be available.

Remember: Attending a conference is an investment in time and money. By devising a strategy before embarking on your journey, you'll get more value out of the price of attendance.

Web Sites and Forums

There are now numerous Web sites that provide CRM-related informa-tion, resources, and links to other CRM Web sites. If you want to find back-ground information about CRM industry topics and software, we suggest that you peruse the following Web sites:

- IT Toolbox CRM (www.crmassist.com)

- Destination CRM (www.destinationcrm.com)

- CRMCommunity.com (www.crmcommunity.com)

- MyCustomer.com (www.mycustomer.com)

- SearchCRM.com (www.searchcrm.com)

- CRM Daily (www.crm-daily.com)

- InformationWeek.com (www.informationweek.com)

- Computerworld.com (www.computerworld.com)

- CNET.com (www.cnet.com)

- CRMToday (www.crm2day.com)

- eCRMGuide.com (www.ecrmguide.com)

- ISM, Inc. (www.ismguide.com)

Research Companies

There are a number of organizations that publish research about information systems technology, including CRM technology, CRM industry statistics, etc. These organizations include the following:

- ISM, Inc. (www.ismguide.com)

- IDC (www.idc.com)

- Aberdeen Group (www.aberdeen.com)

- Forrester (www.forrester.com)

- In-Stat (www.instat.com)

- Yankee Group (www.yankeegroup.com)

- AMR Research (www.amrresearch.com)

- Beagle Research (www.beagleresearch.com)

Although the quality and price of the published information will vary, many of the analyses provided by these organizations can be useful.

Support/Training References

The following companies can provide support/training for members of your organization. Some also provide integration services for selected CRM software products.

- Cambridge Technology Partners Headquarters, acquired by Novell (www.ctp.com)

- Novell, Inc. (www.novell.com)

- C3i Inc. (www.c3i-inc.com)

- MICOR Solutions LLC (www.micorsolutions.com)

- Tech Resource Group, Inc. (www.trginc.com)

- Clarkston Consulting (www.clarkstonconsulting.com)

- AnswerThink Consulting Group (www.answerthink.com)

- Extraprise Group (www.extraprise.com)

- BearingPoint Inc. (www.bearingpoint.com)

Application Service Providers

Broad-Based ASPs

EDS (www.eds.com)

EDS provides strategy, implementation, business transformation, and operational solutions for clients managing the business and technology complexities of the digital economy.

IBM (www.ibm.com)

IBM specializes in the creation, development, and manufacture of the industry's most advanced information technologies, including computer systems, software, networking systems, storage devices, and microelectronics.

Jamcracker (www.jamcracker.com)

Jamcracker is the first pure-play application service aggregator. It is assembling a portfolio of pretested offerings from several ASPs and Internet-based software vendors, which it will offer to enterprises through their own customized application portal. The environment provides secure, single sign-on, 24/7 global support, and full accountability for service levels. The choice of applications covers finance, human resources, CRM, and other business operations. Jamcracker offers IT services such as remote access, desktop management, and infrastructure monitoring.

Oracle On Demand (www.oracle.com/ondemand)

In September 1998, Oracle became the first major applications vendor to offer ASP services based on its own applications and database technology. While many of the software vendors have been trying to negotiate deals with as many ASPs as they can, Oracle has decided that if you want an Oracle solution, you will have to come to Business OnLine for the hosting.

Oracle does not rent the applications. It requires that users purchase the software and an annual maintenance contract before Oracle On Demand will host it. Customization and implementation fees are also required.

Concur (www.concur.com)

Concur provides ASP applications in the areas of CRM, financial management, executive productivity, human resources management, travel, and expense reporting. The company targets Fortune 1000 companies in the retail, publishing, manufacturing, professional services, high-tech, and healthcare fields. Concur supports Siebel for CRM, ATG for customer service, and Microsoft Great Plains for financial management.

USi (www.usi.net)

USi has its own data centers and touts this as a strategic business advantage unlike other ASPs that say they focus on their core competencies and application hosting. In addition to being an ASP, USi has a program that application developers and other ASPs can use to become an instant ASP. For its CRM offerings, USi has teamed with Siebel Systems.

USi has two different ERP offerings: Lawson and PeopleSoft. The company has also teamed with BroadVision for its ecommerce offerings, and Ariba for eprocurement offerings that provide a full end-to-end solution.

For publishing high-value B2B business data on the Web, USi has partnered with Actuate, and for internal data mining and business intelligence, Group 1 software is offered. USi fuses the Group 1 software modules for data extraction, transformation, and loading.

Small- and Mid-Sized Business ASPs

NaviSite (www.navisite.com)

NaviSite provides outsourced enterprise application solutions for CRM, ERP, ebusiness, and productivity applications. The company's service offerings include application deployment, upgrade services, secure hosting, and application management. NaviSite deploys and hosts applications for midmarket companies. NaviSite's customers include manufacturing, professional services, financial services, healthcare, distribution, and trade services firms.

TeleComputing (www.telecomputing.com)

TeleComputing Enterprise, which offers applications for the midmarket, has also begun to design service offerings for larger companies that have multiple offices. In addition to the CRM and ERP offerings, this organization is also one of the first to offer the full complement of Microsoft products via the Web.

The representative list of applications currently includes MS Office, MS Outlook, MS Exchange Server, MS Access, MS Project, SalesLogix CRM, and Microsoft Great Plains ERP.

NetSuite (www.netsuite.com)

Since NetSuite's first online accounting application launched in 1999, the company has surpassed the 7,000-customer milestone, making it the leading provider of integrated online ERP/CRM application services for the small and medium business market. The company has expanded its product offerings by delivering completely integrated ERP and CRM suites, including Oracle Small Business Suite, along with the NetSuite and NetCRM applications.

Specialized CRM ASPs

CrystalWare (www.crystal-ware.com)

CrystalWare, which was formed as a software development and professional services provider, expanded into providing ASP offerings. Today, it provides a suite of CRM applications for small- to mid-sized enterprises via the Internet. CrystalWare has developed CRM applications including several of the other specialized CRM ASPs.

Onyx (www.onyx.com)

Onyx is a "traditional" packaged CRM solution that offers functionality in CRM such as contact, account, sales, time, marketing, and lead management. The Web-based Onyx CRM application is sold on a licensed model to customers.

Pivotal (www.pivotal.com)

Pivotal is another traditional packaged CRM solution with tight integration to Microsoft products for the front and back office. The Pivotal CRM application provides comprehensive CRM functionality to its users. Although the software is generally sold as a licensed model to customers, Pivotal offers its CRM application on the ASP model via third-party ASP provider USi.

Salesforce.com (www.salesforce.com)

The Salesforce.com business model is designed to provide a comprehensive CRM application that can be used to get a sales organization up and running within days. Founded in March 1999 by Marc Benioff, a former Oracle executive, Salesforce.com has put together a well-known management team. The online application provides forecasts by employee, contact and account management, and reporting.

RightNow (www.rightnow.com)

RightNow is a Web-based CRM ASP that offers sales force automation (SFA) tools, including account and contact management, forecasting, and reporting, primarily to small companies. The company has also entered into agreements with business content and service providers, including Dow Jones & Co. and Hoover's Inc. The site provides support for PDAs and scheduling tools such as MS Outlook. Import tools for ACT! and GoldMine are also integrated into the site.

Glossary of Terms

ACD. Automatic Call Distributor or Distribution. Procedure of automatically routing an incoming call to the next available rep.

ActiveX. A segment of binary codes that can run only on the platform for which it was compiled. Developed by Microsoft. Formerly known as Network OLE control.

ADSL. Asymmetric Digital Subscriber Line. A method of sending high-speed data (digitized movies) over the existing pair of wires from a telephone company's central office to most residences.

AJAX. Asynchronous JavaScript and XML. A Web development technique used for creating interactive Web applications. The intent is to make Web pages act more responsive by exchanging small amounts of data with the server behind the scenes, so that the entire Web page does not have to be reloaded each time the user requests a change.

ANI. Automatic Number Identification. A telephone service that provides the telephone number of the incoming call.

AppCenter Server. A Microsoft product that provides features to manage a large cluster of Web servers and application servers, including load balancing, fault tolerance, replication, and testing tools.

Applets. Software components that work with other software components to create or make up a full application.

Application Server. In local area networks, a node that is dedicated to hosting a networked application; this server usually does not host database applications, email, or any other enterprise application.

API. Application Program Interface. A set of formalized software calls and routines that can be referenced by an application program to access underlying network services.

ASP. Application Service Provider. Uses the Internet or private extranet to host, manage, and support applications for companies. Also known as SaaS, or software as a service.

Authentication. The function of ensuring that the receiver can positively identify the sender to prove identity before access to network resources is granted.

Authorization. A method of establishing access privileges for users.

Backbone. A transmission facility designed to interconnect low-speed distribution channels or clusters of dispersed user devices.

Bandwidth. The data-carrying capacity of a communications channel measured (in Hertz) as the difference between the highest and lowest frequencies of the channel.

Baud. As a unit of signaling speed. The speed in baud is the number of line changes (in frequency, amplitude, etc.) or events per second.

BizTalk. An initiative from Microsoft to spearhead XML usage; the BizTalk Framework provides a special set of XML tags that provide a common transport envelope for wrapping XML documents for B2B and application-to-application interoperability.

BizTalk Server. An integration product from Microsoft that combines elements of messaging middleware and Web-based application servers.

BlackBerry. A handheld wireless email device manufactured by Research in Motion (RIM) that integrates with email servers and groupware applications such as MS Exchange.

Blogs. A Web site where entries are written in chronological order and commonly displayed in reverse chronological order; many blogs provide commentary or news on a particular subject.

Bps. Bits per second. The basic unit of measurement for serial data transmission capacity: Kbps for kilo (thousands of) bits per second; Mbps for mega (millions of) bits per second; Gbps for giga (billions of) bits per second; Tbps for tera (trillions of) bits per second.

Broadband PCS. The new implementation of Personal Communication Services (PCS) using digital technologies such as GSM, CDMA, and TDM.

Bulgy Client. A term for computer clients that maintain more information than "thin client" computers such as network computers.

Business Intelligence. A broad category of applications and technologies for gathering, storing, analyzing, and providing access to data to help enterprise users make better business decisions.

Byte. A unit of information used mainly when referring to data transfer, semiconductor capacity, and data storage; can also refer to a character or a group of eight (sometimes seven) bits used to represent a character.

C#. C Sharp. An object-oriented programming language from Microsoft that is based on C++ with elements from Visual Basic and Java.

Cable Modem. A device that enables a user to hook up a PC to a local cable TV line and receive data at about 1.5 Mbps, which is faster than telephone modems.

Call Back. A system security procedure that calls back an incoming dial-up caller and verifies the validity of the caller, usually via password before granting access to the system.

Call Blending. Occurs when call center reps are trained to handle incoming and outgoing calls.

Call Center. A central place where customer and other telephone calls are handled by an organization, usually with some amount of computer automation.

CCITT. Comite Consultatif Internationale de Telegraphique et Telephonique. An international consulting committee that set worldwide communications standards (such as V.21, V.22, and X.25); was replaced by the ITU-TSS.

CDE. Common Desktop Environment. An email platform common to UNIX platforms that is also becoming a standard platform for Java-based environments.

CDF. Channel Definition Format. An XML standard used in conjunction with Microsoft Active Channel and Smart Offline Favorites technologies. It is used to define a Web site's content and structure.

CDMA. Code Division Multiple Access. An improvement on AMPS and TDMA cellular telephone that uses a technology called direct sequence spread spectrum to provide more conversations for a given amount of bandwidth and digital service.

CDPD. Cellular Digital Packet Data. An industry standard for data communication at 19,200 bps across unused portions of analog cellular voice channels.

Cellular. Telephone and data networks that divide an area into regional cells, each of which has its own central transmission facilities.

Centralized Data Warehouse. A data warehouse implementation in which a single warehouse serves the need of several business units simultaneously with a single data model that spans the needs of the multiple business divisions

CGI. Common Gateway Interface. A standard for interfacing external applications with information servers, such as http or Web servers.

CICS. Customer Information Control System. A transaction server that runs primarily on IBM mainframe systems under z/OS or z/VSE; CICS on distributed platforms is called TXSeries and it is available on AIX, Windows, Solaris, and HP-UX.

Circuit-switching. A technique in which physical circuits are transferred to complete connections.

Client. A device or entity in a distributed computing architecture that requests services and information.

CO. Central Office. The building in which common telephone carriers terminate customer circuits.

Collaborative Browsing. A software-enabled technique that allows someone in an enterprise contact center to interact with a customer by using the customer's Web browser to demonstrate.

Collaborative Computing. Software that enables users to set up a workgroup and exchange documents with version control, chat on project issues, and update schedules.

COM. Component Object Model. A model for binary code developed by Microsoft. A broad set of object-oriented technology standards enables programmers to develop objects that can be accessed by any COM-compliant application. Both OLE and ActiveX are based on COM.

Communication Protocol. The rules governing the exchange of information between devices on a data link (such as TCP/IP, IPX/SPX, NFS, X.25, and others).

Communication Server. An intelligent device (a computer) providing communications functions; an intelligent, specially configured node on a LAN that enables remote communications access and exit for LAN users.

Contact Management. A software application that keeps track of clients; this has grown over the years from a PIM (personal information manager) to a CRM (customer relationship management) and ERM (enterprise relationship management) application, which includes sales, customer service, and marketing, and the internal activities of the organization.

CORBA. Common Object Request Broker Architecture. A standardized blueprint worked out by the OMG (Object Management Group) defining how application objects and ORBs can cooperate to deliver services or perform processes independent of platform, network, or location.

CRM. Customer Relationship Management. An enterprise integration of the following 11 components: sales/sales management; time management; telemarketing/telesales; customer contact center; emarketing; supply-chain management; business analytics; multimodal access; data-sharing tools; ebusiness; and field service support.

CTI. Computer Telephony Integration. Enables computers to know about and control telephony functions such as making and receiving voice, fax, and data calls, phone directory services, and caller identification.

Customer Contact Center. A central point in an enterprise from which all customer contacts are managed.

Data Cleansing. Refers to the elimination of anomalies or mistakes in data that will otherwise impede with its intended usage.

Data Completeness. An indication of whether all the data necessary to meet the current and future business information demand are available in the data resource.

Data Extract. Data that normally reside on an operational system and are removed from that system to load into a data warehouse.

Data Loading. Periodically updating and loading data, once they are mapped and cleansed, into a single repository where they will be used by the organization.

Data Mapping. Merging databases into single consistent structure, requiring transformations, calculations, and other "mappings" from one context to the other.

Data Mining. A process of analyzing large amounts of data to identify hidden relationships, patterns, and associations; the process of using the results of data exploration to adjust or enhance business strategies; or a technique using software tools geared for the user who typically does not know exactly what he's searching for, but is looking for particular patterns or trends.

Data Rate, Data Signaling Rate. A measure of how quickly data is transmitted, expressed in bps.

Data Warehouse. A collection of data designed to support management decision making.

Database Marketing. A term describing the art/science of selecting a database of a potential set of customers for a given product or need.

Database Server. In local area networks, a node dedicated to providing mass data storage services to the other stations on the network.

DCOM. Distributed Component Object Model. An extension of COM that provides support for objects distributed across a network. DCOM was developed by Microsoft and submitted to standards bodies.

DES. Data Encryption Standard. A scheme approved by the National Bureau of Standards that encrypts data for security purposes.

DHTML. Dynamic HTML. HTML documents with dynamic content; the three components of DHTML pages are HTML, JavaScript, and cascading style sheets. The three components are tied together with DOM, the Document Object Model.

Digital Certificate. An electronic "credit card" that establishes a user's credentials when doing business or other transactions on the Web.

Digital Data. Information transmitted in a coded form from a computer that is represented by discrete signal elements.

Digital Service. High-speed, digital-data transmission services offered for lease by telecommunication service providers. Services include ADSL, HDSL, ISDN, Frame Relay, T1, and dedicated or switched 56-Kbps transmission lines.

DNS. Domain Name Services. Directory naming convention used for IP addresses, network user names, locations, etc.

DOM. Document Object Model. A programming interface specification developed by the World Wide Web Consortium (W3C) that lets a programmer create and modify HTML pages and XML documents as full-fledged program objects.

EAA. Enterprise Application Architecture. The structure of enterprise application components, their interrelationships, and the principles and guidelines governing their design and evolution over time.

EAI. Enterprise Application Integration. Translating data and commands from one application format into another.

Ebusiness. The conduct of business on the Internet or extranet. Derived from such terms as email and ecommerce.

Ecommerce. The buying and selling of goods and services on the Internet, especially the World Wide Web.

EDI. Electronic Data Interchange. The intercompany computer-to-computer transmission of business data in a standard format.

EIP. Enterprise Integration Portals. Web-based portals that use the features of a consumer information portal to distribute mission-critical enterprise data, applications, and processes to employees and partners connected to the Internet.

EJB. Enterprise JavaBeans. A component software architecture (from Sun Microsystems) used to build Java applications that run in the server.

Encryption. The function of ensuring that data in transit may only be read by the intended recipient. Encryption disguises/scrambles the contents of a message as it travels over a network.

Enterprise Data. Data that is defined for use across a corporate environment.

ERP. Enterprise Resource Planning. A business management system that integrates all the back-office business functions of a business (inventory, sales, marketing, planning, manufacturing, finance).

ESBs. Enterprise Service Buses. A new breed of middleware products that offer XML and SOAP-based integration platforms to be deployed pervasively in the enterprise network.

Ethernet. A network standard first developed by Xerox, and refined by DEC and Intel, that interconnects personal computers and transmits at 10 megabits per second.

Exchange. A unit established by a common carrier for communications administration services in a specific geographic area, such as a city.

Extranet. An intranet that is partially accessible to authorized outsiders.

Fast Ethernet. Any 100-Mbps ethernet-based networking scheme.

Fat Client. A term for PCs that have internal storage and are connected or occasionally connected to the network.

FDDI. Fiber Distributed Data Interface. An American National Standards Institute (ANSI) specified standard for fiber-optic links with data rates up to 100 Mbps.

FFA. Field Force Automation. Term for applications and devices that allow mobile employees easy access of inventory management data, work orders, dispatch components, history, and other multiple features.

File Server. In local area networks, a node dedicated to providing file- and mass data-storage services to the other stations on the network.

Filtering. In LAN technology, discarding packets that do not meet the criteria for forwarding.

Firewall. The gatekeeper used to qualify users or limit access to files; can either be hardware or software applications.

Firewire. A high-speed serial peripheral interface invented by Apple to replace SCSI.

FLEX. A digital transmission protocol developed by Motorola that allows better control for one-way and two-way paging networks.

Follow-the-Sun Support. Support options that are available to users worldwide regardless of time zone.

Fractional T-1. A service aimed at customers who don't need or can't afford all 24 channels of a full T1 line.

Frame Relay. A packet network service that relies on the data integrity inherent in digital transmissions to speed up transmission.

FTAM. File Transfer, Access, and Management. An OSI application utility that provides transparent access to files stored on dissimilar systems.

FTP. File Transfer Protocol. An upper-level TCP/IP service that allows files to be copied across a network.

G3. Third Generation. The latest generation of cellular services that is based on larger bandwidth to allow transmission of data, voice, and limited video.

Gateway. A hardware-software combination that connects two LANs (or a LAN and a host computer) that operate different protocols.

GPS. Global Positioning System. A system of 24 satellites, each of which orbits the Earth every 12 hours at a height of 20,200 km; when receivers view three satellites simultaneously, latitude and longitude can be calculated.

Groupware. Software designed for network use by a group of users working on a related project; applications might include sales team selling, calendaring, bulletin boards, project management, and other global software application environments.

GSM. Global System for Mobile Communications (previously Groupe Spécial Mobile). The current Pan-European (also Pacific Rim and South African) digital cellular telephone standard developed by the European Telecommunications Standards Institute's (ETSI) Groupe Spécial Mobile.

GSTN. General Switched Telephone Network. See **PSTN.**

GUI. Graphical User Interface. A graphics-based user interface that incorporates icons, pull-down menus, and a mouse; now the standard way users interact with a computer.

Handshaking. Exchange of predetermined signals between two devices, establishing a connection or providing flow control.

HDSL. High-Bit-Rate Digital Subscriber Line. A technology developed by Bellcore that provides full-duplex T-1 service (using two twisted pairs of cable) over greater distances than the alternate mark inversion encoding that is traditionally used by T1.

Header. The control information added to the beginning of a message; contains the destination address, source address, and message number.

HTML. Hypertext Mark-up Language. A platform-independent resource definition language that specifies interfaces and graphic representations and assembles applications from components.

HTTP. Hypertext Transfer Protocol. Protocol that enables Web browsers to interact with other applications or applets.

Hz. Hertz. A measure of frequency or bandwidth; 1 Hz equals one cycle per second.

IDE. Integrated Development Environment. A software application that provides comprehensive facilities to computer programmers for software development.

IDL. Interface Definition Language. A descriptive language that is independent of any programming language; the IDL defines object interfaces and lets an object reveal to potential clients what it can do.

IEEE. Institute of Electrical and Electronic Engineers. An international society of professional engineers that issues widely used networking standards.

IETF. International Engineering Task Force. A large, open, international community of network designers, operators, vendors, and researchers concerned with the evolution of the Internet architecture and the smooth operation of the Internet.

IFC. Internet Foundation Classes. A set of Java classes that help speed development of complex, robust, network-based applications.

IIOP. Internet Inter-ORB Protocol. An open industry standard for distributing objects that will allow browsers to interact with enterprise-wide legacy systems based on the CORBA distributed objects standard.

IMAP. Internet Mail Access Protocol. Provides robust messaging.

IMAP4. Internet Message Access Protocol, Version 4. Allows a client to access and manipulate email messages on a server; permits manipulation of remote message folders or mailboxes in a way that is functionally equivalent to local mailboxes.

Intranet. Widely used term to describe the application of Internet technologies in internal corporate networks.

IP. Internet Protocol. The protocol used in gateways to connect networks at the OSI Network Level (Layer 3) and above.

IPCC. Internet Protocol Contact Center. A feature-rich contact center application that routes customer contacts—phone, email, Web, and fax—to customer service agents located anywhere on the enterprise network.

IPX. Internet Packet exchange. A communication protocol in Novell NetWare that creates, maintains, and terminates connections between network devices, such as workstations and servers; an early competitor to TCP/IP.

ISAPI. Internet Server API. A replaceable, dynamic-link library (DLL) that the server calls whenever there is an HTTP request.

ISDN. Integrated Services Digital Network. A CCITT standard for a network that accommodates a variety of mixed digital-transmission services.

ISDN BRI. ISDN Basic Rate Interface. Referred to as 2B+D, provides two 64-Kbps digital channels to the user's desktop.

ISDN PRI. ISDN Primary Rate Interface. An ISDN service that provides 23 B channels plus one D channel in North America and Japan, and 30 B channels plus one D channel in Europe and Australia.

ISP. Internet Service Provider. A company that provides end users and companies with access to the Internet via POPs (points of presence).

IVR. Interactive Voice Response. An automated phone answering system that responds with a voice menu and allows the user to make choices and enter information via the keypad.

J2ME. Java 2 Micro Edition. Sun Microsystem's Java programming environment for mobile devices such as smartphones.

Java. A platform independent programming language similar in nature to C++ developed by Sun Microsystems; also called applets, which are different from ordinary applications in that they reside on the network in centralized servers.

Java Beans API. An application programming interface that integrates Java, ActiveX, OpenDoc, and Live Connect objects into a new cross-platform framework.

Java OS. A highly compact operating system that runs Java applications on devices (network computers, cellular phones, PDAs).

Java/RMI. Relies on a protocol called the Java Remote Method Protocol (JRMP); Java relies on Java Object Serialization that allows objects to be marshaled (or transmitted) as a stream.

Java Servers. Server software designed to support Java applications and clients.

Java Virtual Machine. A layer of software embedded in computer operating systems such as UNIX or Windows that enables the computer to run Java applications.

JDBC. Java Database Connectivity. A protocol that provides SQL-oriented connectivity to databases.

Jini. A programming language that Sun Microsystems calls "spontaneous networking." Using this architecture, users are able to plug printers, storage devices, speakers, and other devices directly into a network, and every other computer, device, and user on the network knows that the new device has been added and is available.

JIT. Just-in-time Compilation. Used in the Java computing environment. Where the Java application code is dynamically downloaded from server to client on demand and compiled upon arrival at the client.

Kbps. Kilobits per second. Standard measurement of data rate and transmission capacity (1 Kbps equals 1,000 bits per second).

Kilobyte. A standard quantity measurement for disk and diskette storage and semiconductor circuit capacity (1 kilobyte of memory equals 1,024 bytes or 8-bit characters of computer memory).

L2F. Layer 2 Forwarding. A protocol created by Cisco Systems that is designed to tunnel the link level of higher-level protocols over the Internet.

LAN. Local Area Network. A data-communications system confined to a limited geographic area (up to 6 miles or about 10 kilometers) with moderate to high data rates (100 Kbps to 50 Mbps); the area served may consist of a single building, a cluster of buildings, or a campus type of arrangement.

Language Mappings. Rules that specify how IDL is translated into a programming language, such as Java, C++, or Inferno, as defined in the IDL mapping for that programming language.

Latency. The interval between the time a network station seeks access to a transmission channel and when access is granted or received (equivalent to waiting time).

Layer. Refers to a collection of related network processing functions in the OSI reference model; one level of a hierarchy of functions.

LDAP. Lightweight Directory Access Protocol. A protocol used to access a directory listing; LDAP services are seamless across all operating environments and applications on the intranet and Internet.

LDPA. Lightweight Document Printing Application. Proposed IETF standard for printing across the Internet and corporate intranets.

Leased Line. A telephone line reserved for the exclusive use of a leasing customer without interexchange switching arrangements.

LEC. Local exchange, local central office. The exchange or central office in which the subscriber's lines terminate.

Link Layer. Layer 2 of the OSI reference model, also known as the Data Link Layer (preferred usage).

Linux. An open-source version of the UNIX operating system.

LMS. Learning Management Systems. A term used to describe software tools designed to manage user learning interventions; goes far beyond conventional training records management and reporting.

MAN. Municipal Area Network. An extended network or cluster of networks serving a city, an academic or business campus, or any site featuring several widely separated buildings.

MAP. Manufacturing Automation Protocol. A suite of networking protocols that track the seven layers of the OSI model; originated by General Motors.

MAPI. Messaging API. Messaging transport layer developed and promoted by Microsoft.

Mbps. Millions of bits per second (bps).

Megabyte, Mbyte, MB, Meg, or M. 1,048,576 bytes is equal to 1,024 kilobytes; basic unit of measurement of mass storage.

Metadata. Data that describes other data; data dictionaries and repositories are examples of metadata.

MHS. Message Handling System. The standard defined by the CCITT as X.400 and by the ISO as Message Oriented Text Interchange Standard (MOTIS).

MHz. Megahertz. A unit of frequency equal to 1,000,000 cycles per second.

Middleware. A general term for any programming that serves to "glue together" or mediate between two separate and often already existing programs.

MIME. Multipart Internet Mail Encoding. SMTP extension that allows audio, binary, and visual data to be included as part of a mail message.

MNP. Microcom Networking Protocol. Networking protocols that include standards for error correction and data compression. MNP is used primarily in modems.

Modem. Modulator-demodulator. Used to convert serial digital data from a transmitting terminal to an analog signal suitable for transmission over a telephone channel, or to reconvert the transmitted analog signal to serial digital data for acceptance by a receiving terminal.

MPEG. Motion Picture Experts Group. A standard for glossy compression of full-motion video.

MSMQ. Microsoft Message Queuing. Provides messaging services to support online transactions between users and programs and between programs.

MTBF. Mean Time Between Failures. A stated or published period of time when a user may expect a device to operate before a failure occurs.

MTS. Microsoft Transaction Server. Provides the transaction services to support online transactions between users and programs and between programs.

Multicast Bit. A bit in the Ethernet addressing structure used to indicate a broadcast message (a message to be sent to all stations).

NAMPS. Motorola's initiative to digitize the AMPS infrastructure so more channels would be available for cellular communications.

NC. Network Computer. Represents a different approach to desktop computers, based on the Java language and Web protocols; it has no permanent local storage.

NDIS. Network Driver Interface Specification. A standard established by Microsoft for writing hardware-independent drivers.

NDMP. Network Data Management Protocol. Proposed IETF protocol that ensures interoperability between different file servers, tape drives, and management software.

.NET. A Web-based development platform from Microsoft that includes tools to develop and deploy Web-based applications that can be accessed from anywhere (browsers, handhelds, cell phones, etc.).

NetWare. A LAN operating system from Novell.

NFS. Network File Server. An extension of TCP/IP that allows files on remote nodes of a network to appear locally connected.

NFS. Network File System. A method of mapping or "mounting" shared remote disk drives so that they appear to be local; developed and licensed by Sun Microsystems.

NNTP. Network News Transport Protocol. An open protocol that allows Internet and intranet servers to interact with ongoing newsgroups.

Notebook. A small portable computer about the size of a standard letter-size notebook.

N-PCS. Narrowband PCS. Two-way paging or enhanced paging.

N-Tier. An application program that is distributed among three or more separate computers in a distributed network.

Object Interface. Defines an object's boundaries and all the operations performed on that object.

Objects. A reusable packet that contains related data (called variables) and procedures (called methods) that can operate on the data.

ODBC. Open Database Connectivity. Microsoft's effort to provide a single API for database (called data sources) access.

OLAP. Online Analytical Processing. Decision support software that allows the user to quickly analyze information that has been summarized into multidimensional views and hierarchies.

OMG. Object Management Group. An organization with 600-plus members formed in 1989 by vendors and users whose mission is "establishing industry guidelines and object management specifications to provide a common framework for distributed application development."

ORB. Object Request Broker. Acts as a middleman connecting objects that request services or functions with objects that can satisfy the request.

OSI. An ISO standard for worldwide data communications; the standard is a framework for implementing communication protocols in seven layers.

Packet-switched Network. A data-communications network that transmits packets.

PAN. Personal Area Network. Refers to a wireless network that operates in the 1- to 5-foot area; either RF or infrared technology is used in this environment.

PBX. Private Branch Exchange. An in-house telephone switching system that interconnects telephone extensions to each other, as well as to the outside telephone network.

PCMCIA. Personal Computer Memory Card International Association. The name of the group that produced the specification for the credit card-sized plug-in boards known as PC cards (initially) for laptop computers.

PCS. Personal Communication Services. The name for a new wireless voice and data communications system with lower transmit power (than standard AMPS cellular telephones), so the telephones can be smaller and lower-cost (since smaller batteries and less-powerful components are needed).

PDA. Personal Digital Assistant. A small, handheld, battery-operated, microprocessor-based device that stores telephone numbers, addresses, and reminders; sends and receives email and faxes (wirelessly); receives pages (just like an alphanumeric pager); and recognizes handwriting.

PMO. Project Management Office. A business or professional enterprise that is the department or group that defines and maintains the standards of process, generally related to project management, within the organization.

Pocket PC. A handheld Windows-based computer that runs the pocket PC operating system (formerly Windows CE).

POP. Point of Presence. An Internet service provider's (ISP) point of entrance into the Internet.

POP. Post Office Protocol. Internet mail server protocol that provides basic message transfer capabilities using SMTP.

POTS. Plain Ordinary Telephone Service. The only type of telephone service available 20 years ago and the lowest common telephone service available everywhere.

PPP. Point-to-Point Protocol. Standardized dial-in protocol for Internet access from client to Internet Point of Presence (POP) equipment.

PPTP. Point-to-Point Tunnel Protocol. Developed by the PPTP forum, a collaboration between Microsoft Corp. and a group of several leading manufacturers of Internet Service Provider (ISP) equipment that enables implementation of secure, multiprotocol Virtual Private Networks (VPNs) through public data networks such as the Internet.

Predictive Dialer. A database with appropriate software that is integrated with a phone system that automatically dials the phone number and routes any "successful" connections to the phone rep(s).

Preview Dialer. A dialing system where the user can see the contact information prior to making or accepting the call.

PRM. Partner Relationship Management. Allows for a more seamless relationship with partners through the management of channel programs, opportunities, sales, marketing, and lead.

PSDN. Packet-Switched Data Network. Provides connections to computers in other parts of the world using the X.25 protocol. The interface between a PSDN and a PSDN user normally operates over a data communications link (an ISDN link). Each PSDN interface is capable of supporting multiple virtual circuits.

PSTN. Public Switched Telephone Network. The telephone system over which calls may be dialed.

QoS. Quality of Service. The ability to define a level of performance in a data communications system; for example, ATM networks specify modes of service that ensure optimum performance for traffic such as real-time voice and video.

RAID. Redundant (or Reliable) Array of Inexpensive Disks. A disk subsystem (that appears as a single large, fast, super-reliable disk drive) composed of more than one (usually equal-sized) disk drives (called an array) to provide improved reliability, response time, and/or storage capacity.

RAS. Remote Access Services. A method used to allow remote computing users to access multiple computing environments from a dial-up connection.

RBOC. Regional Bell Operating Company. One of the regional Bell telephone companies created when AT&T was dismantled in 1984.

Real-Time Enterprise. A new business model for the 21st century where all company departments, customers, suppliers, and partners are electronically connected via internal and Internet applications (the e-enablement of all business functions).

Remote Access. The ability of a computer to reach a device that is some distance away.

RF. Radio-Frequency Modulation. The electromagnetic format in which broadcast and cable TV signals are transmitted.

RFID. Radio Frequency Identification. An automatic identification method, relying on storing and remotely retrieving data using devices called RFID tags or transponders; an RFID tag is an object that can be applied to or incorporated into a product, animal, or person for the purpose of identification using radiowaves.

Router. A network device that examines the network addresses within a given protocol, determines the most efficient pathway to the destination, and routes the data accordingly; operates at the Network Layer of the OSI model.

RSA. A de-facto standard for untappable public-key encryption developed by RSA Data Security Inc.

RSVP. Resource Reservation Protocol. A standard for reserving resources required in each network along an end-to-end path so that an application (likely multimedia) receives the required quality of service.

RTSP. Real Time Streaming Protocol. A proposed standard that was submitted to the IETF for delivery of real-time media over the Internet; RTSP is a communications protocol for control and delivery of real-time media.

SaaS. Software as a Service. A software application delivery model where a software vendor develops a Web-native software application and hosts and operates (either independently or through a third-party) the application for use by its customers over the Internet. Also known as an ASP, or application service provider.

SFA. Sales Force Automation. The first generation of automating the sales force with contact management, forecasting, sales management, and team selling (SFA has evolved into CRM).

SET. Secure Electronic Transactions. A single method, developed by MasterCard, VISA, and several other technology vendors, for consumers and merchants to conduct bankcard transactions securely and easily in cyberspace.

S-HTTP. Secure Hypertext Transfer Protocol. A method that is used to support the encryption and decryption of specific documents sent over the Internet; S-HTTP uses RSA public-key encryption.

Smartphone. A telephone with advanced information access features that is typically a digital cellular telephone providing normal voice service as well as any combination of email, text messaging, pager, Web access, and voice recognition.

S/MIME. Secure Multipurpose Internet Mail Encoding. A standard way to send and receive secure email.

SMS. Short Message Service. A text-message service that enables brief messages (generally 140–160 characters) to be sent and transmitted from a cell phone.

SMTP. Simple Mail Transfer Protocol. Dominant email messaging protocol for use on TCP/IP networks.

SNA. Systems Network Architecture. IBM's proprietary data communication protocols.

SNMP. Simple Network Management Protocol. Services that allow centralized, replicated, and secure management of user information, access control parameters, and server configuration information.

SOA. Service-Oriented Architecture. An architectural style whose goal is to achieve loose coupling among interacting software agents.

SOAP. Simple Object Access Protocol. A protocol from Microsoft, IBM, and others for accessing services on the Web that employs XML syntax to send text commands across the Internet using HTTP.

Social Networking. A group of people that primarily interact via communication media such as letters, telephone, email, computer network, or Usenet rather than face to face. It is also a social structure made of nodes (which are generally individuals or organizations) that are tied by one or more specific types of interdependency, such as values, ideas, friends, kinship, dislike, conflict, trade, Web, Web links, etc.

SONet. Synchronous Optical Network. A synchronous data framing and transmission scheme for (usually single-mode) fiber-optic cable based on multiples of a base rate of 51.84 Mbits.

SQL. Structured Query Language. An English-like, ASCII text, standardized language used to define and manipulate data in a database server.

SSL. Secure Sockets Layer. A security protocol that provides communications privacy over the Internet.

Sub-notebook. A small portable computer that is usually smaller than a standard letter-size notebook and less than 5 pounds.

TAPI. Telephony Application Programming Interface. Microsoft's and Intel's method of integrating phone services and computers so that the user's computer can control the user's phone.

TCP. Transmission Control Protocol. UNIX's connection-oriented Layer 4 protocol (also called transport) that provides an error-free connection between two cooperating programs typically on different computers.

TCP/IP. Transmission Control Protocol/Internet Protocol. A layered set of protocols that allows applications to be shared among PCs, hosts, or workstations in a high-speed communications environment.

TDMA. Time-Division Multiple Access. A high-speed, burst mode of operation that can be used to interconnect LANs; TDMA was first used as a multiplexing technique on shared communications satellites.

Thin Client. Refers to NC, or Network Computer.

TSAPI. Telephony Services Application Programming Interface. AT&T's and Novell's method of integrating phone services and computers.

Tunneling. A technology that allows a network transport protocol to carry information for other protocols within its own packets (for example, IPX data packets can be encapsulated in IP packets for transport across the Internet that isn't normally possible).

UAN. Universal Application Network. An XML-based Web services architecture designed to enable software developers to write code in such a way that if one element changes in inventory, that element is changed across the enterprise's financial, inventory, distribution, manufacturing, and sales systems.

UM. United Messaging. The integration of different streams of communication (email, SMS, fax, voice, video, etc.) into a single, or unified, "message store," accessible from a variety of different devices (e.g., common computer application, telephone).

Unicode Character Set. A character-coding scheme designed to be an extension to ASCII (by using 16 bits for each character rather than ASCII's 7). Virtually every character of every language, as well as many symbols (such as "&"), can be represented in an internationally standard way, and the current complexity of incompatible extended character sets and code pages should be eliminated.

UNIX. A powerful operating system developed at the Bell Technical Laboratories used as the primary operating system on all available computing platforms; presents a competitive alternative to the Microsoft operating system products.

URL. Uniform Resource Locator. The address that is used to specify a Web server and home page (for example, http://www.yourcompany.com indicates that the host's address is www.yourcompany.com).

VCalendar. An industry standard format developed by the Versit Consortium for exchanging scheduling and activity-recording information electronically.

VCard. An industry standard format developed by the Versit Consortium for the exchange of an electronic business (or personal) card.

VCS. Version Control System. A software management scheme that keeps software up-to-date on clients connected to the server.

VoIP. Voice Over Internet Protocol. The two-way transmission of audio over a TCP/IP channel; can be transmitted over the Internet, private intranet, or WAN.

VPN. Virtual Private Network. Uses a public network such as the Internet as a secure channel for communicating private data; allows the creation of a secure link between a corporate LAN (local area network) and a remote user's PC.

VRML. Virtual Reality Modeling Language. An extension of HTML to support 3-D views, simulation, and modeling.

VXML. Voice XML. An extension to XML that defines voice segments and enables access to the Internet via phones and other voice-activated devices.

W3C. World Wide Web Consortium. An organization dedicated to keeping open standards as part of the Internet infrastructure.

WAN. Wide Area Network. A data communications network that spans any distance and is usually provided by a public carrier.

WAP. Wireless Application Protocol. An open, global specification that allows mobile users to use handheld wireless devices to instantly obtain and make use of real-time information.

Web 2.0. A perceived second generation of Web-based services that emphasize online collaboration and sharing among users. It is in a world where computers and other technology have shifted from a means of one-way static communication to platforms for interaction and community building.

Web Analytics. The process of analyzing the behavior of visitors to a Web site. The use of Web analytics is said to enable a business to attract more visitors, retain or attract new customers for goods or services, or increase the dollar volume each customer spends.

Web Services. Self-contained, self-describing, modular application that can be published, located, and invoked across the Web; Web services perform functions that can be anything from simple requests to complicated business processes.

Webtop. Refers to a desktop environment that can run Java or Windows CE applications.

Wideband. A system with multiple channels access a medium (usually coaxial cable) that has a large bandwidth, greater than that of a voice-grade channel; typically offers higher-speed data-transmission capability.

Wi-Fi. A wireless technology brand owned by the Wi-Fi Alliance intended to improve the interoperability of wireless local area network products based on the IEEE 802.11 standards.

WiMAX. Worldwide Interoperability for Microwave Access. A telecommunications technology aimed at providing wireless data over long distances in a variety of ways, from point-to-point links to full mobile cellular type access. It is based on the IEEE 802.16 standard.

Windows CE. A streamlined version of Windows from Microsoft for hand-held PCs (HPCs) and consumer electronics devices; runs pocket versions of popular applications such as Microsoft Word and Excel as well as many applications that are geared specifically for the smaller platform.

Windows DNA. Distributed Internet Architecture. Microsoft's framework for building a new generation of highly adaptable business solutions that enable companies to fully exploit the benefits of the Digital Nervous System (a new generation of computing solutions that dramatically improve the responsiveness of the organization). Microsoft's umbrella term for its enterprise network architecture built into Windows 2000.

WWW. World Wide Web. The network of servers on the Internet, each of which has one or more home pages, that provide information and hyper-text links to other documents on that and (usually) other servers; servers communicate with clients by using the Hypertext Transfer Protocol (HTTP).

XML. Extensible Markup Language. A new Internet language that will make the World Wide Web smarter; as an ISO-compliant subset of SGML, HTML is a markup language, consisting of text interspersed with a few basic formatting tags; XML is a metalanguage containing a set of rules for constructing other markup languages.

XSL. Extensible Stylesheet Language. A stylesheet format for XML documents. It is the XML counterpart to the cascading style sheet (CSS) language in HTML, although XML also supports CSS1 and CSS2 as well.

About the Author

Barton Goldenberg, president of ISM, Inc. (www.ismguide.com), founded the Bethseda, Maryland-based company in 1985. Today, ISM is one of the leading customer relationship management (CRM) and real-time enterprise (RTE) strategic advisories, offering consulting and research services to Global 2000 companies, nonprofit organizations, and government agencies.

Barton's vision to integrate sales, marketing, customer service, ebusiness, and business intelligence has been central to today's CRM industry success. With his bottom-line, results-oriented-style, he has become popular with chief executives as well as a sought-after speaker and writer internationally. He was co-chairman and co-founder of the CRM and RTE conferences and expositions sponsored by DCI, Inc. and currently chairs the annual destinationCRM conference produced by Information Today, Inc. He also conducts CRM and RTE management briefings in the U.S., Europe, and Asia. He has helped companies worldwide successfully implement CRM and has recently turned his sights on finding ways to assist the digital client.

Barton is also the author of *CRM Automation* (Prentice Hall), which provides a step-by-step process for successfully implementing a CRM program, and the benchmark *Guide to CRM Automation* (now in its 15th edition), which features ISM, Inc.'s selection of the Top 15 Software Solution packages. A columnist and member of the Editorial Board for *CRM Magazine,* Barton also contributes to *eWeek* and *Sales and Marketing Management* magazine. He is a frequent quotable media resource in *Business Week, CIO, Information Week,* and *Selling Power.*

In 1999, Barton was recognized by *CRM Magazine* as one of the Ten Most Influential People in Customer Relationship Management for his leadership in galvanizing the CRM industry. In 2002, *CRM Magazine* named him one of the 20 Most Influential CRM Executives of the Year, and in 2003, he was among the premiere inductees in *CRM Magazine's* CRM Hall of Fame.

Before founding ISM, Barton held senior management positions at the U.S. Department of State and Monsanto Europe S.A. He also holds a BSc (Economics) with honors from the Wharton School of Business and an MSc (Economics) from the London School of Economics.

A